SHE FOR GOD

Also by Katharine Moore:
Victorian Wives

SHE FOR GOD
Aspects of Women and Christianity

Katharine Moore

Allison & Busby
London

First published in Great Britain 1978 by
Allison and Busby Limited,
6a Noel Street, London W1V 3RB.

ISBN 0 85031 245 0

Set in 11pt Lectura
and printed by Villiers Publications Ltd,
Ingestre Road, London NW5 1UL

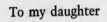

To my daughter

Preface

This book has a dual aim: first, to trace the significance that Christianity has had for women throughout the centuries and, secondly, the significance that women have had for Christianity. To deal with the whole history of women in Christendom at all adequately would have demanded a team of scholars, so I have confined myself almost entirely to the British woman, except for one chapter on the cross currents that were at work between England and America, particularly in the nineteenth century. Even within these limits, it has only been possible to select representative individuals and movements, especially in the later periods, and I can only say that I am as unhappily aware of omissions as anyone else can be. Some of the women included have been chosen for their outstanding personalities, some for their particular opportunities or influence and others simply because they reflected most clearly the trends of thought and of action characteristic of their age. I hope that thus, through particulars, general patterns will emerge which may help to clarify the past, illuminate the present and point the way to the future.

Contents

Foreword

by
Joyce Grenfell

If the first chapter of Genesis is the acceptable metaphysical account of creation — "male and female created he them", "and God saw everything that he had made and behold it was very good" — then the equality of men and women is established. But the second chapter tells a different story and confusion sets in. I abide by Chapter I and I rejoice in Paul's conclusion in Galatians 3:28 that "there is . . . neither male nor female; for ye are all one in Christ Jesus". In spite of these clear statements, sex discrimination has long been practised in religion as in most other ways of life and although it is diminishing there is still some way to go before the truth of equality is wholly accepted.

Katharine Moore's book SHE FOR GOD is a fascinating and intelligent review of the splendid regiment of women who, from Jesus's time to the twentieth century, have witnessed and proved through their spiritual perception, selflessness, and their experience of the practical power of God in us that He is no respecter of gender. Portraits of women who were inspired by their understanding of good that is holy, and therefore whole (rather than moral and inconsistent), are many and vivid. Continuing discoveries down the ages of timeless and infinite truth in situations and under conditions of uncomprehending animosity and resentment toward women illumine the book. I found it both interesting and moving. I see it as an unfolding tapestry of portraits linked by one important thread — the love of God as a practical way of living.

The courage and vision revealed in these brief histories is an encouragement and the account will appeal to anyone who is interested in belief (varied), faith and true understanding of what Jesus came to tell us about our relationship with God.

9

Saints are notoriously difficult to live with and some of these women must have been trying to have about the house. (Margery Kempe is one of them.) All are clearly drawn and the light shed by the brightest stars in Katharine Moore's firmament shines on untouched by time. SHE FOR GOD is a book to keep and return to.

London, 1978

1
Introduction

At the time of the birth of Christ, the state of women throughout the civilised world was little better than slavery.

Among the agricultural settlements of ancient times, where fertility was all-important, the role of women as life-givers was revered as mysterious and powerful, and this remains the attitude among some primitive tribes up to the present day: "Women are able to bring forth, they are able to command the seed they sow to be productive," records a missionary report on the Orinoco.

The Earth-mother under various names was duly honoured and her symbolic marriage with the tribal chief or king was carried out each year, her priestess providing a mortal substitute. She was no gentle deity and sometimes demanded sacrifice; on occasions even the king himself had to die. It was believed that without this marriage the crops would fail and the people perish. The local significance of this female deity was great and if her shrine was desecrated and her image stolen she must be recovered and reinstated or the community was doomed. Hence the significance of the Trojan War, for Helen was more than woman, though by Homer's time she had become a little less than goddess.

Among nomadic pastoral tribes, on the other hand, hunting and warfare and the ceaseless struggle for feeding-grounds were the determining factors of existence. Women and children were a burden in such a way of life: so many more mouths to feed and no use in battle. Abraham belonged to a nomadic pastoral people and the Mosaic law, as it took shape, favoured men. Jaweh, the Jewish god, is unmistakably and uncompromisingly masculine, and alone among the gods he had no consort. The fact that Wisdom, or Sophia, is alluded to in a passage in Proverbs as feminine seems of little consequence, and though there are redoubtable Old Testament women characters, just as there are in Greek tragedy, in neither case do these seem to have any effect on the general status of women in the community; the masculine element was

11

dominant in Judea. The Law was taught only to boys and few Jewish girls were able to read. (It must however be acknowledged that in certain respects Jewish law was more favourable to women, for instance with regard to divorce and to property rights, than was the custom in pagan societies.) In strict orthodox Jewish communities today women are still not allowed to read the Torah. Orthodox synagogues count only male heads as members. While Abraham spake with the angels, Sarah got the dinner. Similarly in Milton's *Paradise Lost*, Adam conversed with the Archangel Raphael while Eve prepared their meal.

Homeric Greece and Republican Rome, founded on agricultural settlements, treated women with some respect but as these simpler communities developed a more ambitious way of life, politics and militarism took over. Pericles's ideal for women was that they should "not be talked about for good or for evil among men".[1] During the great period of Greek history, women were excluded from Athenian public life, and in Sparta where they were allowed a relative freedom this was only to enable them to become strong mothers of soldiers. Aristophanes held women's aspirations up to ridicule, and although in Plato's Republic they were admitted to share in the education and vocations of men this was because Plato believed that the masculine element in life was the only truly valuable one and that girls thus trained would become as like men as it was possible for them to be and therefore of more use to the body politic. Neither as individuals nor in their feminine function as wives and mothers were they to count for much, since marriage partners and children were to be held in common and strictly controlled by the State.

Aristotle classes women with slaves and considers them to be definitely inferior to men in moral, physical and intellectual power. He is even doubtful whether women have souls.

In Roman law a woman was either in the power of her father, husband or some male relative and possessed no rights over her children (this law remained unaltered in England until the nineteenth century); although under the Republic family life had been held in high regard and in the home the Roman matron often exercised much influence, during the growth of the Empire to its huge dimensions, the position of women in Rome speedily declined.

12

Into this world, where among Jew and Gentile alike women counted for little or nothing, Christ was born and grew up trained in the Mosaic Law with all the weight of its fierce and puritanical traditions. He began his short ministry and, from the little we know of it, his treatment of and whole attitude towards women was so immensely creative, revolutionary and dynamic that although the Church, following a long way after in this respect, comprehended him not, neither did it wholly deny him. The Gospels remain. In them we read that Christ actually treated women as worthy of serious attention, worthy of argument, worthy of friendship, worthy of compassion, worthy of praise. In St Luke alone seven specific miracles of healing were concerned with women. That Mary was commended for behaviour so utterly foreign to women's supposed proper role as to leave her domestic tasks in order to listen to a Rabbi who was willing to teach her (in itself an offence against the Law) was of much greater significance than appeared on the surface. Jesus's defence of Mary Magdalene must have astonished as well as appalled the men who heard it. It is quite likely true — although only mentioned in the Gnostic Gospel of Marceon — that one of the accusations brought against Jesus by the Sanhedrin was that he led women astray by teaching them. Women were not meant for such things. As for his talking to the women of Samaria and the Syro-Phoenician women, perhaps the extreme unusualness of this behaviour accounts for the inclusion of such episodes in what is after all a very short and highly selective narrative. Most of all, to be treated as individuals in their own right would have astonished the women themselves. They came to realise that Jesus thought them to be of equal importance as men in the eyes of the Father, "joint heirs" to his kingdom. In return they gave him devotion and faithfulness to the end, and it was to women that Jesus first revealed himself after the Crucifixion. All four evangelists agree about this, which is a curious and interesting point, for the resurrection story, as has often been pointed out, has many discrepancies. No Jewish woman was considered reliable as a witness and indeed could not legally be accepted as such. Therefore, if a concerted account of the resurrection was being *invented* to convince the authorities, to insist that women were the first and thus the most dramatic witnesses to such an extraordinary event would have been enough to discredit it at once. Yet it is just this which is narrated by all the Gospels.

At that time and in that place it would have been impossible for a woman to become an itinerant disciple, but that they were included in the Pentecostal experience is certain and very soon we hear of their work for, and influence on, the early Church. When the nucleus of this began to take shape and its members to meet together in each other's houses, the hostesses of these home-churches were necessarily important, for the home has always been the woman's province. Then, too, when the second coming of Christ was expected so confidently and so soon, distinctions of sex, as of race and status, seemed of less consequence. Moreover, attracted by the assurance of a relative dignity in the present and of complete equality in the hereafter, women and slaves hastened to become Christians and made up the majority of the early converts. The women were by no means all of low birth and many wives succeeded eventually in converting their husbands. Persecution, when it came, ennobled women equally with men — a martyr's crown could be worn by either. A certain slave girl by the name of Felicitas before her martyrdom defined the new faith in one sentence. As Charles Williams records in *The Descent of the Dove*:

> "She lay in prison, there she bore a child. In her pain she screamed. The jailers asked her how, if she shrieked at *that*, she expected to endure death by the beasts. She said: 'Now I suffer what *I* suffer; then another will be in me who will suffer for me, as I shall suffer for him.' In that, Felicitas took her place for ever among the great African doctors of the Universal Church."

Thus, in the first years of Christianity, women are found to be playing a far from insignificant part, but the great formative influence of St Paul in shaping Christian thought must be reckoned with in relation to the role women were expected to fill hereafter. There is no doubt that certain of St Paul's sayings, taken out of their context, as they invariably are, had a disastrous effect upon this role from which the Church has suffered even up to the present day. Succeeding preachers and writers have built into these sayings their own prejudices and doctrines, making them more restrictive than St Paul ever intended. It was not to be expected that he could in this matter follow without qualification such a completely unique and revolutionary master as Jesus, but he was in fact ahead of his times in his attitude towards women. After all, it was he who wrote: "There is no such thing as Jew, Greek, slave, and freeman, male and female: for you are all one person in Christ Jesus." (Galatians 3:28). That he had many friends among them whom he held in high esteem is obvious from the Acts and the Epistles. Euodias and Syntyche "who laboured with me in the Gospel", Priscilla at Corinth, Phebe, who held the office of deaconess at Cenchrea, Rufus's mother "who is a mother also to me", Lydia, Damaris, Rhoda and Dorcas. There is scarcely a personal message in his Epistles which does not contain some particular reference to a woman. It is clear, too, that besides including many women among his friends, Paul recognised and welcomed their work for the Church in all sorts of ways, including the exercise of that special gift of spiritual intuition, or prophecy, for which women are noted both in Jewish and classical tradition. His views on marriage were comparatively favourable to women. Although in the early days of expectation celibacy seemed to be the better way of life since all were looking for a quick transit to that other world "where there shall be no marrying or giving in marriage", St Paul obviously modified his views as time went on and we find him emphasising the importance of the Christian family. He put forward the revolutionary idea that it is the duty of husbands to love their wives, and that husband and wife have equal rights over each other's bodies. His condemnation of divorce was aimed at the protection of women, for desertion by husbands was an abuse widely practised throughout the Empire. Though women are told they must live in subjection to their husbands (and indeed it would have been held as scandalous among Jew and Gentile alike had the Christians taught otherwise) yet this subjection was exalted by its use as a symbol of the subjection of the Church to God. The Church became the Bride of Christ in a mystic marriage, perhaps unconsciously reflecting the ancient ritual union between the Earth Goddess and the king. Though in later times this symbolism became a stumbling block, in the early days of Christianity, when husband and wife were drawn together by the new vision, it may well be that each found joy in the intermingling of love, obedience and worship implied in this idea.

It seems then that though the attitude of the early church

towards women fell short of Christ's own teaching, it was much in advance of contemporary practice and proved a strength to the expanding Christian community. Divorce, exposure of girl babies and abortion were all forbidden and the state of marriage exalted.

Mithraism, at one time the greatest rival of Christianity, was a religion orientated towards militarism and had no use for women; Gnosticism, a powerful heresy, encouraged either extreme asceticism or unbridled licence — both destructive of marriage and family life. Neither Mithraism nor Gnosticism survived but Christianity, which however inadequately aimed at achieving a certain creative relationship between the sexes, continued to spread.

So far, so good; but there are certainly incriminating passages in Paul's writings which have done much harm. They were written, however, in particular circumstances. There are signs that the woman convert, poor creature, who felt herself for the first time valued as an immortal soul, began to behave with an immoderate freedom. Her show of independence was too much for St Paul for whom it was important that the Church should not offend unnecessarily the local way of life. For an Eastern woman to remain unveiled in public was doubly improper; first it was an assertion of equality with men and it was also a custom among the Greek Letairai, a number of whom in Corinth and Athens had become Christians. Actually it is not St Paul's injunctions but his argument that offends:

> "A man has no need to cover his head, because man is the image of God, the mirror of his glory, whereas woman reflects the glory of man. For man did not originally spring from woman, but woman was made out of man, and man was not created for woman's sake, but woman for the sake of man."

What follows — "and therefore it is a woman's duty to have a sign of authority on her head, out of regard for the angels" — has never been satisfactorily explained. Nevertheless, the drift of the whole passage is regrettably clear and its influence potent enough to impel an Anglican verger, more than nineteen hundred years later, sternly to rebuke a small girl of ten for venturing into Canterbury Cathedral with head uncovered.

Paul the Jew could hardly be expected to ignore the Scriptures, and Paul the Roman citizen had been brought up from childhood

16

to despise women. All the more is it to his credit that Paul the Christian ends the above passage thus:

"And yet in Church fellowship, woman is as essential to man as man to woman. If woman was made out of man it is through woman that man now comes to be; and God is the source of all." (I. Corinthians 11:8-12.)

Nonetheless, those sentences from Genesis backed up by St Paul's authority have proved a stumbling block to every Christian woman from this day to our own.

As to the vexed question of whether women should teach or preach in public, here again St Paul's words taken from their context have done much harm. On examination they seem to be contradictory. Corinthians 11:5 declares that a woman if she prays or prophesies bareheaded brings shame upon herself, which indicates that she might, and indeed did, officiate publicly in these capacities. Yet Corinthians 14:30 states unequivocally that women should never be allowed to address the congregation. And this was enlarged by future generations to include a total ban on women opening their mouths in any official capacity whatever within a church, so that until quite recent times women and girls were debarred from singing in choirs (except in convents) — thus St Paul is indirectly responsible for choirboys.

Maybe the distinction between prophesying or praying and addressing was more clearly defined in the early Church than seems practical to us, or it has been suggested that this second passage is a later interpolation. But the letter to Timothy, though its authorship is doubtful, also stresses the argument from Genesis as a reason for forbidding women to speak in public (I. Timothy 2:12):

"I do not permit a woman to be a teacher, nor must woman domineer over man, she should be quiet. For Adam was created first and Eve afterwards and it was not Adam who was deceived."

It is a great pity that the second detailed version of the Creation was so often quoted and that one particular sentence in the first account seems to have been ignored, or its significance completely missed:

"So God created man in his own image; in the image of God created he him; male and female created he them."

Here "man" is obviously used as a generic term for humanity and the dual nature of the Deity is clearly implied, male and female both being included in the image of the Godhead. Nor does it seem to have struck those who argued that because Adam was created before Eve he should therefore always have predominance, that the whole animal creation was created before Adam, therefore Eve should logically be the crown and perfection of the creative act.

Both passages in the Epistles dealing with this theme belong to a later date than St Paul's first writings and it is clear from these and from the Acts that he was in the habit of trusting women to carry out important work and he even alludes to them as fellow teachers and missionaries. Too much must not be made of the office known as "deaconess", however, as this seems to have been a fairly restricted one where a woman ministered to her own sex.

As time went on and the expectation of an immediate Second Coming faded and as the organisation of the developing Christian community became more complicated and formalised, contemporary Gentile attitudes and the strength of Jewish tradition combined to decrease the short-lived spirit of equality and partnership between the sexes. An interesting but dangerous example of this partnership, alluded to obliquely by Paul in his discourse on marriage, was a union of affection without intercourse between some men and women. It was an experiment in an interchange of close relationship which aimed at a sublimation of the sexual element into augmented spiritual power. It may have been successful in some cases but by the third century Cyprian pronounces against it:

"We must interfere at once with such as these, that they may be separated while yet they can be separated in innocence."[2]

The harm done by St Paul's later writings was greatly increased by the use made of them by the early Fathers for whom women were not only the scapegoats for the sins of humanity, but also the focus for their own repressions. They reacted fanatically against the increasing immorality of their times. Sex became synonymous with sin and sex was women's fault. Tertullian, for instance, could not forgive himself for his divided nature. So, not much more than a hundred years later than the birth of a new hope for women at

18

Bethlehem, we find a leader of the Christian Church writing like this:

> "You are the Devil's gateway. You are the first deserter of the divine law, you are she who persuaded him whom the devil was not valiant enough to attack . . . on account of your desert that is, even the Son of God had to die."
>
> (Tertullian)

And again:

> "Nothing disgraceful is proper to man, who is endowed with reason, much less for woman, to whom it brings shame even to reflect of what nature she is."
>
> (Cyprian)

Tertullian, Cyprian, and later Jerome, rejoice in the certainty that women depraved enough to adorn themselves "will burn in Hell hereafter for evermore". Even the tolerant philosopher, Clement of Alexandria, writes that a woman attending church "should be entirely covered . . . and she will never fall who puts before her face modestly and her shawl, nor will she invite another to fall into sin by uncovering her face." It is difficult not to think that if only Christ *had* despised the Virgin's womb, it would have pleased and relieved the early Fathers greatly. In fact, during the early centuries of church history there is little mention of Mary. At this period the Queen of Heaven was in eclipse, powerless to redeem Eve or to help her daughters. We have to wait some hundreds of years and to travel northwards to find any explicit recognition or sympathy for women within the framework of Christianity. In *The Twelve Prerogatives of the Blessed Virgin*, Bernard of Clairvaux wrote:

> "Great was the harm, beloved, that a man and a woman caused us, but thanks be to God, *equally* by a man and a woman all was restored, and not without great increment of grace. Thus, the most prudent and clement Artificer did not break the cracked vase, but refashioned it so wisely and perfectly that of the old Adam he formed the new, and transformed Eve into Mary. Truly Christ would have been enough, since as it is, all one sufficiency proceeds from Him, but it was not fitting for us that it should be the man alone. It was much more to our advantage that both sexes should co-operate in our repair, since both worked for our perdition."

19

It would be a mistake, however, to judge the Fathers out of their historical context any more than St Paul. They lived in a disintegrating society in which Gnosticism (that muddle of Eastern superstition), Hellenic philosophy, old traditions and new heresies such as Montanism, were all a threat to the struggling emerging church. Rightly or wrongly this resulted in a tightening up of ecclesiastical authority and a retreat from the world. Fear rather than faith took over and in this life-denying atmosphere women were looked upon almost entirely as sex symbols (something which tends to happen either in times of extreme puritanism *or* of extreme licence). Yet, as Christians, the Fathers could not deny that women possessed souls, however mistakenly it seemed to them that God had arranged matters thus, so that though they were looked upon as enemies, highly dangerous from Eve onwards to all men, they were never denied membership of the Church. In course of time the revulsion against sex among the Fathers resulted in the growth of one-sex communities. These originated in Egypt from the third century onwards when those who fled from the temptations of the world, and also from its persecution, formed themselves into tiny groups. St Anthony, pestered by his famous devils in the shape of women, may be taken as the patron saint of these early desert hermits. From these developed the first monastic institutions and these eventually proved an unlikely benefit to women. For in due course they, too, formed their one-sex communities, thus for the first time offering an alternative to marriage and endowing the professed nun with a distinguished role — that of the living prototype of the Church as the Virgin Bride of Christ. Chastity for women now became a positive and voluntary virtue. The spread of Christianity among the northern peoples of Europe, where a healthier attitude towards women was customary, also helped towards recovering some of the dignity which had been lost to them since the earliest days of the Church.

2
The Saxon Period

An anonymous Elizabethan Catholic writing his *Lives of Early Women Saints* says:

> "Faith decaying in the world and charitie becoming more and more colde, when they at this time shall behold fraile women to have taken up so weightie and greate crosses and to have carried them so cheerfullie, albeit deigntilie bredd and brought up, how many may be confounded that, for onelie mammocks and scrappe in comparison, neglect to serve God. [They] so much the more forcible, in that they have moste been bredd in this land, where we ourselves have been borne, walked on this earth on which we walke. More potent also are they for their sex and number, who, the weaker they were by nature, so much more admirable to excell the perfecter sex by grace. But God's grace maketh little difference of sex and hence the sloth and pride of the perfecter sex may be more confounded, being so outgone by their inferior and the weaker also be more emboldened and comforted in Christ, seeing their infirmitie made so potent by him, above sondrie by nature superior."

This (barring its harping on "the perfecter sex") is on the whole a generous tribute, though not altogether true to history. "Deigntilie bredd" the early women saints certainly were in the sense of highly born, for Christianity in those times was engendered for the most part in royal courts and the convent was a privilege of the ruling class, but far from taking up their cross in dedicating their lives to a religious foundation, the daughters, sisters, and even the wives of the Saxon nobility were often only too glad to escape from the brutality and dangers of the world outside to the peace and order and culture of the cloister. There was besides more scope for the ambitious and able woman as the head of a religious house than she would find elsewhere. It has been suggested that the rapid spread of convent life among the Saxons is due to memories still held of an earlier age when the goddess and her

21

priestess were the tribal centre of power. Certainly the number of outstanding Saxon abbesses far outshine both in quantity and quality those that came after and there were several reasons for this. The traditional role of women both in Celtic and Saxon society was not necessarily considered as an inferior one. Tacitus remarks on the strange fact that among the Germanic tribes "their men conceive that in women there is a certain uncanny and prophetic sense; they neither scorn to consult them nor slight their answer." Among the Celts and the Picts also there was a belief in the practical wisdom of women. They were expected to play their part in the management of affairs (short of fighting) and with the Picts, succession came down through the female line.

Thus, when Britain was Christianised, it is not surprising to find the royal women of the country playing an important part and sometimes a vital one in the process. Bertha of Kent worshipped as a Christian in Canterbury before Augustine came. Her daughter Ethelburga, who married Edwin, king of Northumbria, prepared the way for her husband and his people's conversion and baptism by Paulinus whom she took up north with her. Her granddaughter, married to the king of Mercia, the last pagan stronghold in Britain, managed at last to convert that country with the help of her imported priests. Thus, three chief kingdoms of pre-Conquest England were Christianised by the influence of three devout queens.

The Church was the stronghold not only of religion but of all learning. What was left of the tradition of Greece and Rome was only saved from extinction by the hermits, the monks and the nuns. It was natural that all those of the nobility who cared about the way their daughters were brought up should send them, if they could, to religious foundations whether destined for the veil or not. Before the establishment of any important convents in Britain these girls were sent to France. They returned well qualified to take up posts of responsibility and those who did not marry were able to fulfil themselves in becoming heads of the newly established institutions and in training others there. Even those who married often exerted much influence over those religious houses which in many cases they themselves had founded and they retired there as widows and certainly in two cases, the Queens Aethelthrith and Cuthberg, even left their husbands to take the veil. By the close of the seventh century there were five important religious foundations for women in Kent alone, whose abbesses at the Council of Beckenham ranked in importance next to the bishops and above the male presbyters. But we must look to the north for the most outstanding personality among the great Saxon abbesses.

St Hilda was born in Yorkshire in 613. Her mother, so Bede tells us, on the night before her birth dreamed that she was wandering in a dark wood when she found a jewel suddenly within her hand which gave out a brilliant light illuminating all the darkness around. Poor woman, she was soon to experience that dark wood, for her husband, a relative of Edwin, king of East Anglia, was murdered shortly after. But the baby Hilda became in due course that bright jewel whose radiance is even now not quite forgotten.

Paulinus, chaplain to the Christian Queen Ethelburga (who was related by marriage to Hilda), held a baptism at York and Hilda as a girl of fourteen was among his catechumens. But Penda, the pagan king of Mercia, fought a battle against Northumbria in which Edwin was killed, and his Queen Ethelburga with Hilda and her mother and sister and Paulinus all fled southwards. We do not hear again of Hilda until peace was restored to Northumbria and the Celtic Aidan of Lindisfarne crossed over from his rocky stronghold from which he had watched Penda's fires burning, to re-Christianise the ravished country. He must have known Hilda as a girl and gauged something of her quality for he could hardly have had much contact with her since. But now he wrote to her just in time to prevent her setting out to France to join her sister and begged her to come north instead and help him in his work. She was to establish convents in some of the distressed areas, which she duly did, beginning in a small way and finally ending up at Whitby, where King Oswy, as a thank offering for finally defeating Mercia, handed over to Hilda a parcel of land for the foundation of a new religious house, and with it his little daughter Aelflaed, to be brought up by her. The new order was of the double type of house originating in France, including both men and women, and here, says Bede, Abbess Hilda

"taught the strict observance of justice, piety, chastity, and other virtues and particularly of peace and of charity. No one was rich and none poor. Her prudence was so great that not only meaner men in their need, but sometimes even Kings and Princes sought and received her council."

What a haven, what a paradise after so many years of savage war, to live under such a rule within those strong sheltering grey walls above the tossing North Sea. It was a haven indeed, but, as Bede makes clear, it was by no means a backwater. Here, besides the kings and princes, young men came to be trained, men who afterwards made their mark in the world. Five of them became bishops, a large percentage of the total of fourteen in Britain at that time. They went on to Lindisfarne to complete their course but "ever gratefully acknowledge that they had received from Hilda". It was this learned and great abbess who had ears also for the humble Caedmon, he, who most unexpectedly became our first religious poet, with his miraculously inspired Song of Creation. Hilda sent for him, encouraged him to repeat his poem to her, commended it, and made him a lay brother at the convent.

Hilda was also involved in ecclesiastical politics. The famous synod of Whitby was called to meet at her abbey; this was apparently sparked off by the practical objections of the Queen at the inconvenience of having two separate dates for the observance of Easter. The cleavage, however, went a good deal deeper than this and was between the simpler, less ritualistic and authoritarian northern church with its more ancient Celtic origins holding itself independent of Rome, and the church founded in the southern half of the kingdom by Augustine. The most famous of Hilda's pupils, Wilfrid, abbot of Ripon and later Bishop of York, was a turbulent character, and having lived for some years in Kent, France and Italy had become passionately involved on the side of Rome. He saw the Celtic church as out of touch with the mainstream of Christian tradition and power, and as he was one of the most important and certainly the most emphatic of personalities at Whitby, his party carried the day. Hilda appears to have kept silent. Perhaps as a convert of Paulinus she felt her sympathies divided and she laboured under the disadvantage of seeing two sides of the question, but one cannot help suspecting that by early associations, by her friendship with Aidan and by her temperamental independence, she must have mourned the eclipse of her native church. Perhaps also Wilfrid had been a tiresome pupil in his youth, always arguing and thinking himself in the right. Anyway, years later we find her laying an accusation against him before the Pope!

Hilda died in 680. Her life had roughly coincided with the golden age of the great Saxon religious foundations. She had had the joy of seeing peace and order reign where there had been chaos and war, and of watching the work for which she was responsible prosper under her hands. Though the last six years of her life were spent in physical weakness and pain, she "never failed to instruct her flock most diligently in health to serve God most studiously and in sickness to give him thanks most heartilie". She did not have to worry about who was to succeed her for her niece, that little girl entrusted to her by King Oswy, was waiting to step into her shoes. Her chief anxiety seems to have been lest the discord between the leaders of the Church (so often a fruit of secular peace) should increase. Her last recorded words were: "Have evangelical peace among yourselves."

St Hilda, efficient, brave, selfless, wise and intelligent, as she comes down to us through the loving portrait drawn of her by Bede, is almost an archetypal figure. The "Candle of the Lord", that light of Reason fused with that of the Spirit, lit so long before by the Saxon abbess, has thrown its beam far indeed in "a naughty world". St Hilda has become a sort of patron saint of the many dedicated Christian women, whose lifework has been in the fields of social service and especially of education. Schools and colleges for women have been named after her and at Whitby itself her inspiration lives on in a contemporary order of missionary and teaching nuns whose late head, Mother Margaret, when asked once whom she felt most in touch with among those who had passed to the life beyond, replied unhesitatingly: "St Hilda."

Aelflaed, who became abbess at Hilda's death, was in every way a credit to her upbringing. Under her Whitby retained its influence. When the king of Northumbria was dying he called to his bedside not his captains and his councillors, but Aelflaed and her sister abbess of Hackness and committed to them his last commands. One of these commands concerned that saintly troublemaker Wilfrid, who had been exiled for a time — then allowed home and yet again left the country for Rome to obtain further support from the Pope. "He was a nightingale who sang sweetest far from Home", says Fuller, and the bishops were all in favour of keeping him there. But he was agitating to come back to York and the king, visited by deathbed doubts, had a last minute repentance of his enmity towards the exiled ecclesiastic. So, at a meeting to discuss the matter, Abbess Aelflaed revealed that "the testimony of the late King Aldfrith in that illness which ended his life, vowed a vow to God and to St Peter: 'If I live I will carry out the judgement of the Apostolic See respecting blessed Wilfrith, which hitherto I have refused to carry out. But if I die, say ye to my heir that he carry out the Apostolic decision respecting Wilfrith.'" The abbess's dramatic disclosure carried the day in favour of Wilfrith and he was allowed home to York but with curtailed authority.

Aelflaed is described by Eddi, the biographer of Wilfrid, as "ever the comforter and best counsellor of the whole province" and she was the friend and confidante of Cuthbert of Farne Island. She outlived him and assisted in the bringing of his body to Durham, herself wrapping it up in a "linen cloth of double texture".

But Aelflaed herself dies at the beginning of the troubled eighth century and those walls of Hilda's abbey that had seemed so impregnable are no match for Danes and for decay. Northumbria's old border enemies, the Mercians and the Picts, are ready to pounce at any sign of weakness and across the grey northern seas come in sequence long boat after long boat of land-hungry Vikings. Under constant attack the great kingdom weakened, its centres of Christianity and culture were destroyed or left to collapse from poverty and neglect.

After all its splendid promise there were only to be two abbesses of the famous convent at Whitby, yet neither they nor their herdsman poet were ever to be forgotten.

In the south, however, important foundations for women flourished at Ely, Barking and Wimborne. Ely was founded in 673 by that same Queen Aethelthrith who had left her husband and in spite of her former marriage, or perhaps because of it, took great pride in being praised for her virginity and acquired a reputation for extreme holiness. The concept of virginity and of the nun being the bride of Christ was a favourite theme of religious poetry throughout the centuries. Here was a romantic appeal lacking in the dedication of a monk to the monastic life. It is connected of course with the ancient magic surrounding the whole idea of the woman as possessing a mysterious power which becomes even more potent when refused to man and devoted to God. Cyprian wrote:

> "Virgins are the flower of the Christian seed. By them doth the glorious fertility of our Mother Church greatlie rejoice and abundantly flourish."

This became more potent a myth as time went on but even in these earlier simpler days of church history, the emphasis is clear. Hildebath, the second abbess of Barking, received a famous letter on virginity from the scholarly and poetic Aldhelm, Bishop of Sherborne, parts of which one may hope were enough to comfort and charm many a pensive young nun, musing over them in her cell. He dwells on the delights of virginity, on the peace achieved by renouncing marriage, on the joys of congenial companionship within the convent walls, but he praises them not only for their purity but for their learning:

> "As bees flit from the marigold to the purple mallow and from the mallow to the yellow blossoms of the willow and the broom, from the clusters of ivy to the flowering lime, so you gather learning from many a page of scholarship.'

He ends by acclaiming these happy nuns of Barking as "Flowers of the Church, sisters of the monastic life, scholarly pupils, pearls of Christ, jewels of Paradise and sharers of the eternal home." Dear Aldhelm, no wonder your letter was lastingly popular in every convent in Europe and was one of the first works to be printed after the invention of the printing press.

Cuthberg, the second queen to forsake her husband for the veil, first joined the scholarly "bees" of Barking and then went on to found Wimbourne in Dorset. This, like Barking, was a double house for both monks and nuns, but they were kept so strictly apart that a wall was built to divide them even when worshipping in their abbey church. At Wimborne Leoba, the friend and cousin of Boniface, was trained. In Boniface's letters we have as valuable a source as Bede for an insight into the lives of these Saxon saints and Leoba seems to have been a second Hilda, though far less well known in English tradition. This was partly because Leoba's work was to lie chiefly in Germany. She was one of the first great mis-

27

sionary nuns. We learn of her not only from Boniface but also from a German monk who wrote her life.

Her first letter to Boniface brings her vividly to light in a role eternally familiar and repeated throughout the history of English women — that of the faithful daughter, doing her duty by her parents, but yearning after a wider sphere and a better education:

"I ask of your clemency that you would deign to remember the former friendship which you made long ago with my father, by name, Dynne, in the West Country, now dead for seven years, and would not refuse your prayers to God for his soul. I commend also to you the recollection of my mother, whose name is Aebbe. She still lives greatly burthened and long grievously oppressed by ill health. I am the only daughter of my parents and I would that I might, though quite unworthy, take you in place of a brother . . . I have composed the few verses which I enclose according to the rules of poetic versification, not from pride, but from a desire to cultivate the beginnings of learning, and now I am longing for your help. I beg too that you will correct the rusticity of this letter and will send me some words, of your graciousness, by way of pattern."

We can take it that Boniface replied kindly for some years later, almost certainly after Aebbe's death, he wrote from Germany, whence he had gone from his native Devon to Christianise the pagan tribes, asking Leoba to join him in his work among the women there. She was given a large foundation at Bischofsheim to mould into good order and gained a reputation for training excellent teachers.

Leoba seems to have been a charming person, good-looking, intelligent, cheerful and such a reader that she "never laid aside her book except to pray or strengthen her slight frame with food and sleep". She also possessed a pleasing commonsense, rather rare in saints. She always took a rest after dinner and made those under her do the same, especially in summer time, and she saw to it that all had sufficient sleep at night, as she was a firm believer that "the mind is keener for study after sleep". Like Hilda, she was much sought after by the secular world. "Princes loved her", so her biographer says, "noblemen received her and Bishops gladly entertained her and conversed with her, for she was familiar with many writings and careful in giving advice." The great Charlemagne sent her presents and his queen tried to persuade her to live with her at Aachen. She went to stay with Boniface at Mainz and he gave her his cloak before setting out on his last journey in 757 to the wild Frisians. He must have envisaged his probable death for he seems to have taken a solemn farewell, asking her to remain true to her work to the end and desiring that he and she should be buried side by side at Fulda. He was killed by the natives on this mission. Leoba lived on near Mainz for many years after, dying in 780.

Leoba is a character in the round. She is convincing and, like Hilda, familiar and realistic in her emotions and achievements and aspirations. Any fine dedicated educational administrator working, say, among African tribes in our own times, might have felt and behaved similarly. With her contemporary, Waltpurgis, on the other hand, we are in the world of fable. She, too, was a missionary nun from England, but she seems somehow to have got mixed up in a maze of folklore — witches, fertility rites and the lot — or to have been confused with an earlier tribal saint of the same name. Goethe commemorates her in his account of the Walpurgisnacht. Miracles and relics protecting from black magic are associated with her name, and German peasants venerating her through the centuries had obviously no idea she was not a national saint of theirs at all. It is an interesting example of the apparently fortuitous mixture of historical fact and folk tradition that her brother Wilibald, who was a great and intrepid traveller, had the luck to be fully documented by an unknown nun at a convent in Heidenhain (one of those looked after by Leoba). This nun was English or she would not find herself in these pages. But she is nameless. She comes down to us as the first woman to write a travel book. Spellbound, she listened to Wilibald's adventures and felt compelled to take up her pen and write them down, and the curious are for ever grateful to her for they contain one of the earliest descriptions we have of the pilgrim's Palestine.

"I am but a woman" — how familiar an apologetic opening throughout the ages! — "I am but a woman," she cries, "weak on account of the frailty of my sex, neither supported by the prerogative of wisdom nor sustained by the consciousness of great power." Yet like all born writers, no matter whether what they write is good or bad, for the private or the public ear, she *has* to do it and

29

there follows Wilibald's experiences, from Waltham Abbey to Rouen, and from Rouen to Lucca, and thence to marvellous Rome for the winter, and from Rome to Sicily and from Sicily to Ephesus and Syria. Travelling *was* travelling in those days. Three times on the way he was cast into prison and the whole trip took seven years. But he describes the site of the nativity at Bethlehem before it was transformed out of all possible imagining. Wilibald saw just a square little cave-like dwelling in a rock "over which a little chapel is built". But he also saw hell, which excited our nun dreadfully. It was on the island of Lipari:

> "And when they arrived there they left the boat to see what sort Hell was — and Wilibald was prevented by cinders from going close. The cinders rose from the black gulf and sank again. As snow settles falling from the sky and the heavenly heights in thick white masses, so these cinders lay heaped on the summit of the mountain and prevented Wilibald's ascent. But he saw a blackness and a terrible column of flame projected upwards with a noise like thunder from the pit, and he saw the flames and the smoky vapour rising to an immeasurable height."

How the nun as she listened must have secretly bewailed her fate as being "but a woman" and therefore deprived of such incredible sights. But she rejoiced at the chance which had brought Wilibald to her convent and enabled her to commit his story to paper in her quiet cell at Heidenhain.

To return to Boniface. He had other close women friends besides Leoba. There was Abbess Eadburg of Thanet, who wrote out for him the Epistle of Peter in letters of gold. It was an age in which the holy *Thing,* the book, the relic, the altar covering, was becoming of more and more significance. Writing the Scriptures in letters of gold upon parchment and embroidering vestments and altar cloths were acts of worship in themselves and were part of the training of all nuns who showed any aptitude for these crafts. Boniface was duly grateful. "Beloved sister," he wrote, "with gifts of holy books you have comforted the exile in Germany with spiritual light, for in this dark remoteness among German peoples man must come to the distress of death had he not the Word of God as a lamp unto his feet and as a light unto his path. Fully trusting in your love I beseech that you pray for me."

Another abbess in Kent called Bugga (which, improbably, seems to have been a favourite Saxon name for women) also sent Boniface gifts of books, money and an altar cloth. Bugga was not a contented nun. She resigns from her rule to live privately for peace and quiet, but next we hear of her consulting Boniface about going to Rome. He advises her thus:

> "If you gave up the charge you had of the servants of God and your own monastic life for the sake of securing quiet and the thought of God, in what way are you now bound to toil and wearing anxiety? Still, if you cannot find peace of mind in your home in secular life among seculars, it seems right that you should seek it in a pilgrimage. Our sister Wettburg found the quiet she longed for near the threshold of St Peter."

He then advises her to wait till the attacks of the Saracens should subside and for a letter of invitation from Wettburg, and ends by asking for her prayers in his distresses "which are more of the mind than of the body." Bugga did go to Rome and Boniface met her there and they enjoyed themselves sightseeing and walking and talking together. Finally Bugga returned apparently refreshed enough to settle down for life in her old monastery again.

Boniface appears to have had a real and intimate friendship with these intelligent women and he was increasingly worried about worsening conditions for nuns in the north. Their convents were no longer safe refuges and many faced real hardship and danger. The Abbess Eangith from Durham writes to him complaining of

> "the poverty and scantiness of our temporal possessions and the smallness of the cultivated part of our estate and of the hostility of the King. There is no one else for us to rely on (but you) . . . so we are weary of our present life and hardly dare to continue it, (but) we believe that in you we have found the friend whom we longed for."

It is poignant to think how far away, infinitely further than he would seem today, was this one friend. Through long days and nights, by horse and by foot, through forests and swamps and across stormy seas, facing hazards from the hands of lawless men, from pestilence or fire, the letters travel bravely to and fro passing from country to country, carrying with them bright tokens of friendship, gifts, and counsel, encouragement and sympathy and

31

the assurance of mighty prayer. "Pray for us, pray for me", they continually ask and the promise follows: "We will pray."

Boniface did all he could, writing to expostulate with kings and with bishops and smoothing the way for those who understandably tried to escape by way of pilgrimage from the restraints and difficulties of their native settlements.

Rome had become the Mecca of Christians, the city of God, as a compensation for yielding up the secular glory of the Empire to Byzantium. In Rome the Pope had taken over the ancient pomp and glory of the emperor. Pilgrimages thither were becoming more and more popular. Boniface encouraged those among his women friends in whom he had trust to make this holy journey, and there is a letter from a deacon in Rome, informing him that "the sisters and maidens of God, who have reached the threshold of the Apostles, are being looked after by him, as you have desired." Some such guidance and help was certainly needed as other troubles beside the Saracens were apt to befall the pilgrims. Prison and persecution and ravage were not unknown. None the less presently the popular urge to leave England for pilgrimages abroad became too much of a good thing. Boniface is forced at last to write to Cuthbert of Canterbury:

> "that it were an honour and credit to your Church and a palliation of evils if the Synod and your princes forbade those who have taken the veil to travel and stay abroad as they do, coming and going in the Roman states. They come in great numbers and few return undefiled."

By the ninth century these pilgrimages had become such a scandal that steps were taken to put a stop to them. The ninth and tenth centuries were altogether a dark time for Christianity in Britain. Like an engulfing wave the Scandinavian invasions swept westward and southward from the north and nuns fled from their cloisters or were killed or ravished while their churches and monastery buildings were destroyed.

By the tenth century only a few of the religious foundations for women remained and these were almost all in Wessex. The revival of the monastic orders when it came under Dunstan did not give the convents the same pre-eminence that they once enjoyed. But the tradition of royal Saxon saintliness among women still per-

32

sisted. St Edith, a friend of Dunstan's, refused to be made a queen and devoted herself to the service of the sick. It was said of her "that in doing so she was a Martha, but in spiritual solitude with Christ she was a Mary".

The total roll call of these royal women is a long one and I have confined myself to those with an authentic historical identity. There are those others who come down to us as obvious inheritors of pagan traditions of tribal goddesses and whose behaviour is sometimes somewhat dubious, but most are clad in indistinguishable garments of inviolable piety, purity and miraculous powers. Their insubstantial radiance is like moonlight that takes all colour away. This monotonous portrait gallery is lit here and there, however, by gleams of individuality, such as the pleasant wit of St Mildred, which persisted even after her death, for when a bell-ringer at her Abbey of Thanet fell asleep over his duties, she appeared and boxed his ears, exclaiming before she vanished: "Understand, fellow, that this is an oratory to pray in, not a dormitory to sleep in." Yet all these legends that cluster round those early fabulous saints do contribute, if only faintly, to the undeniable evidence that in Saxon Britain women *were* a powerful spiritual force.

This chapter began with three great Christian queens who played a large part in the conversion of England. It shall end with another queen who may be said to have re-Christianised Scotland.

St Margaret was the granddaughter of Edmund Ironside and was born about 1045 in Hungary, where her father had been sent as a boy to get him safely out of the way of Canute. He had married into the royal house of Hungary but when Margaret was about twelve he and his wife and family were invited back to the court of Edward the Confessor. There she continued what had apparently been a peaceful upbringing and in due course she was married to Malcolm of Scotland, that same Malcolm who with Donalbain, his brother, appears in Shakespeare's *Macbeth*. Queen Margaret was her husband's superior in culture — this was not uncommon when the nobility educated their girls in the convent and their boys on the battlefield. Possessed of a determined character she set about civilising Malcolm, his court and, as far as was possible, his kingdom without delay. The Church was in a poor way, the lamp which St Columba had once kindled was almost extinguished, and there was only one bishop left in the whole country. Margaret built churches and saw that people used them, founded monasteries, restored Iona, and tried to end the slavery that had grown up out of the constant feuds and raids, gave generously to the poor and though she could not teach the king to read, read to him out of her holy books, which he afterwards kissed devoutly and ordered to be rebound splendidly in her honour. He seems genuinely to have been devoted to her — at least he let her do what she wanted to a very large extent.

We have a vivid account of her written by Turgot, Prior of Durham, and afterwards Archbishop of St Andrews. He knew her well and allowing for the inevitable adulation the picture he gives is convincing enough. "Others may admire the indications of sanctity which miracles afford," he says refreshingly, "but I admire much more the works of mercy which I perceived in Margaret." These works of mercy included feeding three hundred poor men every day and bringing up numerous orphans at her own expense. Also, with that flamboyance, which in simpler ages than our own seems a necessary part of sanctity (the best way, perhaps the only way in an illiterate age, to make your point) she insisted on waiting on twenty-four beggars every morning before she took her own breakfast.

Shakespeare in three gripping lines gives us *the saint*:

> "The Queen
> Oftener on her knees than on her feet
> Died every day she lived."

(In the play for obvious reasons he assigns this description to Malcolm's mother instead of his wife, but the portrait is obviously of Margaret.) Turgot, however, gives us the active determined administrator as well — she knew what she wanted and saw that her wishes were carried out. He says that she made her husband "most attentive to the works of justice, mercy, alms giving and other virtues". It cannot be denied that she sounds like the ideal headmistress:

> "She united so much strictness with her sweetness of temper, so great pleasantries even with her severity, that all who waited upon her loved her, while they feared her, and in fearing loved her."

She encouraged foreign industries to start up in Scotland, hung the grim walls of her castles at Edinburgh and Dunfermline with silken coverings and introduced civilised manners from the south. It is noticeable that she called four of her sons by Saxon names — Edward, Edgar, Edmund, Ethelred — and the other two David and Alexander, names of Biblical and classical origin which have remained most popular in Scotland up to this day. Her children were notable. One daughter became a scholarly nun, one married Henry I of England, and her son David was one of Scotland's few satisfactory monarchs, and the two others didn't do so badly as kings either. But for all her strength of character, she could not keep her husband Malcolm from carrying on his endless warfare with the English, and it was on one of these disastrous raids he was killed and his eldest son with him. Edgar, the second son, arrived to break the news to the Queen who was lying ill at Edinburgh Castle. After hearing of the disaster, she exclaimed: "All praises be to Thee, Almighty God, who has been pleased that I should endure such deep sorrow at my departing and trust that by means of this suffering it is Thy pleasure that I should be cleansed from the stains of my sins." They were her last words. She was buried at Dunfermline in the church which she herself had founded there, but which was later splendidly rebuilt in her honour by her son David, so that a more immediate link is the little Norman Church which she raised up on the Castle hill at Edinburgh. She was canonised in 1250, no mean achievement considering that she was neither martyred nor a virgin, nor had she left her husband to take the veil, but had died more or less peacefully in her bed, the mother of eight children and a devoted wife.

Thus, from the sixth century till the Norman Conquest there seems to have been an unbroken line of great Christian women leaders who were in touch with both the secular and the religious life. They were often scholars and were the friends of princes and of bishops, who indeed frequently consulted them on matters of importance. Their golden age was the seventh century but their tradition and influence lasted on through succeeding ages. The Saxon society in which they lived, in spite of its turbulence, afforded its women a sphere of greater importance than that which followed.

3
From the Conquest to the Reformation

The Normans were a masculine and war-like people and allowed little place to women in their society. Under their law women could not inherit property, so there were no longer great heiresses to bring wealth to the convents nor to become patrons of church property. The number of foundations for women had declined during the troubled ninth and tenth centuries and few new ones were instituted. For the most part, too, these were ruled over by a prioress instead of an abbess, a less powerful official in her own right and one who was always subject to an abbot. Most of the convents now were small and poor. One of the new and more prosperous to be established after the Conquest was that of St Mary's at West Malling, Kent, founded by Gundulf, the friend of Lanfranc and of Anselm, who was always well disposed towards women. (Its fine Norman tower still remains besides a thirteenth-century cloister, and it is one of the few convents in England still fulfilling its original purpose.) Whitby and Ely were restored but as monasteries only. Indeed there seems to have been no provision for nuns in the north until the time of Gilbert of Sempringham. Gilbert (1083), a native of Lincolnshire, was educated in France where he became familiar with the idea of joint houses for monks and nuns such as had in Saxon times been instituted at Barking and Wimborne. There was a famous one at Fontevraud, ruled by an abbess, where even poor working women were included, though all the nuns without exception were expected to take Martha as their model rather than Mary. When the nunnery at Amesbury was refounded in the reign of John, nuns were brought from Fontevraud to help to start it. The French continued to be the main influence on English convent life till the Reformation. Gilbert felt called to establish a double house in Yorkshire and hoped to affiliate this with the new Cistercian order that had taken root in France, but this was not approved and he had to invent his own rule for his canons, lay brethren, nuns and lay sisters. Unlike Fontevraud and the earlier double houses, the headship was divided, the men being subject to a prior and the women under three prioresses. The nuns did all the domestic duties but they were allowed a library and reading time. However they were forbidden the use of the Latin tongue — except of course in the Liturgy. Men and women worshipped together but in separate parts of the church.

Gilbert deserves to be remembered as one "who devoted his energies to the control and government of religious women". His foundation was successful and the idea took root in other parts of the north, Walton Priory, for instance, where there were 140 women and 90 men. At first the nuns were considered of greater importance in these foundations but gradually the monks got the upper hand and by the time of the Reformation none of them remained as double houses. Gilbert of Sempringham shows the influence of the French renaissance of faith and of holiness inspired by Bernard. Its spiritual influence came to England by way of the Cistercians, but their rule was found to be too exacting and the work on the land by which they lived too physically wearing for the nuns (still almost exclusively drawn from the wealthy classes) and so they followed only a modified order of simplicity, poverty and labour.

One important link with pre-Conquest times carried on into the twelfth century, a last trace of the noble Saxon influence. Matilda, daughter of St Margaret and King Malcolm of Scotland, received her education at Wilton nunnery in the charge of her aunt Christina, and narrowly escaped an enforced profession. The question of her marriage to Henry I came up and objections were raised that she was a nun. The fighting spirit inherited from both parents was aroused in Matilda:

> "But that I did wear a veil, I do not deny. For when I was quite a young girl and went in fear of the rod of my Aunt Christina, she, to preserve me from the lust of the Normans, used to put a little black hood on my head and when I threw it off, she would often make me smart with a good slapping . . . that hood I did indeed wear in her presence, chafing at it and tearful, but as soon as I was able to escape out of her sight, I tore it off and threw it on the ground and trampled on it . . . In *that* it was, and only in *that* way I was veiled."

Her case was brought before all the dignitaries of the Church called together by Anselm and judgment was given in Matilda's favour. "So having obtained an interview with Anselm and his blessing she departed, and a few days later became . . . a wife and Queen," as we learn from Eadmer's History.

Matilda carried on the tradition of noble Saxon ladies, for though she rebelled against the veil, she was deeply involved with the Church, a friend of Anselm's, and practised great personal piety. There are letters of hers to Anselm urging him not to injure his health by too much fasting. She compares his literary style to that of Cicero, Quintilian, Jerome and Gregory, thus giving us some insight into her own learning and, obviously unhappy at his exile, she writes on her own account to the Pope to defend him. When Anselm's quarrel with Henry was at last resolved and he returned to England, the chronicler Eadmer relates that "no earthly concerns, no pageantry of this world's glory, could keep the Queen from going on before to the different places to which Anselm was coming . . . and by her careful forethought (she) saw to it that his various lodgings were richly supplied with suitable furnishing."

Matilda founded the Hospital of St Giles in London and made the care of the sick her special concern. With a touch of histrionic holiness reminiscent of her mother, the Queen would wash the feet of lepers and kiss them. But this sort of performance in public of certain symbolic acts had an important role to play in an age when few could read or write. We are told that her brother, King David, found her one day surrounded by these miserable beings and remonstrated with her but she answered that "she was kissing the feet of the Eternal King". But she was also always the royal consort of England's monarch. She presented the famous church at Cluny with a splendid seven-branched candlestick — "a candelabra, like a great tree of brass, fashioned with wonderful skill and glittering as much with jewels as with the lights they hold", wrote Bernard, the founder of the simpler Cistercians, in protest against its magnificence.

Queen Matilda was the last for a long while of outstanding influential Christian Englishwomen. Here no such powerful voices were raised as those of Hildegard of Bingen (1098-1130) or Elizabeth of Schonau (1129-88) of whom it was written: "In these days God made manifest his power through the frail sex." These two Benedictine nuns, says Evelyn Underhill, "were the first of that long line of women mystics, visionaries, prophetesses and political reformers – combining spiritual transcendance with great ability, of whom Catherine of Siena is probably the greatest example."

But it was not until the time of Julian of Norwich that England produced anything comparable. Nor was there any convent to rival in scholarly learning that of Helfta in Saxony, where the nuns studied the liberal sciences and which produced some notable women religious writers. On the contrary, by the fourteenth century in England the majority of nuns knew no Latin except that which they chanted parrot-like in their offices.

"Therefore I thynke one gret dirisiown
To heir the Nunnes and systeres night and day
Syngand and sayand psalms and orisaun
Nocht understandying what they syng nor say."
(Sir David Lyndsey)

They read no books but their service books and practised no arts but embroidery, so that it is not surprising that there is no record of any scholastic achievement or any religious writing of note by English nuns from the time when a nun, under the guidance of Abbess Dame Mary Becket (sister of the famous Thomas) wrote a life of St Catherine of Alexandria in French until the works of Julian of Norwich in the fifteenth century. We look in vain for any great spiritual heads of houses during this period. The names that stand out are those of eminently practical women, such as the Abbess Euphemia of Wherwell (1226-57) under whose rule the numbers in the convent doubled. She built new farm buildings, dug out a stream to carry away refuse, made gardens and planted vineyards and trees. She also built a new chapel dedicated to the Virgin and repaired those manor houses which belonged to the convent. Another later building prioress was Joan Wiggenhall of Crabhouse, Norfolk.

A good capable manager could make her convent a true centre of the whole parish, for the medieval nun was often a very busy woman. As well as offering up continual praise to God and prayer for those who, labouring from sunrise to sunset, had no time for their soul's welfare, she practised the rudiments of medicine and surgery, was the only available nurse and teacher and knew not a little about husbandry and all the domestic crafts.

The convents maintained themselves by their farms which fed them and from which they sold their surplus produce, by taking in guests, by boarding and educating children (not very adequately) and by their dowries. Widows retired to them and noblemen found them a cheaper provision for their daughters than a husband, or an even greater convenience for ridding themselves of illegitimate or unmarriageable girls.

The convents generally housed at least three very distinct types of nuns. There were the ambitious, mostly of high birth, who looked upon the cloister as a career leading, if possible, to a position of authority in which they could exercise power, or at least win for themselves a considerable amount of freedom and ease. Then there were those for whom it was a refuge from a harsh world, outcasts from social life through some physical or mental disability, and some few because they possessed a vocation for the life, for there were always some of these, however unfavourable the environment for its true development. Lastly there were the rebels, condemned from childhood to a life they hated, or driven to it by widowhood, desertion or the fortunes of war. It was no wonder that among such a mixed community the vows of chastity, poverty and obedience were continually broken and continually having to be reinforced.

First, as to the heads or potential heads. These often lived in some luxury with a separate suite of rooms and servants, the excuse being that they had to entertain. They broke many a convent rule with impunity. In 1284 the Abbess of Romsey and Wherwell was keeping pet dogs and monkeys and "fared splendidly while her nuns went short". They could be impatient of control. Isobel Stanley, the prioress of Kings Mead, Derby, refused to pay rent to the Abbot of Barton, declaring: "I am a gentlewoman of the greatest of Lancashire and Cheshire, and that they shall know full well."

Many heads evidently took every opportunity of escaping into a merrier life, visiting friends and relations, attending marriages, and making pilgrimages or the business of the convent an excuse for travelling. Frequent are the admonitions to stay within the cloister walls, but these were gaily disregarded and bishops, abbots

40

and priors were forced to be content with demanding that they should always be accompanied by a nun or two on their journeys, ostensibly to act as chaplains, but also to see that they behaved themselves.

Chaucer was no caricaturist, nor was he prejudiced either for or against the Church. His keen and quizzical eye can be trusted, and in his Madame Eglentyne we probably get a true picture of an average prioress of the times, not corrupt, yet certainly not exemplary. She is much shrunk in stature from the great Anglo-Saxon abbesses, as she rides complacently on her enjoyable pilgrimage to Canterbury when she should have been attending to her nuns at home. She has her attendant chaperone as chaplain and conducts herself prudently, but her clothes are of a cut and a quality that would not have commended her to Gilbert of Sempringham, and her brooch with the motto "Love conquers all" could carry a secular as well as an ecclesiastical significance. Poverty and chastity are suspect and she keeps pets and obviously enjoys travelling, thus breaking at least two rules of obedience. She is of gentle birth and probably a little above the average in learning as she speaks French, though not with a good accent, and has some knowledge of music. There is no mention of Latin. It is easy to conclude that under her gentle lax rule her nuns did pretty well as they pleased.

A great deal depended on these heads of the religious foundations; if they were competent and conscientious, the tone of the community throughout was good and the average nun probably led a more or less contented busy life, divided between the duties of Martha and Mary. But given an unprincipled or lazy prioress, a disproportionate number of rebels, bitterness, intrigue and immorality were often rife.

Langland has none of Chaucer's detachment. He writes as a reformer and his picture of convent life is horrific:

> "all one chapitere it wiste
> of wijcked wordes. Wrath here wortes imade
> Til 'thow liest', and 'thon liest', lopen out at ones
> And eyther hitte other under the cheke
> Hadde they had knyves by Chryst, her eyther had killed other."

Langland concentrates on hatred within the cloister but there are more frequent witnesses to a laxity that seemed to increase in spite of all efforts. William of Wykeham wrote in 1387 of Romsey that the nuns brought pets of all sorts into the church and maintained hounds with the money that should have been given to the poor. This craving for pets came, of course, from stifling the natural instincts in those who were forced into convent life. The difficulty of how to avoid contamination with the outside world is always cropping up. Visitors could not be controlled and besides they brought much needed money with them, but they were always a disturbing influence. The Prioress of Langley in the fifteenth century complained about a certain Lady Audley who brought a great number of dogs with her when she came to stay and who also apparently took them in to the church — and, even back in the thirteenth century, Agnes de Vescy at Walton brought "with her a great number of women and dogs and other things which have interfered with the devotions of the nuns."

Besides the guests the practice of taking in children as boarders and pupils was discouraged because of its distractions. It became more and more difficult to impose chastity. Some nuns were regularly locked in at nights. During any time of national disturbance such as the Wars of the Roses, disorder and corruption increased and continual border warfare between Scotland and England disrupted the northern convents to a disastrous extent. Immorality and laxity increased until the Reformation, though in England it never reached such excess as in some foundations on the Continent.

The French poem "The Land of Co Kayne" satirises this laxity and immorality. The writer places his imaginary land in Spain, and there

> "Another Abbey is thereby
> Forsooth a great fair nunnery
> Up a river of sweet milk
> Where is plenty great of silk.
> When the summer's day is hot
> The young nunnes taketh a boat
> And doth them forth in that river
> ....
> They maketh them naked for to play
> ....

The young monks that hi seeeth
They doth them up and took they fleete
And cometh to the nuns anon.
And each monke him taketh one
And snellich beareth forth their prey
To the mochel grey abbey.
And teacheth the nuns an orison
With jamblence up and down."

And at Wennigsen near Hanover, the nuns used, so it was said, to chant the Black Mass lying on the floor of their choir with their arms and legs stretched out in the blasphemous mockery of the cross.

The chief trouble throughout arose from the considerable body of bitter and unhappy prisoner nuns. The strong-minded among these either became wilful and disobedient heads, or remained to disrupt the community by self-indulgence. Some few managed to escape into secular life. In 1290, for instance, "Agnes of Sheen, Joan of Carra, and a certain kinswoman of the Lady Ela, Countess of Warwick, professed nuns of Godstow, have fled from their house and casting off their habit, are living a worldly and dissolute life." But their escape was usually short-lived. The Church condemned them to excommunication, their families who had placed them in the convent were against them, the lovers for whom they had risked their souls often deserted them. They could not bear the weight of both divine and human condemnation, and most of them crept back to their cloister penitent and submissive.

Nevertheless there were many who sympathised with the plight of the prisoner nun as we learn from the literature of the period, for example the allegory "The Court of Love" (attributed to Chaucer):

"Se howe thei crye and wryng here handes white
For thei so sone wente to religion . . .
'Oure frendes wikke in tender youth and grene
Ayenst oure wille made us religious.'
And yet agayne warde shryked every nonne
The pange of love so strayneth heir to cry.
'Now woo the tyme,' quod they, 'that we be bourne!
This hatefull order uyse will done us dye!' "

The anonymous fifteenth-century poem "Why I can't be a

43

Nun" expresses the less usual point of view of the girl with a vocation who longs to take the veil but is warned by a dream that the convent has become too corrupt for any true bride of Christ. She is shown the inmates: Dame Pride, Dame Ypocrite, Dame Slowthe, Dame Veyne Glory and Dame Envi, "and a nother lady was there

<blockquote>
wonnyng (dwelling)
That hyzt dane love unordynate.
In that place bothe erly and late
Dame Lust."
</blockquote>

There was also Dame Disobedience, who distressed the girl more than all the rest so that: "I sped at great speed out of the gates, to escape from that convent so full of sin." The end of the poem is a contrasting nostalgic hymn of praise to the great and noble women saints of old.

Yet in spite of all the abuses satirised in the literature of the times, undoubtedly there were many who served God truly, though possibly more of these were to be found without rather than within the convent walls. Chaucer's "poore Parson" is as vivid and trustworthy a picture as his worldly Prioress and probably he could number among his parishioners hearts as humble and as holy as his own. There were besides those who felt called to a life of great simplicity and contemplation than could be found either within the cloister or in the secular world. These became anchorites or anchoresses and dwelt alone or in twos or threes in cottages or hermitages hard by a church — "anchored under the church as an anchor under a ship, so firm that the devil's storms . . . may not overwhelm it."[3] They were bound by no special ecclesiastical rule and varied in the amount they mixed with the world, but we know about their way of life from two famous contemporary sources. Sometime during the twelfth or early thirteenth centuries three anchoresses, who appear to have been sisters, applied to a friend (presumably a bishop or abbot or prior) to provide them with a Rule by which to govern their lives. The result was that appealing book *The Ancrene Riwle*, which became the most popular manual in use by anchoresses and also by many nuns right up to the Reformation, and the second source of information about anchoresses comes from the pen of the most famous of them all — Julian of Norwich.

The fact that the *Ancrene Riwle* was so popular and for so long is, in itself, a sign that all medieval nuns were not lax, hypocritical or power-seeking, for the standard of conduct here laid down is high indeed. It exhibits the very strong obsession with sin and temptation reminiscent of the early Fathers. Human nature is frail and is not to be trusted. The senses must be feared. Sight is dangerous:

"Love your windows as little as possible and see that they be small."

Speech is dangerous:

"Let our anchoress, whatsoever she be, keep silence as much as ever she can and may. Let her not have the hen's nature. When the hen has laid, she must needs cackle and what does she get by it? Straightway comes the chough and robs her of her eggs . . . and just so the wicked chough, the devil, beareth away from the cackling anchoresses, and swalloweth up all the good they have brought forth."

Hearing is dangerous:

"People say that almost every anchoress hath an old woman to feed her ears."

Above all, of course, should indulgence in seeing, speaking or hearing lead to any but a purely business communication with a man, that is a prime offence against their calling. "Take good heed now," saith our Lord, "if thou knowest not thyself, that is, if thou knowest not whose spouse thou art — Queen of Heaven."

The anchoress should be careful "not to draw upon her any capital sin with her five senses". She must fight temptation by prayer and meditation and "if she thinks that she shall be most strongly tempted in the first twelve months" she is mistaken. "For in the beginning it is only courtship, to draw you into love, but as soon as Jesus Christ, your spouse, perceives that he is on a footing of affectionate familiarity with you, he will now have less forebearance with you, but after the trial — in the end — then is the great joy."

There is wisdom and tenderness in this, as in many passages of the *Riwle*, for if, at times, the author seems to show a desert father negativism, his common sense, humour and affection keep breaking through. He is always courteous towards his three "dear sisters", carefully exonerating them from his strictures on anchoresses in general. For instance, when he is warning them against gossip, he exclaims:

"Christ knows, this is a sad tale, that a nunnery, which should be the most solitary place of all, should be amongst those in which there is the most idle discussion."

But he hastens to add: "Would to God . . . that all the others were as free as ye are of such folly." Or again, in talking of the sins of the flesh he says:

"Ye, my dear sisters, of the anchoresses that I know, are those who have least need to be fortified against these reputations . . . There is much talk of you, how gentle women you are; for your goodness and nobleness of mind beloved of many; and sisters of one father and of one mother, having in the bloom of your youth, forsaken all the pleasure of the world and become anchoresses."

The author bears in mind throughout that he is writing for women. He takes as illustrations to his homilies women from the Bible: the three Marys "who denote three bitternesses" — remorse, the ceaseless struggle against temptation and the longing for heaven. The analogies he chooses are also specially fitted for women to understand.

"And was not our Lord shut up in a maiden's womb. These two things belong to an anchoress, narrowness and bitterness. For a womb is a narrow dwelling where our Lord was shut up. And this word Mary, as had often been said, signifieth bitterness. If ye, then, in a narrow place endure bitterness, ye are like him – shut up as he was in Mary's womb."

Of course he is almost bound to expatiate on the frailty of woman, calling Ish-bosheth from the Book of Kings stupid to act so foolishly as to "appoint a woman to be his gateward, that is a feeble warden", but he does it with compassion and, refreshingly, Eve is only mentioned as being too talkative with Satan in contrast to Mary "who told the Angel no tale but asked him briefly that she wanted to know"! He is besides very sympathetic with women's physical weakness and though he warns the anchoress that she must be willing to suffer hardship for "let no one think that he can ascend to the stars with luxurious ease",

46

yet the *Riwle* is full of good advice as to the treatment of their bodies. "Whoever is infirm they may eat potage without scruple and no one is to fast upon bread and water except ye have leave." The sisters are to be sure to wear good thick shoes in winter but may go barefoot in summer and they are to have comfortable clothes, though of course without any ornament. If they are bled for any disorder, they ought to do nothing irksome for three days, or if they are dispirited or grieved about some worldly matter or sick, they should talk to their maids and "divert yourselves together with instructive tales. Thus wisely take care of yourselves . . . that ye may labour the more vigorously in God's service . . . for it is greatly folly, for the sake of one day, to lose ten or twelve." They may also wash as often as they please. Obviously masochism was no part of this monastic rule, in fact the wearing of "iron or haircloth or hedgehog skins" next to the flesh is expressly forbidden — moderation in all things should be aimed at, even in prayer: "Often, dear sisters, ye ought to pray less, that ye may read more. Reading is good prayer." Then, when praying the sisters should regularly remember those in distress, for it is possible to be absorbed in self even in the very act of spiritual meditation:

> "At some time in the day or night think upon and call to mind all who are sick or sorrowful, who suffer afflictions and poverty, the pain which prisoners endure who live heavily fettered with iron."

The occupations necessary to the nuns of a busy self-supporting convent, but dangerous as distractions from the spiritual life, are both needless and wrong for the anchoress who, once for all has chosen Mary's rather than Martha's role. She must never busy herself with husbandry, she may keep a cat but not a cow, as the cow would produce milk and butter and cheese, and this would be the thin edge of the wedge of secular business. For the same reason she must not take pupils, though an anchoress's maidservant can, if she wishes, teach "a little girl concerning whom it might be doubtful whether she should learn among boys". These maidservants must be carefully selected and looked after. Their rule of life is scarcely less rigorous than that of the anchoress. The laxity of convent servants was a constant source of trouble, so a strict discipline must be enforced especially where any man is concerned, but though firm it should be mild, "for such ought the instruction of women to be — affectionate and gentle and seldom seen".

The true anchoress then must be wholly devoted to prayer and meditation. She should "give her thoughts to God only" then joy and comfort is in store for her and all her hardship and pains will be as nothing: "Love makes all this easy." It is this positive bliss rather than the negative sense of sin and shame which is at the heart of the book. The author begins and ends on the same note of Divine Love. He is ravished by its glory and so his *Riwle*, for all its prohibitions, is a joyful book. His final word however is less exalted and brings him vividly to life, not as the medieval mystic, but as someone akin to any and every one who has finished an arduous job with a mixture of thankfulness and misgiving. He hopes he has done something that will be of use, if not he has certainly wasted a lot of time and

> "God knows, it would be more agreeable to me to set out on a journey to Rome, than to begin to do it again."

And for all his pains he begs his anchoresses

> "as often as ye read any thing in this book, gret the Lady with an Ave Mary for him who made this rule and for him who wrote it and took pains about it. Moderate enough I am, who ask so little."

It is worth noting that the four chief English books of mystical devotion which have come down to us from the Middle Ages were written either for women or by women. Richard Rolle, sometimes called the father of English mysticism, wrote for the nuns at Hampton. His works are purely devotional but probably were read in company with *The Ancrene Riwle* by most women contemplatives, among them the two with whom our next chapter deals, Julian of Norwich and Margery Kempe of Lynne.

4
Julian of Norwich and Margery Kempe of Lynne

Julian — or Juliana, as she is often called — of Norwich (1342-1413) was brought up in the Benedictine nunnery at Carrow. Her life corresponded to a time of distress and change. The great Schism and the growing abuse of Indulgences had brought the Papacy into disrepute and Lollardism was rapidly spreading in England. The Black Death and the Peasants' Revolt heralded the break up of the old feudal system. Laxity appears to have been the rule and not the exception among the monastic orders which, especially as far as women were concerned, were becoming fewer, smaller and poorer. But as always at such times of apparent failure, new life and light were stirring, sometimes in unexpected quarters. For many, especially among the laity, the teaching of Wycliff brought fresh inspiration, but for the mystic it hardly seems to matter under what rule or with what creeds they are nurtured. A few are vouchsafed to every age (even our age of Reason brought forth William Blake). In England Julian was immediately preceded by Richard Rolle (1290?-1349) and followed by Walter Hilton, and there was the author of the "Cloud of Unknowing", but although these writers sometimes seem to speak with one voice, there is no evidence of them influencing one another.

Julian chose the life of an anchoress and it was from her obscure little cottage that there flowed forth her *Revelations of Divine Love* which were to inspire succeeding ages, and, in due course, in our own day some of the poetry of T. S. Eliot and the music of Walford Davis and the writings of Evelyn Underhill. Her dwelling was "anchored" to the east end of Corrisford Church. It possessed three windows, one looking into the church itself, hard by the altar, one communicating with her maid's room and one looking out upon the churchyard, whence came the many men and women, rich and poor, to confide in and consult her.

The tension between the authority of the Church and the individual's own beliefs was becoming an increasing problem. Julian managed to resolve that tension, an extreme one for her as regards the wrath of God and the dogma of eternal damnation, for instance. She seems to have accepted, or rather to have bypassed the doctrine of the Church on such matters, but placed her own interpretations upon them. Always her visions, meditated upon and prayed over, were for her the final word. Possibly these were not fully understood, or even known, until after her death, or perhaps her obvious humble holiness had its effect. Otherwise one wonders how she got away with it for she is uncompromising in her repudiation of a revengeful Deity — "God is the Goodness that cannot be wroth, for He is nothing but Goodness" — and this in a world dominated by the fear of eternal punishment. When convinced of the truth of her beliefs her sex and her status are irrelevant.

> "Because I am a woman, ought I therefore to believe that I should not tell you the goodness of God, although I saw at that time that it is His will that it be known."

One reason why she was so sure of her message of Love was that she had waited a long while before pronouncing it: "From the time it was shewn I desired often times to know what was our Lord's purpose. And fifteen years after and more I was answered in spiritual understanding." She had prayed from youth onwards for three wishes to be granted — first that she might be given a vision of Christ's Passion, second that she should be visited by a serious illness through which she might grow in spiritual awareness, and thirdly that she might experience the three wounds: of contrition, of compassion and of longing towards God. These wishes, their classification and the granting of them belong to the framework of medieval thought and emotion but what she made of them during twenty years of contemplation belongs to all time.

Her book is based upon the lessons of Divine Love taught to her by her visions or "showings" and her musings upon them. Julian was no scholar but she possessed a natural and sweet power of expressing herself. She does not use argument or dogma to drive home her meaning. These anyway are of little use to the mystic who like the poet is always trying to express the inexpressible. Her images are clear and simple and remain in the memory. She describes the moment of vision when she saw the world like a little thing, like a "hazel nut lying in the palm of my hand. What may this be?" (she asks) "and it was answered — it is all that is made. I marvelled how it could last for it seemed so little." "It lasteth and ever shall because God loveth it. And so the world hath its existence by the love of God." Elsewhere she says: "I saw God in a point by which sight I saw that he is in all things." This is close to Blake's perception of the world in a grain of sand.

The sense of underlying unity behind all that is made seems to be a common experience of true mystics — so also the taking over by the spirit of the sentient part of being. Julian says of another vision: "And the bodily sight stinted but the spiritual sight dwelled in my understanding and I abode with reverent dread, joying in that I saw." So Wordsworth speaks of being "laid aside in body and becoming a living soul".

Another showing came when Julian was meditating on the saying that "Many waters cannot quench love". Again there is a vivid clarity in her description:

> "One time my understanding was led down into the sea bed and there I saw hills and dales appearing green as if it were moss covered with wrack and gravel. Then I understood thus – if a man or woman were under the ocean, if he could have sight of God just as God is with a man continually he should be safe and take no harm. And more than that; he should have more solace and comfort than all this world can tell."

But whatever shape her visions took, the significance was always the same — "Wouldst thou know thy Lord's purpose on this thing? Know it well. Love was His purpose. Who showed it thee? Love. What showed He thee? Love. Wherefore showed He it thee? For love." How then equate this Love with pain and evil? Suffering does not worry Julian as much as sin. This is because the Church laid so much emphasis on sin and its necessary punishment, dwelling far more on God the Aweful Judge than on God the Loving Father. Fiends were at least as numerous and certainly busier in this world than angels. Julian's preachings on Love were both original and daring. She does not take the easy path of dualism but wrestles with the problem both in herself and without. The sins of which she accuses herself, "impatience, sloth, despair or doubtful dread", are the last of which we can imagine her guilty. Patience, diligence and a singularly joyful serenity are the qualities which impress us most in her writings, but her sincerity is unquestionable and like most true saints, she suffered sometimes "the dark night of the soul". When her visions faded she was sometimes "left to myself in heaviness and weariness of life". We could not trust her if she had not known such weakness or confessed to such sins. She must also, with the sensitiveness of the seer and the poet, have agonised over the sorrows and sins of the world as she came to know them through her churchyard window. Her answer was grounded in belief in God's creative power and in the acceptance of finite limitations. She comes to the conclusion that "Sin is behovable, that it is serviceable for God will turn it to good". It is not part of reality as Love is, though it is always an injury to Love. "I believe it hath no manner of substance nor any part of Being nor could it be known but by the pain it is the cause of." As for the pain, it will not last, besides "He said not thou shalt not be tempested, thou shalt not be travailed, thou shalt not be distressed; but He said Thou shalt not be overcome."

A full acceptance of the mystery of sin and suffering brings peace:

"It behoveth that there should be sin. But all shall be well, and all shall be well, and all manner of things shall be well. For we shall see . . . that we have grievously sinned in this life and notwithstanding this, we shall see that we were never hurt in His love, we were never the less of price in His sight. For strong and marvellous is that Love which may not nor will not be broken for trespass."

Julian's *Revelations of Heaven* seem more inclusive, more satisfying intellectually and morally, more entirely acceptable and more homely than the Revelations of St John the Divine:

"As verily we shall be in the bliss of God without end . . . so verily we have been in the foresight of God, loved and known in His endless purpose from without beginning . . . In which beginning love He made us . . . And therefore when the Judgment is given and we be all brought up above, then shall we clearly see in God the priorities which now be hidden to us. Then shall none of us be stirred to say in any wise: 'Lord, if it had been thus, then it had been full well', but we shall say all with one voice: 'Lord, blessed mayst Thou be, for it is thus: it *is* well'."

Julian would have no truck with the doctrine of original sin: "and what time our soul is breathed into our body, mercy and grace also began working, having care of us and keeping, with pity and love." "For our natural will is to have God and the good will of God is to have us." The harsh fear-inspired tenets of the Fathers, the pitiless logic of Calvinism cannot stand up to this woman's conviction of creative Love. She never falls into the life-denying fanaticism that despises the body and the mind. In a classification which reminds us of the Cambridge Platonists, she speaks of "the natural love of our soul, and the clear light of our Reason and the steadfastness of our mind" (or will). All are necessary. Nor has Julian much trouble about the modern problem of a tension between a transcendent personal God "up there" and the indwelling God or Holy Spirit within. To Julian there was no difficulty in apprehending that God was in all things and yet at the same time "the courteous and dear worthy Lord for it behoveth God to be courteous to man".

This intimate relationship, lovely in its homeliness, is typical of women saints at this time: Julian, Brigitte, Catherine of Siena and later of St Teresa of Avila. It is perhaps something with which women especially enrich their worship. One meets it again and again even after the Reformation, for the rigours of Calvinistic Puritanism cannot altogether stamp it out. Of course without humility, self-discipline and sensitivity, it may easily and often alas did, degenerate into sentimentality, but with Julian we meet it in its highest and loveliest aspect. She never, like Margery Kempe, brings her Lord down to our level but always tries to raise us up nearer to Him — nor does she ever lose sight of His Infinity. With Julian too, in a supremely interesting manner, is stressed another aspect of Deity. Men had satisfied the need for a feminine element in their worship by exalting the Virgin to the rank of godhead. Julian's view of Mary was much more that of the Gospels and of the early Church — "a simple maid and meek, young of age and a little waxen above a child". It is the Son who is the great mother,

"our dear worthy Mother in the solace of true Understanding. All the fair working and all the sweet natural office of dear, worthy

53

Motherhood is impropriated to the Second Person of the Trinity. Our kind Mother, our gracious Mother, for that He would all wholly become our Mother in all things . . . Himself to do the service and the office of Motherhood in all things. The Mother's service is nearest, readiest, safest — nearest for it is most of nature; readiest for it is most of love, and surest, for it is most of truth."

Again Julian has no hesitation in speaking of

"our Mother Jesus – the kindly loving Mother who understandeth and knoweth the need of her child, she keepeth it most tenderly, as the nature and condition of motherhood will. And as it waxeth in age, she changeth her method but not her love."

So much for the views of those who, living more than five hundred years later, object to the ordination of women on the grounds that God is unequivocally and essentially masculine. Julian's "showing" of the twofold nature of the godhead not only provides for a deep psychological need, but also, if one thinks of God in these terms at all, must needs be a revelation of a profound truth. It is natural to her mystic vision of the unity of creation that she finds both male and female elements in the risen Christ, for he who is our dear Mother is also Adam, the universal man and woman, the indwelling spirit of humanity. "For Jesus is all that shall be saved and all that shall be saved is Jesus and he is the longing and desire of all mankind."

In her old age one of the visitors who came to Julian's churchyard window was a claimant to saintly visions of a very different type from the holy anchorite. Margery Kempe belonged to her age as obviously and was as limited by it as Julian was free of it. She has been wrongly classed as a mystic on the strength of her visionary imagination, but she was as egocentric as Julian was self-oblivious. She too wrote, or rather dictated, for she could not write herself, a unique document — a most lively account of her astonishingly different spiritual pilgrimage. She is paradoxically further from us than Julian because she is bounded by time and yet nearer to us because for all her aspirations and devotions, she was no saint but, in many ways, an ordinary very human woman. Her credulous faith, her excesses of tears, screams, howls and writhings, her physical toughness and terrifying vitality, all these are alien as is the world which her book recreates for us, a world of exhibitionism, of supersition, of pilgrimages involving incredible hardships, dangers, disease and filth, but also equally incredible excitement, beauty and emotional satisfaction. Yet as we read on of her husband, her neighbours, her lust for adventure and travel (in this respect she was like a pious Wife of Bath), she takes a humble but assured place among the Immortals.

Margery was born into a prosperous middle-class family about the year 1373. She married a worthy citizen of Lynne and bore him fourteen children. After the first baby's arrival she suffered a period of physical and mental illness not unfamiliar today, tried to take her own life and had to be tied down to her bed. From this unhappy state she was suddenly delivered by the sight of Christ, clad in a mantle of purple silk, who sat down on her couch and began to chat with her. From that moment she was on free and easy terms with Him and with all His heavenly host.

She continued to live out her normal and apparently very happy family life, but she wished to obtain recognition of the truth of her vision. It also becomes clear as we read further in her book that Margery could never resist talking about herself and her miraculous visions. She therefore went first to the vicar of St Stephen's at Norwich and asked for an interview of an hour or two with him. He lifted up his hands and said, "Bless my soul! How could a woman spend one hour or two talking about the love of God. I will not eat my dinner till I hear what she has to say about our Lord God which takes an hour to tell." Nothing could have pleased Margery more. She related to him with gusto the whole story and how subsequently at times she heard divine music and how she would fall down in paroxysms of mingled joy and sorrow. She had no difficulty in convincing the vicar. Two other Norwich notables however Margery felt must also be informed, a Carmelite hermit who was often visited by the Virgin Mary, and the famous anchoress Julian. The Carmelite was as favourably impressed as the vicar. As for the lady Julian, we only have Margery's own account of the visit, but even so we can read between the lines. Her comments on Margery's revelations are ambiguous and she is obviously not so impressed as the two men. "The Holy Spirit never inspires anything contrary to the love of God. I pray God to grant you perseverance. What you need is patience, for in patience you shall preserve your soul." Perhaps there was something so impressive about the old quiet voice speaking through the little window that Margery remembered it word for word long years afterwards for it sounds like Julian's authentic utterance. Patience was not Margery's characteristic virtue, but perseverance certainly was. Fortified by these visits she returned home determined to pursue her cult of holiness by first taking a vow of chastity after embarking on the physically perilous, but spiritually highly rewarding, pilgrimage to Jerusalem, for long and arduous though this was, it guaranteed a correspondingly quick and easy passage to Heaven.

The ever-present fear of what followed death was a dark shadow over the lives of those belonging to the later Middle Ages, the learned no less than the humble. It accounts for the growing number of chantry chapels and for the widespread expenditure on all ways of mitigating the pains of Purgatory. Sir Thomas More in his *Supplycacyon of Soulys* (1529) writes as one from the dead:

> "If ye pity any man in pain, never knew ye pain comparable to ours; whose fire as far passeth in heat all the fires that ever burned upon earth, as the hottest of all those passeth a feigned fire painted on a wall. If ever ye lay sick and thought the night long and longed sore for day, while every hour seemed longer than five, bethink you then what a long night we silly souls endure, that lie sleepless, restless, burning and broiling in the dark fire one long night of many days, of many weeks, and some of many years together."

No wonder pilgrimages were popular and indulgences sold like hot cakes, and wonder indeed that the lady Julian, brought up in such beliefs, familiar with the painted supernatural tortures in church and missal, could write in such utter denial of these and, instead, of the all-loving, all-forgiving, all-tender God.

Margery Kempe, however, though she was always an optimist, accepted the general beliefs of her times. After having borne fourteen children (and from the little or nothing that we hear of them, we may suppose that Margery was not by nature a very maternal woman) we can neither blame nor praise her for her leanings towards chastity. This vow too was held in much esteem as a sign of holiness and it was not uncommon for pious women, after a period of marriage and childbirth, to dedicate themselves forthwith as brides of Christ — it may have been a useful form of birth control. We do not know as a general rule what their husbands thought, but in this case we can make a good guess, for Margery's account is full and frank. The couple "had had gret delectacyn eythyr of hem in us yor of other" and John was not inclined to give up without a struggle. No man, however, could have much of a chance against Margery, backed up as she was by the express approval of Christ and His holy angels. John soon found himself impotent on approaching her and intimidated by this he decided to make the best bargain he could. She was a woman of substance, of which she had managed to keep control and he bargained with her that in return for paying his debts he would agree to a joint vow of chastity and to her Jerusalem journey. Presumably too he undertook to look after the children during her absence.

The pilgrimage was a great undertaking. It meant being away for more than a year, a huge outlay of expenditure and the hazards of bandits, hostile Saracens, rapacious landlords and relic vendors, storms, possible shipwrecks, innumerable delays, dirt, disease and almost perpetual acute discomfort. Nonetheless, as a sure passport to Heaven and as a splendid adventure with all its attendant kudos, there was never any lack of pilgrims. They travelled in companies — a sort of package tour — for safety and economy, and unfortunately Margery was exceedingly unpopular with her companions. At every meal time she told long, boring stories with herself as holy heroine or harangued them as to the state of their souls. She also subjected them to her noisy religious fits of ecstasy or weepings. By the time they reached Constance they could bear it no longer and left her behind. Undaunted she persuaded or bullied an old man into being her companion and together in midwinter without knowing a word of any language but their own, they crossed the Alps on foot and arrived in Venice actually before the others. They were amazed and horrified at seeing her and now began that perpetual questioning which harassed her companions whether at home or abroad. Was she inspired by God or the Devil? It was obviously important to know, for instance, when she decided to journey from Venice to Jerusalem by a certain ship, was it expedient to transfer to her vessel in order to insure a safe voyage notwithstanding the boredom of her company, or was it not? When a storm arose should the captain throw her overboard or ask her to pray for calm weather? It is impossible not to sympathise with their quandary. Usually Margery had such luck that over and over again she was vindicated. When she became too insufferable to be borne, a champion always appeared, a wandering friar falling under her spell, a lady of high degree hoping to make amends for a misspent life by befriending her. Storms abated at her behest and once when she was back home again at Lynne and a great fire had broken out, the people, still undecided whether or not this was the wrath of God descending on her native city to punish Margery for her presumption, in desperation and doubt besought her as a last chance to do what she could to help them. She prostrated herself with shrieks and groans before the altar of the parish church and she hadn't been at it for long before they rushed in shouting, "God hath wrought gret grace for us and sent us a fayre snowe to quenclyn wyth the fyr." From a sky "bryght and clear came cloudys and derkys". In all these cases had God not played up it would have gone ill with Margery, for no one could call her popular.

At Jerusalem she enjoyed herself to the full — rushing round from holy place to holy place, kissing and weeping and screaming and shouting and hearing voices and music without ceasing. Her vivid visual imagination fed on the pictures in the churches, the stained glass and statues, supplied her with solid manifestations. Indeed, she was not capable of distinguishing fantasy from reality and sometimes the evidence of her simple overwhelming faith is suddenly moving:

> "When this creature [herself] saw a crucifix or if she saw a man, or it might be an animal wounded, or if a man beat a child in front of her or struck another animal with a whip, it seemed that she saw our Lord beaten or wounded."

Again, when in Rome, she relates how she was called in by a poor woman once to drink wine with her and as she looked at her suckling her child, she was reminded of the Virgin and sat and wept and felt "This place is holy". It is not possible to call Margery either hypocritical or insane, in fact she only differed from many of her contemporaries in the intensity of her religious preoccupation and in the violence of her exhibitionism. Many of the pilgrims were overcome with emotion on first seeing the Holy Land and at their first sight of Jerusalem and at their vigil in the Church of the Holy Sepulchre. The accounts of their paroxysms recall the quaking of the early Quakers (whose spirituality no one calls in question). Perhaps the physical manifestations of emotion, so suppressed today except in the Pentecostal movements or, outside religion, in the realms of pop singers and football fans, are really a more or less healthy and necessary emotional outlet. Yet it is impossible not to feel that Margery overdid it and enjoyed the effect of, in her own words, "howlyng as it had been a dog". Certainly she was proud that the ecstatic scream vouchsafed to her for the first time at the Holy Sepulchre increased in occurrence from a month to once a week, then to a daily visitation, and once even to fourteen times in one day.

It would seem hardly possible to collect more years off purgatory, more virtue, more holy souvenirs after the Jerusalem tour, yet many pilgrims, Margery of course among them, were determined to go back via Rome where the same pattern was repeated. Rome specialised in early Christian martyrs. It was at this time a desolate and decaying city. A popular saint born only seventy years before Margery was the Swedish Brigitte who had spent years of her life trying to reform the Pope. She died in Rome and had been lately canonised and Margery happened to be in the city for her Saint's Day. Though very different in character, being a quiet self-effacing woman, Brigitte had certain points in common with Margery, as she too had married and had had a large family and had subsequently been vouchsafed visions. Probably stung by a desire to emulate both Brigitte and the more famous Catherine of Siena, Margery seems to have thought it high time to take further steps herself towards sainthood. Catherine and Brigitte were both notable brides of Christ and now Margery, kneeling in one of the Roman churches, heard God declare, "Dowtyr, I wil han ye weddyd to my God hede." It was like a child's dream. There were Saints Margaret and Catherine as bridesmaids and many angels, all one feels with special gleaming wedding wings, and God's voice clearly speaking out: "I take thee, Margery, for my wedded wyf, for fayren, for foweler, for richear, for powern." There is no better way of distinguishing the true mystic from the self-hallucinated aspirant than by the importance they attach to their visions. To Julian, Catherine and Teresa what is significant is the spiritual insight which is sometimes set going by such manifestations, but which depends for its development and continuance upon self-discipline and contemplation. True mystics warn against unquestioning acceptance of visionary experiences. St Teresa says:

> "In such matters as these there is always cause to fear illusion until we are assured that they truly proceed from the spirit of God. Therefore at the beginning it is always best to resist them."

Julian's "showings" led her to a fuller insight into the mystery of God's love for all men:

> "I saw full surely that ere God made us He loved us. . . . In our making we had beginning. But the love wherein He made us was in Him from without beginning – in which love we have our beginning . . . I saw God in a point by which sight I saw that He is in all things."

Margery's holy wedding dream led her only to the conviction that she was singled out by God and the chief preoccupation with which it left her was her determination from henceforth to dress only in white as more befitting Christ's spouse. This gave rise to endless trouble both on her journeys and at home. Anything out of the ordinary, any individual assertion led at that time to accusations of Lollarding. Margery's enemies were not slow to bring charges of heresy against her. Until the danger became uncomfortably close she dreamed of a splendid public martyrdom, but finding the immediate prospect of conviction terrifying when brought before the Archbishop of York, a famous anti-Lollard, she collapsed with one of her fits of fierce weepings and cries. "Why wepist thee so?" asked the Archbishop. Margery, never at a loss for an answer, replied that the day might come when he would wish *he* had wept for the love of God. Of course Margery was no Lollard and was able to refute all the counts against her, but the Archbishop, like most people, was uncertain how to treat her: "I hear seyn thou art a right wikked woman." Not even to save herself could Margery resist the retort based on the Prelate's far from blameless reputation — "Ser, so I hear seyn that ye are a wikkyd man . . . and ye shall nevyr come in Hevyn but ye amende you while ye ben her." Not surprisingly the Archbishop was both taken aback and furious: "Why, thou wrecche, what sey men of me?" But Margery was too much for him: "Other men, syr, can telle you wel anon."

It says much for both of them that the interview ended happily, the Archbishop finding no heresy in her. This was not quite the finish of the story. She was brought before him once again by two Franciscan friars, but this time they met as old friends and the Archbishop only said she must obtain a certificate of orthodoxy from the Archbishop of Canterbury. She could not help laughing as she left his presence. "Holy folke shelde not lawghe," remarked the steward. Little did he know, thought Margery. The Archbishop had tried at one point to make her swear not to teach or argue any more — a vain request indeed to which if she had agreed, she would certainly have broken her word whenever the next opportunity arose. "No, Sir, I will not swear that, the Gospel allows me to talk about God." The attendant clerics immediately weighed in with relief: "Ah, Sir, now we know well that she has a devil inside her because she talks about the Gospel. St Paul says no woman ought to preach." It was the same old story, but Margery was unabashed. "I am not preaching, Sir. I only use conversation and holy talk and I intend to do that as long as I live."

Maddeningly egotistical, self-satisfied, credulous, uncontrolled and a fearful bore, Margery yet had her points. She ranks far above the poor epileptic, visionary "Maid of Kent". She was brave and her faith gave her enormous moral courage and endurance. So, too, in spite of her frequent tears, she was a cheerful soul insisting that "It is full merry in Heaven" and laughing as often as she wept. She was generous, often giving away her money and goods right and left. She was compassionate. Her miraculous healing of a woman possessed by devils was really only the result of her gentle and kindly treatment, and when her husband became senile and incontinent in his old age, she stayed at home and nursed him patiently, remembering that once they had been happy lovers. After his death, when she herself by medieval standards was an old woman, she set out on one more great pilgrimage. She had squeezed in a visit to the Shrine of St James at Compostela only three years after Jerusalem and Rome, and then she had made herself equally unpopular with her fellow pilgrims. And now this last trip was to Aachen and once again her companions found her unbearable and tried to shake her off by going at a pace which in her old age she could no longer manage. "Ye forsakyn me for non other cawse but for I wepe whan I thynke on our Lordes Passyon." But the "wepinge" was far from silent and the homilies were incessant. However, as always, she found helpers, this time among some of the poorest and dirtiest of pilgrims who were glad enough of the company of such an obviously well-to-do and saintly lady. On her way home she made a pleasant stay at Sheen, where there was a newly founded convent of the Brigittine Order, which was a model of piety. It was for these nuns of the Syon Monastery that Thomas Gascoigne, Chancellor of Oxford (1403-58), wrote a devotional treatise, in which he exhorted the sisters to pay special attention to divine service from which once more we gather how widespread was the prevailing laxity:

> "They that have healthe and strength . . . they ought to be full hasty and redy to come to this holy service and loth to be thense. They ought not to spare for any slowth or dulness of the body, no yet though they fele some tyme a maner of payne in the stomacke or in the head, for lacke of sleape or indygestyon . . . For lyke as they that stirre up themselfes with a quycke and a fervent will thyderwarde ar helped forth and comforted by our Lorde's good anngels; right so fiends take power over them that of slowthe kepe them thense."

There follows a highly moral tale of a monk who was too sleepy to rise for matins until one morning he found a company of fiends who had come to fetch him "that cried against hym wyth fearfull noyse and hasty, often saynge and cryyng, 'Take hym, take hym, gete hym, holde hym' ". We may be sure that Margery never spared for any sloth and that she would have relished and believed completely Gascoigne's story.

On reaching home at last she determined to commit her spiritual experiences to paper as a final proof of her special claims to holiness. The project appealed both to her egotism and to her strong didactic urge. She had famous precedents: The Revelations of St Brigitte, St Catherine of Siena's Dialogue, and Julian's very recent *Revelations of Divine Love*. The only trouble was that Margery could not write. Her first scribe, sometimes erroneously said to have been her son, was obviously of German origin, probably a friend of her German daughter-in-law. He wrote in an almost unintelligible mixture of English and German, which his successor, a priest at Lynne, found very difficult to decipher. This, together with the usual uncertainty as to Margery's supernatural credentials (were they from Heaven or Hell?) seems to have put him off until, as usual, a miraculous sign intervened on her behalf. Suddenly in Church he was overcome with such an uncontrollable and inexplicable weeping fit that "he wett hys vestment and the ornaments of the Alter". He was immediately convinced that Margery's outbursts were God-given and he agreed to undertake the task. What with the obscurity of the first part of the book, the struggles Margery had with her memory and her storms of emotion, the book took a long while, probably about ten years, but when finished it seems to have been popular enough. For the next hundred years or so bowdlerised editions were printed with much of the racy secular part omitted. Then it was forgotten. It was not till 1934 that the original manuscript was discovered in Yorkshire and saw the light of a very different world.

Of what value is it to us? What possible contact can we find between Margery Kempe and ourselves? Travellers in time pass through many strange landscapes. In the Middle Ages we feel for the most part that we are in a fantasy world peopled by angels and fiends, apparently as real and as visually apprehended as the human beings with whose lives they are perpetually interfering. The background, too, appears to us rather like stage sets — some beautiful, some horrifying. Our senses are overwhelmed by lurid light, or unearthly unfathomable darkness, there are howls, groans, loud weepings and heavenly chants, powerful stenches and sweet scents, silks, velvets, sackcloth and hedgehog skins. Only here and there we recognise with relief some homely familiar object, such as the anchorite's cat, a child at play, or a meadow full of daisies. Far above, certainly, the eternal Sun of the Mystics shines on us, if we could apprehend it, as it did on Julian and the author of *The Ancrene Riwle*, but that light is not of this earth.

The link between ourselves and the world of Margery Kempe lies in the basic human emotions. Self-love and self-giving, for instance, are the same in any age though dressed up in different clothes and expressing themselves in different ways. Margery's book, for all its credulous beliefs and violently expressed emotion, is a very recognisable human document and it tells us both frankly and simply what she and her neighbours believed and how they behaved. It does for us in fact what Chaucer does for us in fiction, and coming when it did in the first part of the fifteenth century, it is a bridge book between an earlier age of anonymity and sacerdotal authority and the more personal and secular world of the Renaissance and Reformation. Some seventy years later with Margery Paston's letters, we are breathing a different and more familiar air altogether. The angels and the fiends have dematerialised — "Farewell rewards and fairies". Soon the stained glass and the statues will go and the last abbess will ride away from her convent to deliver up her keys. Christian women in Protestant England must henceforth do without their pilgrimages, their relics, their solid supernatural visitations, their ever compassionate Queen of Heaven, and must seek new sources of inspiration and fresh outlets for their faith and their service.

5

The Virgin Mary

The cult of the Virgin Mary from the fifth to the sixteenth centuries is of great importance in any study of women and Christianity. Her influence had been growing throughout the ages and she was by far the greatest of the saints whose worship was swept away by the tide of Protestantism that engulfed England at the Reformation.

It must have been an extraordinarily traumatic experience for the mass of the people who had been accustomed to ascribe to the Virgin divine honour and power, to see the Queen of Heaven deposed and disgraced — her statues broken and banished from her lovely Lady Chapels, which had been increasing in number and magnificence throughout the fifteenth and early sixteenth centuries. In some of them the gilt had hardly dried, in some the craftsmen, in defiance, still carved faces of the Madonna in some obscure unfinished corbel or choir stall. The loss was the more terrifying because there had gradually grown up the belief that it was Mary who stood between the judgment of God and frail humanity. "Perhaps you fear the divine majesty," said St Bernard. "Appeal to Mary. There is pure humanity in Mary . . . and I say it for certain, she too will be heard for reverence of her." And Bonaventura wrote, "She restraineth the Son that he should not punish."

From this "pure humanity" they were now remorselessly separated and women perhaps felt the deprivation more than men, for when the ideal of celibacy as a supreme virtue was destroyed in men's minds, they had less need for the worship of Mary as a sublimation for their passions, whereas the women still yearned for the tenderness of the Mother Goddess.

The sources of Mariology as a cult lie far back in the middle of the fifth century when, at the Council of Ephesus, the title Theotakos, Mother of God, was formally bestowed upon her — though not without some opposition. What had happened was that gradually the worship of ancient fertility deities had penetrated from the East into Christianity. The need for a female goddess was too deeply ingrained to be denied and there was Mary ready to take over.

Apuleius, second-century Roman platonist, prays thus:

> "Whether thou art Ceres, mother of the grain . . . whether thou art heavenly Venus who first united the sexes in love – whether thou art Phoebus' sister, who dost help women in confinement . . . whatever thy name, whatever the rite, in whatever form it is permitted to invoke thee, come to help me . . . O thou holy one, perpetual saviour of mankind . . . thou dost give a mother's sweet affection to the wretched and unfortunate."

The Virgin succeeds to all these titles, honours and duties.

> "Orthodox and heterodox magic were kindled at the same fire and fanned by the same breezes; in Church, the women crowded round Mary, yet they paid homage to the older deities by their nightly fireside."[4]

Through Gnostic influence the Virgin also became identified with Sophia, the Spirit of Wisdom, the feminine counterpart of the Logos. At Ephesus she replaced the famous Diana and the town laid claim to her sepulchre. In many places, among them the Erechthon on the Acropolis, temples dedicated to Athene, Minerva, Isis, Cybele and Juno were re-consecrated to Mary. There is an interesting connection between the willow tree used by Homer and other classical writers as a symbol of chastity and the trees sacred to the Mother Goddesses and the Virgin. The willow was chosen because it loves to be near water, a source of life; yet, too, it was planted near graves, so like the Earth Mother it gives life and receives it back.

But also it does not propagate itself through seeding and fruit and so became a symbol of virginity. At the feast of Demeter women dedicated themselves to chastity by lying on a bed of willow branches. The symbol survives in the cult of Mary. A medieval work in praise of her describes the willow in terms derived from Pliny:

> "Its seed, if drunk, produces infertility. This was fulfilled in the Blessed Virgin for she elected Virginity and so chose an unfruitful life, but as the willow loves to grow by the waterside, so did

the blessed Virgin flourish by the waters of grace and heavenly gifts."[5]

She became the special protector of pregnant women in place of Juno. She was the star of the sea whose duty it was to watch over sailors. In some cases even we have the closest resemblance between the earliest representation of the Virgin and the Infant Christ and those of Isis with Horus upon her knee. In the Coptic liturgy the feasts of Mary in May, August and September correspond to the seasons of sowing, harvest and vintage.

St Gregory wrote to St Augustine of Canterbury not to destroy the pagan temples in Britain but to sprinkle them with holy water and rededicate them — in many cases the rededication of a female deity would have been to Mary, and worshippers would have drawn little distinction at first between the Virgin and the pagan goddess. Sometimes the Virgin's name is directly associated with some particular heathen divinity. In Antwerp up to recent times there was an ancient idol which was hung with flowers by women praying for children. Above it was a figure of Mary. In Germany her name was joined to that of the goddess Sif and in the Mosel district there is a church dedicated to Mariasif.

But Mary had one great advantage over the old goddesses: she was fully human. This made her at once more available, more understanding and, as a last resort, more efficacious. For as a unique being she was not simply one among many female deities, she alone was the Theotakos and could command the ear of the All-powerful.

> "Moder and mayden was never none but she,
> Well coulde such a maiden
> Goddess mother be."

As such she was, for men, nurtured in an ascetic tradition, a necessity as an outlet for their suppressed sexual emotions. Taught by the Church to despise earthly beauty, they could satisfy their natural craving by exalting as a figure of ideal beauty Mary, the Queen of Heaven, because she was also the Holy Virgin, pure Chastity itself.

For women, the despised and exploited daughters of Eve, she could also be a greater comfort through her humanity, for was she herself not a woman, had she not born a child and watched him die; did she not know all the special sufferings that were woman's inescapable sad lot on her earthly pilgrimage? But besides, to both men and women alike, she was the symbol of maternity, the giver of life and of that security for which all humanity yearns.

A medieval engraving shows Mary upon a throne, close to, and only slightly lower than, the thrones of the Trinity "and the four figures are enclosed in the sacred oval of the mandala, symbol of the Unity of God and the Cosmos".[6]

The growth of the worship of Mary was gradual and different aspects were emphasised by succeeding centuries. During the fifth and sixth, when asceticism as a revolt from the decadence of the failing Empire was at its height, it was her virginity which was stressed. Later, the miraculous details of her birth, life and death supplied by a large apocryphal wealth of legend, in lieu of the extremely inadequate information of the Gospels, became of first importance in establishing her as the divine Madonna. She was accepted as more and more on a level with her son in holiness, and the doctrines of the assumption and of the immaculate conception were evolved to free her from the universal stain of sin. By the late Middle Ages her chief role was that of the compassionate mediator and so great was her redemptive power that it was held to reach back even to the first great sin of all, converting it into a blessing:

> "Ne had the apple taken been,
> The apple taken been
> Ne had never Our Lady
> A-been heavenè queen.
>
> Blessed be the time
> That apple taken was
> Therefore we moun singen
> Deo gracias!"
> (Fifteenth-century carol)

St Bernard was the first to expatiate on the theme of Mary as redeemer, drawing the parallel between her as the second Eve, even as Christ was the second Adam. The Cistercians established themselves as the great champions of Mary, but Dominicans and Franciscans also laid claim to her special love and protection.

The Virgin of the Middle Ages was very feminine and in France

68

she became the Grande Dame, whose most marvellous palace was the cathedral of Chartres. She is most particular about the honour which she demands as her due — anyone lacking in this is very soon made aware of his shortcomings, but those who show her particular attention are granted mercy even if they are pretty far gone in wrongdoing. The devil complains with some justification that

> "She it is who doeth us the most harm, seeing that she through her mercy and indulgence brings in and saves those whom her Son in His justice hath damned and given to perdition."[7]

Combined with her function as the compassionate mediator was her role as the All-Beautiful. The sensuous myth of Mary as the perfect ideal of womanhood merged into the chivalric pattern of thought which dominated Europe in the thirteenth and four-teenth centuries. Madonna (My Lady) now became for the first time the name by which the Virgin was most frequently honoured. Knights fought battles in her name. She inspired brave deeds, it seems sometimes even that she herself enjoyed a fight: there is a legend that she once deputised for a knight while he was attending mass. She was also the confidante of all lovers and was the inspiration of all poets, minstrels and jongleurs. There is a well-known charming medieval story of the tumbler who became a monk but did not know how to perform the proper offices. "To leap and to jump, this he knew but nought else," so instead he decided to "serve the Mother of God in her Church after mine own manner. . . . Then he began to turn somersaults, now high, now low, first forwards, then backwards, and then he fell on his knees before the image and bowed his head. 'Ah, very gentle Queen!' he said, 'of your pity and of your generosity despise not my service'." The tumbler did this every day secretly in the crypt but a brother monk discovered him and told the Abbot. The Abbot went with this monk and they hid themselves where they could watch and they saw the tumbler caper and dance until he fell to the ground exhausted. And then "there descended from the vaulting so glori-ous a lady that never had he seen one so fair or so richly crowned, and never had another so beautiful been created. . . . And the sweet and noble Queen took a white cloth and with it she very gently fanned her minstrel before the altar . . . and greatly did the noble and gracious Lady concern herself to aid him".

Nobility, generosity, courtesy — these were the qualities especially of the French madonnas, who were even allowed a little wilfulness and caprice. The worship of Mary became almost a separate religion. Certainly she was far the most loved of any saint. Her popularity probably inspired Dante to make a woman the means by which he attains salvation, for Beatrice in the *Divine Comedy*, like Mary, was both complete woman and divine goddess.

Yet it would be a mistake to equate the chivalric romantic cult with Mariology for there was no exaltation of mother love in the secular literature of the time, whereas Mary, though the Queen of Heaven, was only so in relation to her child. For women naturally the motherhood of Mary made the strongest appeal, and it is in this relationship that they saw her most vividly.

There is one story amongst the vast accumulation devoted to her life and miracles which tells of a mother who besought the Virgin for the release of her only son who was imprisoned. At last she went into the church and stole the Christ child from the Virgin's arms saying, "Holy Virgin, I have begged you to deliver my son and you have not done so. Very good! Just as my son has been taken away from me, so I am going to take away yours and keep him as a hostage." The plan worked and the Madonna forthwith set free the imprisoned boy and said, "Tell your mother, my child, to return me my Son, now that I have returned hers." Such a legend both illustrates the fellow feeling that existed between the humble human mother and the holy "Theotakos" and the simplicity of the medieval worshipper who did not distinguish between the statue and the spiritual being. (Such simplicity is by no means confined to the Middle Ages.)

Perhaps in England the Virgin was honoured more as a mother and rather less as the romantic Queen of Heaven. In the guild miracle plays Mary is depicted as the lowly human maid of Julian's vision. She is Joseph's "sweet dear" and, in the Chester cycle, he even fetches two midwives to help in the birth:

> "For though in thee be God from high
> Coming as mankind,
> Yet a woman should help thee
> For custom's sake as thanks me,"

and Mary welcomes their ministrations — though the baby is born
without pain or travailing.

A little anonymous song of a very poor and humble Virgin
breathes the spirit of universal maternal tenderness:

> "Jesu, sweete sone dear,
> On poorful bed liest thou here
> And that me grieveth sore:
> . . . Jean, sweete, be not wroth,
> Though I n'ave clout ne cloth
> Thee on to folde ne to wrap,
> For I n'ave clout ne lap;
> But lay thou thy feet to my pap
> And wite thee from the cold"

and other English medieval poems in praise of Mary stress her
motherhood:

> "Of care conseil thou art her
> Of alli weary thou art rest.
> Feix fecundata
> Mater honorata."

> "He came all so stille
> There his mother was
> As dew on Aprille.
> That falleth on the grass."

Chaucer's Prioress, in a prologue to her tale, which becomes her
calling more than her habilements, addresses the Virgin as:

> "O Mader Mayde! O Mayde Mader free!
> O bush unbrent, brenninge in Moyses sighte
> . . . .
> That ravisedest down fro the deitee
> Thurgh thyn humblesse, the goost that in th'alighte
> Of whos vertu, whan he thyn herte lighte
> Conceived was the father's sapience
> Help me to telle it in thy reverence."

The humble suppliants of the compassionate Mary did not trouble
about dogma, especially if they were women. They craved aid from
a powerful deity who was at the same time as feminine and as
immortal as the ancient goddesses and yet was more accessible,
more human, and in the mother of Christ they found her. She

was never depicted as an awesome figure, austere and forbidding, even when angry she was so in a thoroughly familiar way and soon appeased by a little extra attention. Mary, then, more than all the other saints put together, and certainly more than the persons of the Holy Trinity, brought relief from that inexorable logic in the matter of salvation or damnation:

" 'Let us go secretly to the Queen and promise a present'. Women felt this need even more than men, for they had most reason to rebel against that priestly rigorism which condemned the dance and all elaboration of dress . . . which even in natural beauty itself often saw one of Satan's deadliest snares . . . Above all, women must have revolted against the doctrine of infant perdition. Was she reconciled to that which Acquinas himself could not attempt to explain away: that it is not her duty even to pray God's mercy for this godforsaken flesh of her own flesh."[8]

It is interesting to note that in a table based on a return of Catholic recusants made in England in 1603, the number of women outnumbers the men by half as much again. This may have been because women are by nature more conservative and cling more to the old Faith, but it may also be because the worship of the divinely human and merciful Virgin still appealed most strongly to women through her shared experience of motherhood.

Universal belief in the Fall through Eve and the subsequent cause of original sin lay like a shadow over all ideas about sex and birth, inextricably confusing these with evil. The psalmist's cry, "In sin did my mother conceive me", originally meant as a general statement of the universality of evil in the world after the Fall, was often given a special significance. Mary had somehow to be freed from all taint while yet remaining human and so the two doctrines of the Assumption and of the Immaculate Conception grew up. The first offered less difficulty, the punishment of death incurred by the Fall could not be avoided, but Mary was held to have been delivered immediately from the chains of death and to have been taken straight up to heaven. Her body did not know corruption. Her conception involved more argument. Anselm held that Mary was not only conceived but born in sin like everyone else, but St Bernard tried to set her apart:

> ". . . celebrate her, who in conceiving knew no concupiscence nor pangs in giving birth . . . [for] she received in the maternal womb the grace necessary that she be born holy."

She was thus not only to be a pure Virgin at Christ's conception and birth but also to be untouched by original sin at her own birth. But then Bernard became tied up in a good many theological difficulties and he ends by asserting that after all only Jesus Christ was conceived without sin.

> "So the glorious one [Mary] will gladly do without this honour with which sin seemed to be honoured or she is to be clothed with a false sanctity."

Thomas Aquinas tried to resolve the question by asserting that Mary contracted original sin at her conception but was cleansed of it before birth. Bonaventura upholds him saying that she suffered the penalty of original sin, i.e. sorrow and death. Arguments continued about this, though all agreed upon her perpetual virginity. Any brothers or sisters to Christ mentioned in the Gospels were dismissed as cousins. Franciscans were inclined to support the immaculate conception as doing most honour to Mary and Dominicans to oppose it because it made Mary equal to Christ, less perfectly human and erred against the Augustine teaching about original sin. (It was not, however, till 1854 that Pius IX declared that the doctrine that Mary was preserved immune from all stain of original sin had been revealed by God "and therefore is to be believed firmly and constantly by all the faithful", and not till the mid-twentieth century that both doctrines of Assumption and Immaculate Conception were established as dogmas. The trend of present-day Catholicism in its new emphasis on Mariology seems to be aiming at a religious form of the popular exaltation of humanism but this concentration on the Virgin is as unacceptable as ever to the Protestant world.) But up to the Reformation men and women were left free to choose between the more holy or the more human Mary. However, there is no doubt that she was both holy and human enough to satisfy the need for a merciful and yet a powerful advocate. What was lost by her overthrow? The exaltation of Mary had saved men and women from the despair engendered by the doctrine of original sin accompanying the belief in a just and omnipotent God Who was bound to punish

73

the wrongdoer. Mankind has always craved both mercy and justice. Christ, who in the Gospels is the merciful one, is after his ascension absorbed into the Trinity and is thenceforth one with God. There remained Mary, the one being who was at the same time and for ever perfectly human and perfectly good, and could therefore dispense mercy alone, leaving justice to the Omnipotent. After the repudiation of Mary by the Reformation, the Virgin's free-for-all compassion was succeeded by the arbitrary gift of grace. Calvinism became the substitute for Mariology, and a difficult harsh substitute it often proved. John Calvin taught the total depravity of the human race, even more uncompromisingly than Augustine. It is the greatest pity that Augustine, perhaps the greatest figure in Christianity since Paul, should have been obsessed by his own lack of chastity.

> "When St Monica drove Augustine's eighteen years' paramour, the mother of his son, back from Milan to Africa, something went with her which Christendom and Augustine needed almost as much as they needed St Monica."[9]

The Augustine view of sex mattered not only to the Middle Ages but through his influence on Calvin it came to present an even more harmful aspect. Calvin wrote in *Christianae Religionis Institutio*:

> "For our nature is not merely bereft of good, but is so productive of every kind of evil that it cannot be inactive. Those who have called it concupiscence have used a word by no means wide of the mark, if it were added (and this is what many do not concede) that whatever is in man, from intellect to the will, from soul to the flesh, is all defiled and crammed with concupiscence. Old writers often shrink from the straightforward acknowledgment of the truth in this matter. . . . Even Augustine is not always emancipated from that superstitious fear."

As man was thus incapable of goodness, he could be saved only by special grace because his own apparent merits were worthless. As obviously not all receive this grace, for Hell (and all then believed in its literal existence) was well populated, so God must exercise an apparently arbitrary choice as to who should be saved and who damned, and the disappearance of Mary, the all-merciful, who need not trouble herself about justice, left a gap which was filled by the doctrine of predestination, a source both of great strength and of great agony. Calvinism took over as the most potent influence after the Marian Protestant exiles returned to England from Geneva. For it was a positive and logical creed and therefore laid hold strongly on men's minds but it was essentially a masculine way of thought. Like all great conceptions, the fruit of some great mind, it became degraded by the lesser minds who adapted it to their own prejudices. John Knox, one of its chief exponents, held women in contempt.

Since St Bernard Mary had been allowed to redeem Eve and her suffering was held to complete the suffering of her Son:

> "Mary's grief gave to Christ's passion an additional intensity and a human quality especially that otherwise would be profoundly lacking . . . Jesus could suffer everything except the compassion for His own sorrow."[10]

So a modern French Dominican expresses what many must have felt as a profound truth, for if the cross is to symbolise the height of suffering for humanity, it must include that of experiencing the death of the beloved and this Mater Dolor was one of the aspects of the Virgin most precious to women. But the Protestant reformers justifiably rejected the apocryphal Mary with her long usurpation of divinity. They could not indeed banish her entirely and at once. Luther himself wrote:

> "She is my love, the noble Maid
> Forget her can I never.
> Whatever honour men have paid
> My heart she has for ever."[11]

In parish churches and cathedrals throughout the land, in stained glass and obscure bits of carving, her emblems — the mystic Rose, the burning Bush, the Ark which contained the treasure — remained, though the statues and pictures were defaced or cast out. Even so devoted an Anglican as George Herbert in the seventeenth century uses her sacred symbolism in his poetry and with a lovely courtesy apologises in "To All Angels and Saints" for being unable to worship her:

> "Not out of envie or maliciousnesse
> Do I forbear to crave your special aid:

        I would address
My voice to thee most gladly, blessed Maid
And mother of my God, in my distress.

Thou art the holy mine whence came the gold,
The great restorative for all decay
                In young and old;
Thou art the cabinet where the jewell lay;
Chiefly to thee would I my soul unfold.

But no, alas, I dare not; for my King
Whom we do all joyntly adore and praise
                Bids no such thing."

Herbert's regret would no doubt have earned him a stern rebuke
from contemporary Calvinists, but it represents a feeling that
some quality was lost when the feminine element represented by
Mary was banished from Christianity. It seems sad that instead
terms such as "the great masculine symbol of the fatherhood of
God . . . inevitable in every living religion's conception which is
not disposed to dissolve itself into abstractions of formal logic"
should emphasise the one-sidedness of established Christianity, or
that a modern Protestant writer can talk of *the contamination*
of the Gospel by the eternal feminine of the cult of Mary". True,
the substitution of the apocryphal Mary for the historic Christ
was fraught with superstition and unreality, but it none the less
represented a real need. We should try and learn more from the
true mystics who "see into the heart of things". If the Reformers
could have shared Julian of Norwich's vision of Divine Love which
combined both the Fatherhood and the Motherhood of God, they
would have taken a step nearer to truth.

6
The Reformation

The fresh inspiration that brought new life to the Christian Eng-
lishwoman in place of her traditional rituals was found first and
foremost in the vernacular Bible. "Mother," wrote a Lincolnshire
squire in 1536, "you have much to thank God that it would please
him to give you licence to live until this time, for the gospel of
Christ was never so truly preached as it is now. Wherefore I pray
to God that he will give you grace to have knowledge of his scriptures." Access to the Bible was an immense and revolutionary
influence in the lives of countless women who for the first time
were able "to read, mark, learn and inwardly digest" the Word of
God for themselves. For the vernacular translations coincided with
the growth of literacy and with the rapid spread of the primitive
press. Thomas Becon, More, Vives and Erasmus were all in favour
of a better education for women. Becon especially wished and
worked for the establishment of girls' grammar schools: "Is not
the woman the creature of God so well as man? . . . they do no
less deserve well of the Christian commonweal." The development
of the Reformation was the direct result of the deepening of individual responsibility and of judgement with the corresponding
weakening of the influence of the priesthood due to the importance
which the Bible assumed in the life of the nation.

The study of the Scriptures by the laity had been sternly suppressed as Lollardism, but Tyndale's New Testament (1526) broke
through the barrier and less than ten years later this was followed
by Coverdale's complete Bible. It is to this that the exultant letter
quoted above refers. The first Authorised Bible, a revision of
Coverdale's with a preface by Cranmer, followed in 1540 and the
first to be divided into chapters and verses with pictures and maps
was the Geneva Bible published in 1560. This, the work of Marian
exiles, was annotated with a commentary strongly Calvinistic in
tone and, because of its manageable size and clearer presentation,
was significantly the most popular of all translations until the

publication of the Authorised Version of James I. It was dedicated to Elizabeth exhorting her to be "bold and strong in God's quarrel with Satan, the old dragon".

The aim of all these translations was to create a scripturally-educated laity so that Erasmus's dream might come true that *"all good wives* should read the Gospel and Paul's Epistles, . . . that out of these the husbandman should sing while ploughing, the weaver at his loom; that with such stories the traveller should beguile his wayfaring. . . ."

Something very like this did come about with tremendous consequences. For centuries the only books to be found in the majority of English homes were the Bible, together with Foxe's *Book of Martyrs* and Bunyan's *Pilgrim's Progress*. Of these the Bible was chief — the guide, the comforter, the encyclopedia of knowledge, the unequalled story book, but above all the Sacred Word of God. Even should the housewife be unable to read, some member of her family or a neighbour would read a daily chapter to her and she would hear it regularly expounded every Sunday at Church, where preaching and reading had taken the place of the Mass as the focus of religious life.

Bible stories ousted the old legends of the saints. The heroines, especially of the Old Testament — Naomi and Ruth, Rebecca and Rachel, Deborah and Hannah — were now better known than Barbara or Ursula, Dorothea or Catherine. Their courage and constancy were a fresh and compelling source of inspiration and women could read about them for themselves in the dramatic Hebrew narratives translated into their own creative prose. Their example was to bear fruit in the days of trial to come. Elizabeth herself liked to be called the Deborah of her people. There was one New Testament saint, however, who in the Reformed Church swallowed up all the other saints. This was St Paul, and the emphasis placed upon his teaching, including his supposed doctrine of the subjection of women, had an unfavourable influence when Puritanism dominated the country. On the other hand, the Gospel story, now so freely and widely read, restored a full humanity to the conception of Christ. The narrative of Jesus's life here on earth, studied first-hand, made clear and undeniable the merciful aspect of his attitude towards women and children. He became for them once again the Good Shepherd and divine Friend. When Mary

Tudor tried to set the clock back she found that the habit of reading the Scriptures in the vernacular was too firmly established in the hearts and affections of her people to be denied. Perhaps more than anything else, this was to destroy her purposes. In the examination of the Marian martyrs, time and again the argument centres on the new knowledge of the Bible. "My Lord, if you speak to me of St Paul, then speak English", and: "She said she believed as much as Holy Scripture agreed unto" (Foxe's *Book of Martyrs*).

Biblical scholarship was not confined to men. The influence of the Renaissance "before the Yoke of Rome had been replaced by the Yoke of Geneva" affected the education of studious girls. Like the Saxon abbesses of old, these Renaissance scholars were either of noble blood or of the aristocracy. The Princesses Mary and Elizabeth, Lady Jane Grey, Lady Jane Howard, Margaret Roper (daughter of Sir Thomas More), Elizabeth Woodford (also of his household), the four daughters of Sir Anthony Cooke, all these had the advantage of being tutored by some of the greatest scholars of the age — Ascham, Aylmer, Cranmer and Foxe. Nicholas Udall, a friend of Erasmus, wrote to Catherine Parr of

". . . the great number of noble women at that time in England, not only given to the study of human sciences and strange tongues but also so thoroughly expert in Holy Scriptures that they were able to compare with the best writers . . . as also translating good books out of Latin and Greek into English . . . It was now no news in England to see young damsels in noble houses and in the courts of princes, instead of cards and other instruments of idle trifling, to have continually in their hands either Psalms, homilies or other devout meditations, or else Paul's epistles, or some book of holy scripture matters."

This ardour comparable to the devotion and enthusiasm of the early abbesses, can partly be accounted for by the spirit of discovery and excitement which a reinvigorated but not yet established faith brings to any age, and also by the fresh access of interest and power the new learning gave to women.

The very first of these Renaissance scholars belongs actually to pre-Reformation times. She was Lady Margaret Beaufort, mother of Henry VII and great-grandmother of Elizabeth I:

"She was a gentlewoman, a scholar and a Saint and after having been three times married, she took a vow of celibacy. What more could be expected of any woman!"

So wrote Elizabeth Wordsworth, the first principal of Lady Margaret Hall, Oxford, one of the foundations to be called after this notable and pious scholar. She was a great friend of Fisher, Bishop of Rochester, and was inspired by him to direct her patronage away from monastic foundations towards the endowment of schools and colleges. She endowed the Lady Margaret Professorship of Divinity, bestowed upon Erasmus — and held today for the first time by a woman, Dr Morna Hooker. It was at Queen's College also, under the patronage of Lady Margaret Beaufort, that Erasmus prepared his revised edition of the New Testament which set the great ball of Biblical scholarship rolling throughout Europe. Christ's College, Cambridge, was extended and established in law by Margaret, who caused a little oratory to be built for her in the Master's Lodge from which she could watch the services in the chapel below. She exercised maternal care over the scholars and is said to have urged the Master to deal "softly, softly, softly" with them. She was one of the noble patrons of Caxton's Printing Press and it was for her that the beautiful and famous first printed edition of Hilton's *Scale of Perfection* was issued. At her death Fisher spoke of her as a "mother to the students of both Universities".

Perhaps the greatest prodigy and the most tragic of the Renaissance and Reformation women scholars was Lady Jane Grey. As a little girl she knew some Latin, Greek, Spanish, Italian and French, and later she taught herself Hebrew Arabic, in order to study the Biblical texts at first hand. She was tutored by Bishop Aylmer. There is the well-known story of how Ascham, visiting Aylmer, found all the company out hunting except the Lady Jane Grey who was reading Plato "with as much delight as some gentlemen would read a merry tale in Boccacio". She herself put her love of learning down to the fact that "one of the greatest benefits that ever God gave me was that he set me so sharp and severe parents and so gentle a schoolmaster". She loved theology and was a firm, and at times a furious, Protestant. She comes down to us in history not as the poor puppet queen of eight days but, for all her youth, as an example of the spiritual strength which a true religious education in the humanities can bring to a woman.

Of Sir Anthony Cooke's four daughters, Katherine became the close friend of Edward Dering, a powerful Elizabethan Puritan preacher. Of her it was written:

"All Greece and Rome did in her numbers shine,
The sacred language too she made her own.
Nor Eastern learning was to her unknown."

Another daughter translated from the Latin a tract on the Sacrament. A third, who became the mother of the great Francis Bacon, was a redoubtable and rather terrifying Calvinist and she too translated an important work, the *Apologia Ecclesiae Anglicanae*. Archbishop Parker hoped that by her example "all noble gentlewomen would be allured from vain delights"! A fourth daughter married Cecil and became the notable Lady Burghley — "a very noble and highly erudite lady, versed alike in Latin and Greek, which she is said to have spoken as easily as English". She was known to have great influence. She left much to scholars and to the poor, thus carrying on the tradition of secularising philanthropy which was begun by Lady Margaret Beaufort.

"She played a major part in Burghley's home life, occupying her powerful intellect and forceful faith in educating her children in religion and in the management of her huge household and in talking and listening to her husband."[12]

Such were some of those great women scholars of the sixteenth century; but undoubtedly the most influential of them all was that extraordinary character Queen Elizabeth I. Elizabeth's effect on the form Protestant Christianity took in England was the result both of circumstance and character. Curiously enough during this crucial period it was the characters of three contemporary queens, reacting most powerfully on each other, that shaped the destiny of the Church in England and Scotland. At this moment of time it was in an unusually direct way that women affected the history of their religion.

Mary Tudor was undoubtedly the most religious of the three, but unhappily both by temperament and early experience she was predestined to bigotry. With all the strength of her simple, sincere and loyal character, she clung to the religion and nationality of her much wronged mother. With the fatality of a Greek tragedy Mary, throughout her sad reign, swept on to disaster. She might conceivably have led the bulk of her people back to a reformed Catholic way of worship had she been content to keep clear of Spain and the Pope. But she chose to marry a Spaniard and was ever a devoted daughter of Rome. Compromise was utterly foreign to her nature and the public martyrdom of three of the most outstanding churchmen in the country was, in itself, enough to ruin her cause. At the same time both foolhardy and timid, she allowed them and other notable preachers to put forward their case forcibly and dramatically which, together with the spectacle of their fortitude and suffering, strengthened the weak and confirmed the doubtful. Mary plunged deeper and deeper into violent reaction. In the last three years of her reign more people were put to death than in all the thirty years of her sister's; many were ordinary humble folk and fifty-five of them were women. The annulment of decrees made by her late father and brother weakened her personal authority. She affronted the pride of her people by her subservience to Philip and the unpopular war that lost Britain Calais. Altogether she could not have played more successfully into the hands of her half-sister Elizabeth, nor ensured more completely the overthrow of all she had determined to accomplish.

Mary Stuart, from very different causes, is an equally tragic figure and her personality also contributed to the religious destiny both of Scotland and of England. Where Mary Tudor was fanatically religious, her cousin was fanatically feminine. Her disastrous marriages and her implication, whether true or not, with the murder of Darnley, her first husband, led to the thunderous denunciations of John Knox and drove the country further towards his Calvinistic form of Puritanism. Her intrigues against Elizabeth led to the tightening up of measures against Catholics in England and confirmed Elizabeth yet more firmly in her people's hearts as the great champion of Protestantism and bulwark against Rome and Spain.

Luckily this third queen possessed all the qualities lacking in the other two and made none of their mistakes. Had she been either bigoted or passionate by nature, the golden age of English history might never have come to fruition, for at her accession the situation was precarious and the country could well have been plunged into bitter religious warfare. Elizabeth, with just as unhappy and indeed an even more insecure childhood and youth as her half-sister, was able to overcome her deprivations and indeed, to turn them to advantage, for she learned to keep her own counsel, to read men's characters and never to give way to despair. She was lucky in possessing a powerful intellect and a balanced temperament. It is a mistake, however, to think of her as merely the successful opportunist or as having no strong personal religious convictions. She was sincerely opposed to extremes and would not allow too drastic changes. The alterations made in the Prayer Book of 1552 were accommodated to a more Catholic attitude towards the Eucharist, and at her bidding. The lines attributed to her may well have been her authentic pronouncement — they so characteristically leave the interpretation open-ended:

"Christ was the Word that spake it,
He took the bread and brake it,
And what his Word doth make it
That I believe and take it."

Kneeling was allowed, much to Knox's disgust. Derogatory references to the Pope were taken out and against strong opposition from many quarters the Queen authorised the use of vestments, and she also changed the title of "Supreme *Head* of the Church" assumed by her father to "Supreme *Governor*", which allowed a certain latitude of interpretation. She is known to have wished to retain the crucifix. Characteristically, she would have liked to have forbidden her clergy to marry, but she had the sense to see that this was not possible. However she could not forbear greeting poor Mrs Parker, the Archbishop's wife, with: "Madam I may not call you and Mistress I am ashamed to call you, so I do not know what to call you." Sandys said, "She will winke at the marriage of her clergy but not establish it by law, which is nothing else but to bastard our children."

Elizabeth had a personal liking for ritual and disliked the breaking of stained glass and statues. She protected the Marian bishops as well as she could, even if they did not conform. For instance, Bonner, who was responsible under Mary for the persecution, ended his life peacefully in "protective custody". Her leniency to Catholics is well-known until the menace of Spain and the plots against her life forced her hand. The Emperor Ferdinand thanked her for this leniency and even asked her to set aside one church in every city for the Catholics — a remarkable request considering the bitterness of the quarrel between Catholics and Protestants abroad. But Elizabeth, whatever her private views, was too much aware of the general temper of her people to agree to this. Her reply is a model, not only of tact but also was probably a sincere avowal of her own convictions:

> "We and our people – thanks be to God – follow no novel strange religion, but that very religion which is ordained by Christ, sanctioned by the primitive and Catholic Church and approved by . . . the most early Fathers. But to form Churches expressly for diverse rites . . . would be but to graft religion upon religion to the distraction of good men's minds."

This distraction was what she wisely determined to avoid. She tried to treat all who did not conform to her settlement with tolerance, privately though not legally. She really disliked forcing men and women to go against their consciences. Her attitude was pragmatic, if you like, but it was not therefore insincere and shallow. She was one of those far too rare characters who are able to preserve a sense of balance above all else and this was of immense value in stabilising the religious settlement in England, enabling us at that time to avoid the bloodshed that was deluging Europe. On the eleventh anniversary of her accession, Bishop Jewel, the author of the *Apology for the Church of England*, preached at Paul's Cross a sermon on the story of the fall of Jericho: "Upon this day God sent his handmaid and delivered us — then was our mouth filled with laughter and our tongue with joy." A year later, Foxe, preaching on Good Friday soon after the Pope's excommunication of Elizabeth, again referred to England as "great Jericho" and Elizabeth herself as a God-given queen "so calm, so patient, so merciful, more like a national mother than a princess . . . such as neither they nor their ancestors ever read of in the stories of this land before."

A community does not suddenly grow out of a whole way of thought and the objective symbolic use of images and allegory, so strange to us, so natural to them, persisted though in different forms, well into the seventeenth century. The secular nobility took on much of the ritual significance that had formerly belonged to the religious hierarchy. In churches and cathedrals their coats of arms and splendid effigies replaced the pictures and the statues of the saints. Abstractions continued to be given visible form and personality and especially was this the case with the monarchy. In the Termine portrait of Queen Elizabeth, for instance, every detail of the costume is symbolic — the ermine of chastity, the serpent of wisdom, the embroidered ears and eyes for omniscience. The secular Virgin Queen, though far from saintly, did much to fill the gap left by the dethronement of the Virgin Queen of Heaven.

It was much more than the fate of the martyrs that Foxe was concerned with. It was indeed "the stories of this land before" — a view of the working out of the purpose of God for England, His second Chosen People, and culminating in the Marian persecution with Elizabeth herself as the Royal Martyr delivered at the last moment by Divine Intervention to be a saviour to her country. In trying to account for the religious history of sixteenth- and seventeenth-century Britain, the enormous influence of Foxe cannot be ignored. It was second only to the Bible. On into the next century we find the saintly Mrs Ferrar reading to her little son Nicholas from the *Book of Martyrs* the stories which probably, more than anything else, kept him securely within the Anglican fold, in spite of his obvious attraction to the great Catholic personalities of the Counter Reformation. It was Foxe who, by keeping alive the sense of shared suffering and shared privilege (the holy nation), bound together the Protestants of both extremes under Elizabeth and James in an emotional bond that kept the balance between their mutual dissatisfactions, so that, even when the Puritan Revolution occurred, the Elizabethan Anglican settlement was too firmly established to be overthrown. As Foxe himself says: "If there cannot be an end of our disputing and contending one against another, yet let there be a moderation in our affections." It was, of course, not necessary for Foxe to be historically accurate to attain his ends, though there is evidence that for his age he was both honest and painstaking in collecting his material. His first volume stresses the point that Christianity was brought to this country in its pure form not by Rome but by Joseph of Arimathea — an argument used by Elizabeth herself to disown allegiance to the Roman Church.

The events in Foxe's history are all centred upon religion. The invention of printing, for instance, is described as: "Then the Lord began to work for the Church, not with sword and target, but with printing, writing and reading." Thus in the last volume, the stories of the martyrs are presented in the large perspective of the glorious narrative of God's Elect — Foxe himself was a humane man. He commends the mercy of Edward VI in pleading with Cranmer against the burning of the Anabaptist Joan Boucher and contrasts his compassion with Gardiner's condemning of Anne Askew, "the first of the Protestant women martyrs". Gardiner and Bonner rather than Mary are condemned by Foxe for cruelty and they, not she, are given the name of "bloody". Perhaps as a woman, perhaps as a queen and half-sister to the great "Deborah", he wished to spare her as much as he could. He seems to have a special feeling for women: "They showed a stouter mind and were as ready of speech, quick to act as men," he said. He includes in his stories the stirring accounts of many women martyrs drawn from both high and humble walks of life. These are given with such vivid touches and in language so alive, it is no wonder they fired the imagination of many in years to come, deepening their faith and their courage.

Here is Elizabeth Folkes:

"When she came to be burned she plucked off her petticoat and would have given it to her mother, but the wicked there attending would not suffer her to give it. Therefore taking the said petticoat in her hand, she threw it away from her saying 'Farewell the world, farewell faith, farewell hope', and so taking the stake in her hand said 'Welcome, Love'."

Here again is Alice Driver answering two priests:

"Have you no more to say? God be honoured. You be not able to resist the spirit of God in me, a poor woman. I was an honest poor man's daughter never brought up in the University as you have been, but I have driven the plough before my father many a time, I thank God. Yet notwithstanding, in the defence of God's truth and in the cause of my master Christ, by his grace I will set my foot against the foot of any of you all in the maintenance and defence of the same, and if I had a thousand lives, it should go for payment thereof . . . and so went she to prison again as joyful as the bird of day."

Joan Waste was born blind and supported herself by knitting "hosen and sleeves". In no case would she be idle:

> "She went to Churche daily to hear the Bible read in English and saved up money to buy a New Testament — and would pay a prisoner from the debtors' prison or some other poor person to read a chapter to her daily. She thus became convinced that the Roman observance of the Mass was not according to Christ's meaning in the Gospels and was led away to her burning 'holding her brother by her hand.' "

Humble Joan's judging for herself from the Bible is typical of the new spirit of independence engendered in women from Anne Askew onwards. She "victoriously confuted every argument quoting many texts". When the Bishop of Winchester threatened her with burning, she answered: "Neither Christ nor his Apostles put any creature to death." Elizabeth Young was accused under Mary of bringing Protestant tracts into England and distributing them. She too was able to more than hold her own in argument. She gave her age as forty years. "Twenty of those years thou wentest to Mass," said her accuser. "Yea," she answered, "and twenty more I may, and yet come home as wise as I went thither first, for I understand it not." When faced with the rack she exclaimed: "Here is my carcase, do with it what you will. And more than that ye cannot have, and if ye take away my meat, I trust God will take away my hunger." Her defiance was such that her accuser shouted: "Twenty pounds, it is a man in woman's clothes! Twenty pounds it is a man." She was reproved by the Bishop of London's chancellor in words which are significant enough: "What shouldst thou meddle with the Scripture? It is more fit for thee to meddle with thy distaff than to meddle with the Scriptures." Unabashed, she quotes to him, "It is the spirit that quickeneth, what meanest Christ by that?" To which the chancellor hastily replied: "O God forbid. Would you have me interpret the Scriptures? We must leave that for our old ancient fathers which have studied the Scriptures a long time and have the Holy Ghost given unto them." It is the age-old rift between authority and personal responsibility.

Sometimes the women are more resolute than the men. William Dangerfield of Wootten-under-Edge recanted to save his wife and new-born child, but his wife cried, "Alack! thus long have we continued one and hath Satan so prevailed to cause you to break your first vow made to Christ in Baptism?" So he took back his recantation and both died together in prison. Though Foxe was obviously prejudiced in favour of the martyrs, many of the sayings reported in his stories ring so true that we cannot but believe them, from the immortal words of Ridley downwards, and besides them, there are authentic written documents and letters which have come down to us. These are often addressed by the prisoners to their wives, who bore no little part in preserving them and in sending them secretly abroad. Rowland Taylor's famous resistance was recorded by his wife, and John Bradford also wrote from prison to his wife epistles which were of great influence in strengthening the "elect". There are more moving personal letters too; Lawrence Saunders wrote:

"Dear Wife. Be merry in the mercies of our Christ. O remember always my words for Christ's sake be merry and grudge not against God and pray, pray. We be all merry here. Pray, pray. The Spirit is ready but the flesh is weak. God will bless thee, good wife, and the poor boy also. Pray, pray, pray."

For, spiritual merriment though there may have been, there was also very human heartbreak.

Foxe's history was acknowledged as the one great authoritative account of the true Church, and was appointed to be read "in all orphanages and City companies". It was rightly taken for granted that it would be widely read in private. Copies were provided in cathedrals for the use of the Chapter and also in parish churches and colleges. Drake took a copy round the world and read it to his Spanish prisoners, no doubt enjoying this experience to the full. Of course there was another side to Foxe's account. Those who prosecuted were not all the wicked blind men that they appeared to him. Many were unhappy and bewildered at the role thrust upon them. "Why, Sir, have you not the Holy Ghost given and revealed unto you?" enquired the redoubtable Elizabeth Young of the Chancellor. "No, God forbid that I should so believe," he replied, "but I hope." Most were as sincere Christians as those they opposed but their point of view had ultimately no chance against the moderation of Elizabeth's rule. It would have needed a counter persecution to raise up a Catholic Foxe. Meanwhile for generations the *Book of Martyrs* remained virtually unchallenged.

In addition to those who actually gave up their lives at the stake or in prison, there were a group of women who suffered a period of unpleasant, if not painful, existence under the Marian persecution. The Reformation had brought into being a quite new category — the clergy wives. These were to exert great influence in times to come, not least in training women in responsibility and Christian service of all kinds. But to begin with their lot was hard. Celibacy had been enforced on priests by Pope Gregory VII. In rare cases a licence to marry was granted but a married priest was despised. Mistresses were another matter and these were certainly winked at. Wolsey himself had illegitimate children, but although Henry VIII was against legitimising the marriage of clergy, public opinion was veering that way and at the dissolution of the monasteries, when monks often became parish clergy, many of them did marry, and often dispossessed nuns. An effort to check this was made in the Act of Six Articles in 1539, but the penalties were not strictly enforced. The fact that Cranmer had married before the Act was passed caused some embarrassment, especially to poor Mrs Cranmer who is said to have travelled about with her husband more or less secretly, confined for journeys in a chest and once nearly stifled when it was turned the wrong way about thus blocking up the air holes. She was of German birth and Cranmer had married her when he was envoy to the Emperor. When he was recalled to become Archbishop at Warham's death, he was forced to keep his wife in seclusion at Ford near Canterbury. The change of attitude was, however, having a good effect among the laity, and this was bound to influence the clergy eventually. Luther himself set the fashion and writes with horror of the old ideas: "When I was a boy, the wicked and impure practice of celibacy had made marriage so disreputable that I believed I could not even think about the life of married people without sinning." The better relationship now possible between husband and wife is finely illustrated in Shakespeare's plays.

At Edward VI's accession, Convocation recognised the marriage of clergy but this did not become law. But all the clergy wives emerged into respectability until Mary repealed the Convocation Act when the poor things again lost their status. Mrs Cranmer fled back to Germany but some wives, as we have seen, staunchly suffered with their husbands, some went into exile with them, some were deserted and publicly repudiated, many only temporarily, and some bided their time in seclusion and poverty. Among these last was Mrs Parker. Her marriage had only taken place at Henry VIII's death after a seven-year wait, but then there was a period of happiness when Parker was Master of Corpus Christi College, Cambridge. Mrs Parker was an intelligent woman who made her house a centre for scholars from Europe, among whom was that Nicholas Udall who had so admired the scholarship of English women. He says that she "was capable of conversing in Latin and Greek upon Godly matters" and the famous Ridley was said to admire her. She was obviously a woman of character, for she was nicknamed Parker's "Lady Abbess", and it must have taken some courage to entertain Queen Elizabeth, knowing as she did the Queen's views on the marriage of her clergy. She seems also to have been a good housewife (her cookery book is still to be seen at Cambridge) and she was a loved and respected mother.

The Parkers were very much luckier than most well known Protestant dignitaries and their wives for, although he was of course deprived of his office, both he and she were left in peace in their seclusion. He had been chaplain to Anne Boleyn and this secured him Elizabeth's friendship, so that she chose him as her archbishop, but the choice was also a wise and successful one as there was a natural affinity between their balanced and tolerant minds. Parker, however, made no concessions with regard to his marriage. He refused to keep his wife in the background and probably it was this firm stand on the part of her archbishop which induced the Queen "to wink" at a practice she would have preferred to have forbidden. As it was, legal recognition of clergy marriages did not come till James I's time, since when the parson's wife has filled an important religious and social role. That wise and fine poet and clergyman, George Herbert, sketched out this role as he saw it in his little book *The Country Parson*:

"His wife is either religious, or night and day he is winning her to it. Instead of the qualities of the world, he requires only three of her; first, a trayning up of her children and mayds in

90

the fear of God, with prayers and catechizing and all religious duties. Secondly, a curing and healing of all wounds and sores with her owne hands; which skill either she brought with her, or he takes care she shall learn it off some neighbours. Thirdly, a providing for her family in such sort as that neither they want a competent sustentation, nor her husband be brought in debt."

His own wife fulfilled all these requirements. She was Jane, one of the nine daughters of a Mr Danvers, who had set his heart on Herbert as a prospective son-in-law. More successful than most parents in such a case, he had "so much commended Mr Herbert to her that Jane became so much a Platonick as to fall in love with Mr Herbert unseen", and happily when they met:

> "a mutual affection entered into both their hearts as a conqueror enters into a surprised city and love having got such possession, governed and made there such laws and resolutions as neither party was able to resist; insomuch that she changed her name to Herbert the third day after this first interview".

Isaak Walton, who obviously delights in recounting this love story, goes on to justify its precipitateness by the result, which was so happy that it "was only improvable in Heaven, where they now enjoy it". George Herbert was still a courtier when he married but his wife made no complaint when, at his changing his sword and silk clothes into a canonical coat he said to her:

> "You are now a Minister's wife, and must now so far forget your father's house as not to claim a precedente of any of your parishioners; for you are to know that a Priest's wife can challenge no precedence or place, but that which she purchases by her obliging humility; and I am sure, places so purchased do best become them."

It is obvious from Walton's account that she shared her husband's sensitive care for the poor of the parish and for the renovation of church and parsonage house at Bemerton.

> "He made her his almoner and paid constantly into her hand a tenth penny of what money he received for Tythe and gave her power to dispose of it."

They had no children of their own but adopted two little orphan nieces and a third came later also to look upon Bemerton Parsonage as a home.

George Herbert died in 1633. Jane married again six years later and lived on through the Civil War and the Protectorate. One wonders if she often looked back regretfully to that peaceful time when she was the ideal country parson's wife, at a period when there was still possible a harmony within the Anglican Church while the Elizabethan compromise still held. But the tensions between the Calvinistic Puritans and the traditionalists were becoming more and more strained.

7
The Growth of Puritanism and the Civil War

As soon as power passed from Elizabeth Tudor to James Stuart, trouble ensued. The Calvinist section of the Anglican Church had high hopes that James would purge it of what they considered were Popish practices still allowed by Elizabeth's settlement. They were mistaken. James hated the Calvinistic Presbyterians and hated them all the more because in Scotland he was powerless against them. He was determined to rid himself of any such influence in England and therefore returned an unequivocal "No" to practically all the proposals of the Puritan Divines who waited on him with the Millenary Petition of 1603: "Away with all their snivelling, I will make them conform or I will harry them out of the land," which is exactly what began to happen. The Puritan movement ceased to be contained within the Anglican fold and turned to sectarianism and the more extreme among the sectarians betook themselves to Holland and to the New World with their wives and families.

The Pilgrim Mothers had a grim time of it. Those that survived the voyage were faced with "a hideous and desolate wilderness". Added to the physical hardships were fear and loneliness. The maternal and infant mortality was appalling, perhaps one or two surviving out of sixteen babies. It was imperative to populate the new settlements and women were compelled to constant child-bearing, those wives who died were replaced within a month or so. Marriages for nearly a hundred years were not sanctified but were performed by a magistrate as being "a wholly civil thing upon which questions of inheritance doth depend". And for this, as indeed for all things, justification was sought for and found in the Bible where "it was nowhere mentioned that marriage was to be laid on God's ministers". No graces softened the harsh male Puritan world. Women's duty towards God and man was to bear children and work incessantly in the home and in the fields. They were no better than slaves; worse off than the indentured servants the settlers brought with them, for these at least could quit eventually. It is significant that the Covenant agreed upon and signed by the Mayflower Pilgrims on landing, though it included a few of these servants, excluded all women.

Gradually conditions improved. In 1623 the first harvest was garnered that deserved the name and it is recorded that now "women went willingly into the fields", implying that before they had to be driven there. Of course, even in the worst times, love must have lightened the load in some families, but the general state of the "Desires", "Fears", "Patiences", "Humilities" (the names might have come straight out of an old morality play or from Bunyan's *Pilgrim's Progress*) was a degraded one. Among the "saints" of Plymouth, "the libel" was indignantly denied that women had been granted any "rights or privileges" and in the northern provinces, which were even more fiercely puritanical, women were held to be the greatest source of sin, by which, as among the early Fathers, was meant first and foremost the gratification of sexual desire (unless for the lawful purposes of procreation within marriage). The Quakers, when they arrived on the scene, were at first persecuted by their fellow Nonconformists more harshly than they had been at home, primarily because they admitted women to an unprecedented degree of equality, even encouraging them to speak in their meetings. The few allusions to individual women in the chronicles of the settlers are generally derogatory. The governor of Hartford is rebuked because "owing to his indulgence his wife was allowed to give herself over to reading" instead of "attending to such things as belong to a woman, meddling in such things as are only proper to men". She appropriately lost her wits, poor woman. Mrs Hutchinson was killed by Indians and this was held to be a just punishment for "broaching heresies" and supporting the hated Anabaptists.

So much of the animosity towards women in strict religious communities seems always to have been inspired by fear. Milton, the supreme poet of Puritanism, faithfully reflects this attitude. The inexplicable power of woman's beauty over man, which he himself had obviously experienced, is discussed and deplored in *Paradise Lost* and in *Samson Agonistes*:

"Therefore God's Universal Law

94

Gave to man despotic power.
Nor from that right to part an hour,"

and the inferiority of woman as a spiritual being is summed up in the lines:

"He for God only.   She for God in him."

As the Puritan movement grew in strength and intolerance, so did the denigration of women increase. Punishment for sexual offences were stepped up and in 1650 a law was even passed allowing the death sentence for adultery. It was also in this period that the persecution of witches reached its height. This had always been rife in Europe but was not really bad in England before the return of the Calvinist exiles and it is, perhaps, the most cruel and unsavoury chapter in the history of the relation of Christianity to women. Originally witchcraft developed from the old fertility rites, rooted in the belief that women were able to bless or curse the crops. But from Augustine onwards the cult was held to be a blasphemous parody of Christianity. At first those who believed in witches were held to be heretics, a doctrine set forth in the ninth century Canon Episcopi, but later those sensible enough *not* to believe in them were persecuted by the Inquisition. Unfortunately by the seventeenth century this was the one subject upon which Catholic and Protestant agreed — the only difference being that the Calvinistic Protestants based their belief upon random texts from the Bible and were the more thorough and whole-hearted in their witch hunts.

James I had a national prejudice against witches as he believed Bothwell had set to work a covey against him. His *Demonologie* (1597) however only reflects the general widespread belief. Witches were taken for granted. Reginald Scot's humane and sensible book *The Discoverie of Witchcraft* (1584) fell on deaf ears and was more than a hundred years before its time. During the Civil War the general state of unrest made matters worse. Essex, Fairfax and Cromwell all had witch cases connected with their families. Between 1645 and 1647 two hundred witches were executed in the eastern counties alone, an enormous proportion of the then sparse population. Even such tolerant and wise writers as Richard Baxter and Sir Thomas Browne thought witchcraft an obvious and undeniable evil, and Browne wrote in *Religio Medici*:

95

"For my part I have ever believed and do now know that there are witches, they that doubt of these do not only deny them, but Spirits and are . . . Atheists."

What was it that led to this widespread and pitiless obsession in seventeenth-century England? There were the old smouldering superstitions and these were reinforced by the puritanical fear and hatred of sex with its inevitable anti-feminism — warlocks counted for little beside witches in the popular imagination. Then there was the general inhumanity against the poor, the old and the help-less. Perhaps most insidious of all was the distrust of women with any pretensions to learning, almost as if it were an aberration or hateful abnormality.

Of course such a climate of opinion gave rise to a certain amount of real mispractice. Grudges among neighbours were common enough and some spiteful or misused old women cashed in on their supposed powers which often had the desired psychological effects upon their victims. Some no doubt even resorted to poison. Evil begets evil. But these must have been a tiny minority — the vast number of those who suffered were undoubtedly entirely innocent. With the Restoration and the dawn of the Age of Reason, the per-secution subsided, except in Calvinistic Scotland, where it con-tinued until the eighteenth century was well advanced. In 1687 Sir John Reresly attended a witch trial at York and wrote of it thus:

"A poor old woman had the hard fate to be condemned for a witch. Some that were more apt to believe these things than me, thought the evidence strong against her but the judge thought fit to reprieve her."[13]

In 1696 Judge Sewall in New England publicly acknowledged with shame his part in the notorious Salem trials when nineteen poor creatures (six of them warlocks) were executed — all of them protesting their innocence to the end. The swing of educated public opinion reached its climax in 1736 when the law con-demning witches to death was repealed. But many country people continued to believe in witches for long after that and, in remote places, even up to the beginning of the present century. This age-long deep-rooted association of anti-Christian black magic with women was due in part to suppression of the female element in worship and the fear and aggression which such suppression produced.

So much for the darker side of Puritanism. The Church during the seventeenth century encouraged the hateful persecution of so-called witches and undoubtedly diminished the general status of women by its Calvinistic theories. Yet, within its framework, many found their only joy and the fortitude and discipline they needed during the stress of the Civil War that often divided father from son, husband from wife or sister from brother. In the record of those heroic women whose lives have come down to us from these times, it is not possible to guess from their spiritual confessions which side they supported. All are suffused with an ardent and sacrificial devotion. Each seems to order their lives by a self-discipline as strict and as regular as any professed nun. There is little or no doctrinal comment and there is nothing to choose between them with respect to personal dedication and devotion. It is only when they speak of political and general matters that we gather that Lady Warwick kept the date of Charles I's execution as a fast day, that Mrs Godolphin was lady-in-waiting to Charles II's queen, that Lucy Hutchinson's husband was a colonel in Cromwell's army and Margaret Baxter wife to a nonconformist minister.

Mary Rich, Countess of Warwick, sister to Robert Boyle, the famous scientist (1625-78), combined the transports of a mysticism, almost medieval in its simple objectivity, with a strong Calvinist conviction of responsibility and of guilt. At times she experienced a ravishing joy in the sense of Jesus's presence and of an intimate relationship with him, reminiscent of a true "bride of Christ", and the importance she attaches to the actual physical manifestation of weeping is like a page from Margery Kempe. Yet she was haunted by a strong Puritanical burden of sin. She had married without her father's consent and though the succeeding deaths of two near relatives soon raised her chosen husband to the peerage and hence to his father-in-law's favour, this early act of filial disobedience so haunted her that, when she lost her own son from smallpox, she believed it a just punishment. Both her children died while she was still young, and pitifully and mercilessly she told herself that her hopes of more children were disappointed because, after two quick conceptions in her early married life, she was "troubled of a proud conceit I had that if I childed so thick it would spoil what my great vanity then made me to fancy was tolerable in my person: and out of a proud opinion too, that I had, that if I had many to provide for they must be poor, because of my lord's (then) poor estate. . . ."

The Warwicks, like many a moderate liberty-loving family, were sadly divided in their loyalty. At first Mary's father-in-law was opposed to Charles and his home was actually once invaded by Royalist troops, but the execution of the King changed their allegiance — "the news of that barbarous and wicked action was of a sudden told me, which endangered my life, for I had a great abhorrence to that bloody act". Yet her nephew Robert married Cromwell's favourite daughter.

Mary seems to have had a continual longing after solitude for which the cares and duties of a large ducal establishment left little room. The Restoration brought uncongenial company:

> "This day while I was entertaining my guests, some of them made a mock of sin, and said that great ones were no sinners. I was mightily grieved and offended to hear such wicked discourse; showed openly my dislike of it . . . and begged to hear no more."

Complaints of "vain and idle discourse" and of the hurry and bustle of London, from which she was always thankful to escape, are frequent. She was a country-loving person, whose close observation of trees and flowers, birds and insects lighten her otherwise undistinguished *Meditations*, though it is of interest as being one of the earliest devotional books written for publication by a woman. She could not concentrate upon her religious devotions in town and this distressed and humbled her. As usual she is full of self-reproach:

> "I found my heart broken for the strange, dull and distracted temper I was in, as to spiritual things, that week I was so hurried at London."

She would have loved, like the ladies of the Port Royal, to have turned her back upon the world, but her duty to her husband forbade such indulgence. It was no light burden. Besides entertaining her unwelcome friends, she had for years to put up with the violent and uncertain temper of a man in almost ceaseless pain from gout and other ailments. Also, though they were always lovers at heart, it is difficult sometimes to live with a saint and often it looks as though her husband was spurred on to see if he could induce her to lose her self-control. It was a painful pastime for, whether successful or not, it reduced her to a misery of contrition:

> "My lord, having been full of passionate expressions to me, I found myself troubled, and when I was retired before going to bed, I wept exceedingly, but afterwards was troubled that I shed so many tears for anything but my sins."

As he frequently blasphemed and swore before her, she was also concerned for his spiritual welfare and spent hours "mightily crying to God for him". He had his times of repentance when he would thank her for nursing him, but he does not ever seem to have done much to please her and even cut down the trees in her favourite retired walk, which he knew she loved, and this she found hard to forgive. Yet they were faithful to one another in an age when conjugal affection was unfashionable — her painful self-reproaches included that of loving him too much and taking more care to please him than to please God, while he, towards the end of his life, became gentler towards her, begging her pardon for his fits of anger, and he showed his trust in her by leaving her unconditionally the possession of his entire estate.

The moral tags attached to her observations of nature and country life illustrate the puritanical discipline of this seventeenth-century Anglican aristocrat:

> "Upon observing a mower to go sometimes to a whetstone to wet his scythe and then presently return again to his mowing — O Lord, most humbly I beseech thee, let me never use lawful recreations, but when I find absolute necessity of them, to be as the mower's whetstone, to make use more fit to return with more vigour and cheerfulness of spirit to the work thou hast sent me into the world to do."[14]

Lucy Hutchinson (b. 1620), who wrote her own autobiography of which, alas, only a fragment remains, was also the author of a singularly well-composed biography of her husband, *Life of Colonel Hutchinson*, which includes a lucid and vigorous account of contemporary affairs.

Her father was Sir Allen Apsley, Lieutenant of the Tower when Raleigh was imprisoned there, and her mother was one of those notable women produced by the early post-Reformation days. She paid, out of her pockets, for Raleigh and his friend and fellow prisoner Mr Ruthen, to pursue "rare experiments" in medical science. This "brought them great solace", but Lady Apsley's aim was not only to help them but to teach herself so that she could "succour such poore people as were not able to seeke phisitians" and this candle lit in the darkness of prison threw far its beams, for she passed her knowledge on to her daughter "who dressed wounds as well as any man's surgeon" and, moreover, insisted on attending to the wounded of both Roundheads and Cavaliers alike during the Civil War.

Lucy, like her mother, was a born scholar; she describes how as a child, she eagerly devoured books but "as for musick and dancing, I profited very little in them and for my needle, I absolutely hated it."

We are not surprised to find her less emotional in her approach to religion than Lady Warwick, though no less firm in her beliefs. She had a clear head and a brave decided will. When Colonel Hutchinson, in danger of imprisonment at the Restoration, refused to take precautions for his own safety, Lucy resolved to disobey him and "with her unquietness she drove him out of her own lodging into the custody of a friend". She then wrote a letter in his name but without his knowledge, promising that he would be ready to appear when summoned and begging for his parole. She was successful in this but she could not persuade him to fly the country and eventually, in spite of her efforts, he was imprisoned first in the Tower, and then in Sandown Castle, Kent, where his health suffered so much that he died from the bad conditions there.

It is from her account of those last sad months that we get some idea of her own character as seen through the mirror of her husband's words to her:

> "He would very sweetly and kindly chide her for her sadness and tell her that if she were but cheerful, he should think this suffering the happiest thing that ever befell him. He was sure that the case (of the Commonwealth) would revive because the interest of God was so much involved in it. He bade her let his son keep clear and take heed of rash attempts and keep free from all faction, making the public interest *only* his."

She was walking every day in all weather from Deal to Sandown and back, but he begged the authorities to allow him

> "to have her in his chamber so that they shall not pluck her out of my arms and then in the night she shall collect and write down for him his work upon the Epistles which he had been thinking on during his imprisonment."

They both spent hours in studying the Bible together.

Pathetically, she was not with him when he died but in London on one of her wearisome, unsuccessful attempts to plead for release, or better treatment, or a change of prison, but he left her this message:

> "Let her, as she is above other women, shew herself on this occasion a good Christian and above the pitch of ordinary women."

There is no doubt that she did so shew herself and was upheld in her courage and hope both by his faith and by her own.

The Restoration debased women in a different way than the Calvinistic Puritans had done. They were not shunned and feared as so many tempting Eves, but exploited as one of the chief means to men's pleasure. Wine, women and song were on a level and just as in a time of extreme strict morality, so with the swing of the pendulum, when immorality took over, the status of women suffered equally.

> "For we courtiers learn at School
> Only with your sex to fool
> Y'are not worth the serious part,"

wrote William Habington. The sober-minded, whether Anglican or Nonconformist, escaped if they could. Lady Falkland, widow of that brave leader whose heart was broken between king and country, betook herself to her "cottage" to spend her time in good works "with a book, a wheel and a maid or two".

Margaret Blagge (1652-77) was less fortunate. As a child, her father being Groom of the Bedchamber to Charles I, she was sent to France when the troubles began, where Henrietta Maria tried her best to convert her to Roman Catholicism, but she was destined to be an Anglican saint under the discipline of her own conscience instead of a Catholic one under the discipline of Holy

Church. She came back to England as a young woman to a dissolute Court and her private diary gives a moving picture of the rules she laid down for herself in the isolation of a self-dependent integrity. But she would have denied this vehemently for she felt in all things dependent upon God.

> "I must, till Lent, rise at half an hour after eight a clock; while putting on morning clothes, say the prayer for Death and the Te Deum. When I go to the withdrawing roome lett me consider what my calling is: to entertaine the Ladys, not to talk foolishly to Men, more especially the King. Lord assist me . . . goe to the Queene allwayes att nine. If I find she dignes late, come downe, pray and read: and think why I read, to benefit my soule, pass my tyme well and improve my understanding — O Lord assist me. Sitt not up above halfe an hour after eleven att most and as you undress, repeate that prayer again . . . being in bedd repeate your hymne softly, ere you turne to sleepe."

John Evelyn tells how she attached a long packthread to her wrist at night which went through her keyhole to the sentinel at the entrance to the royal palace, with instructions that he should pull it very hard at the hour she wished to wake for her devotions. Playing-cards, the curse of the period, were a constant source of boredom and distress to her. She joined in when required to do but made stern and brave resolutions to resist high stakes:

> "I will never play this halfe year butt att 3 penny omber . . . I will not; I doe not vow, but I will not doe it . . . Three pounds would have kept three people from starveing a month: well, I will not play."

To live a double live — that of a nun within and of a Restoration beauty without — called for no little courage, ingenuity and self-command. Margaret was no more than sixteen when she apparently managed to conduct herself so that she neither offended her conscience nor any of her companions at Court. She had to take part in a fashionable masque and to consort with such well-known characters as the Duchess of Monmouth. We find neither scandals nor sermons in her diary but only self-imposed rules of conduct:

"To go not to the Duchess above once a week if possible and allways to be armed with a book to read when I don't act. Talk little when you are there; if they speak of anybody I can't commend to hold my peace, what jest so ever they make, be sure never to talk to the King, when they speak filthily, tho I be laughed att, looke grave. Never meddle with other's business."

According to Evelyn she was too pleasing a little actress to be spared, "there was no retreating". Appropriately enough, she was cast for the part of Diana, goddess of chastity, which it is to be hoped slightly mitigated the unwelcome privilege of appearing "with near twenty thousand pounds value of Jewels on her". Unfortunately a diamond lent by the Countess of Suffolk was lost or stolen during the performance which "extremely concerned her" but the King, obviously bearing no grudge for her avoidance of him, "understanding the trouble she was in, generously sent her wherewithall to make my Lady Suffolke a present of soe good a Jewel" — as characteristic a piece of generosity as his undesirable conversation.

But it was evident that, in spite of what might have been condemned as priggishness, she was, on the contrary, a general favourite at Court.

"She would sing and play and act and recite to recreat old and melancholy persons and divert the younger."

Her goodness seems to have been of that appealing nature which allied with loveliness and wit was irresistible. Evelyn says she looked like a flower and his son describes her as "my pretty pious pearly governess".

At any rate she served a long seven years without a stain on her character, "nor did her piety eclipse her pretty humour . . . when she was sometymes provoked to Railly then was nothing in the world soe pleasant and inoffensively diverting". No wonder she captured the heart of the Earl of Godolphin and retained it through nine long years of courtship, a short idyllic period of married life and thirty-four years of loneliness after her death. The courtship was thus long because Godolphin was despatched abroad on various missions, but also because his young love was torn between him and her early determination never to marry:

103

"No, no, I will remain my Saviour's. He shall be my love, my husband, my all. I will keep my virginitie and present it unto Christ and not put myself into the temptation of loving everything in competition with my God."

It is the ancient sacrificial cry, but her own natural, honest heart forswore it and together with the sound advice of John Evelyn, won the day for Godolphin, though there was a mysterious business of an apparently quite unnecessary secret marriage and an almost immediate separation while Margaret, in pursuance of some mistaken idea of duty, carried out a promise of companioning Lady Berkeley to France. "This is a strange proceeding," wrote Evelyn sensibly; "find it a name if you can, for I confess I understand it not . . . nothing is so repugnant as love and absence . . . goe back, goe back then and be happy for this course will weare you both out." The only name she could have given it was an overscrupulous sense of honour coupled perhaps with a Calvinistic fear of her own happiness, but "goe back" she did not, instead enduring four long months of tedious court tittle-tattle and the boredom of cards. She refused to visit the French Court at St Germain, but she went to see "a cloister of nuns" and it is not surprising that their way of life did not displease her but "God knows the more one sees of their Church, the more one finds to dislike in itt," she wrote; "I did not imagine the tenth part of the superstition I find in it, yett still could approve of their order." Her own self-imposed order was not relaxed by marriage, but she found with joy she could love Christ and her husband too.

It is heartrending to learn of the shortness of her exultant delight in her own home and freedom after so many years of servitude — "my tyme my owne, my house quielt, sweete and prety and in private, how happy in my Friend, Husband, relations, servants . . . none to waite or attend on but my Dear and my beloved God . . . what a melting joy runs through me." The one thing wanting was a child, but after two years she adopted a little orphan girl and soon after came the ultimate joy and the ultimate sorrow. She died in childbirth at the age of twenty-five.

Considering the high rate of maternal mortality, it is not surprising that many a young mother's hopes were haunted. Margaret, for all her happiness, was apprehensive enough to write a farewell letter to her husband to be opened in case she did not survive childbirth. It is full of love and commonsense, the balance she maintained between self-discipline and what Evelyn calls "a wonderful complacency towards others" while a young girl at Court is present still though softened by happiness:

> "My deare, not knowing how God Allmighty may deale with me, I think it my best course to settle my affairs, soe as that, incase I be to leave this world, noe earthly thing may take up my thoughts. In the first place, my dear, believe me, that of all earthly things you were and are the most dear to me, and I am convinced that nobody ever had a better, or halfe soe good a husband."

There follows clear instructions as to her property and what she would like done for the child and then, at the last:

> "Now, my deare child, farewell; the peace of God, which passeth all understanding, keep your heart and mind in the knowledge of God, of his Son Jesus Christ our Lord."

The same mixture of affection, religion and good sense appears in a letter she wrote to two girls about to follow in her footsteps as ladies-in-waiting:

> "Dear Children . . . As to your dressing, I can't belive that there should be any neglect of that beauty God has given you, soe it be done with this caution. As to your conversation, there is nothing forbidden butt what is either prophane, or unjust . . . 'Tis true, wee should not preach in the Withdrawing Roome, butt wee must, by our lookes shew that wee fear God, and that wee dare not hear anything filthy, or that tends to the prejudice of our Neighbour: wee may divert people, and be innocently merry; butt then wee must not please our selves in the thoughts of it . . . calling to mind that saying of St Paul 'What hast thou which thou didst not receive?' As to your retirement . . . if you have been faulty . . . read some Chapter . . . that doe most divinely sett forth the Love of God to us . . . that your sorrow for sin may proceed from the sense you have of God's great mercy and love and not from fear of Hell which terrifyes and damnation amazes, and I am never the better for those reflections."

Such balance was obviously lacking in the young Margaret Charlton (1641-81) who became the wife of the famous nonconformist divine, Richard Baxter. Their love story was a strange one. Margaret was a child when her father's castle was besieged and burnt by Cromwell's troops. The experience haunted her with terror and all her life she suffered from nightmares of great fires. She was sensitive, timid and emotional, but also possessed of a good mind and a strong will. Once again family loyalties were conflicting. Her father was killed fighting for the king, but her mother had strict Puritan ideals and as a widow went to live at Kidderminster where she came under Baxter's influence. At first Margaret reacted against her mother and against the miseries of her insecure childhood. In Baxter's words: "She had a great aversion to the poverty and strictness of the Kidderminster circle, glittering herself in costly apparel and delighting in romances."

But her need of a father figure fastened upon Baxter himself, and her emotional nature soon made of the relationship a source of anxiety to the middle-aged celibate minister. A serious illness complicated things still further for Baxter, who, putting great trust in intercessory prayer, called a special meeting on Margaret's behalf, which was successful, for she recovered miraculously and firmly believed that he had saved both her life and her reason. She was now, whether consciously or unconsciously, deeply in love with him and this was not in the least affected by his efforts to detach himself. He used a severity in his advice to her as her spiritual guide, accusing her of too great a love towards her mother (but was it her mother he really meant?) — "too strong a love to any, though it be good in kind, may be sinful and hurtful in the degree," exhorting her to pull herself together: "If your trouble of soul is sin, why do you not repent and thankfully accept your pardon? . . . If you grieve for it, why are you not willing to leave it and be holy!"

At length he welcomed a convenient summons to London on ecclesiastical business. Margaret's private diary tells its own tale:

> "When the Lord shall take our carkasses from the grave, and make us shine as the sun in glory, then shall friends meet and never part, and remember their sad and weary nights and days no more! Then may we love freely!"

Baxter did not escape his fate, however, by removing himself from Kidderminster. In direct opposition to his wishes Margaret and her mother followed him to London. Then the mother died and he felt himself even more responsible for the daughter. But the Restoration had brought him into difficulties, and though an outstandingly moderate man (he had been offered a chaplaincy by Cromwell and a bishopric by Charles II and had refused both), he lost his living. He had always believed that a clergyman in charge of a parish should not marry, but now he had no settled parish and his defences against Margaret were at last overcome. He drew up certain conditions, the most important of which were that he was to have no claim upon her estate and that she was to have but a secondary claim upon his time — his work was always to take precedence over everything else in their partnership. He notes with a wry humour, "I think the king's marriage was scarce more talked of than mine."

It was no wonder. A Puritan minister of humble origin, though a notable figure in ecclesiastical politics, turned out of his church for nonconformity, a bachelor of forty-seven who had preached celibacy, marrying a girl just twenty, of aristocratic birth and of a highly romantic and emotional disposition — it seemed to be courting ridicule and disaster. Yet it brought to both nothing but joy and contentment: "We lived in inviolated love and mutual complacancy, sensible of the benefit of mutual help." For Margaret proved no helpless parasite. She devoted herself without any possessive jealousy to her husband's strenuous and difficulty ministry. The passing of the Conventicle Act and the Act of Uniformity brought Baxter into trouble and he was fined and sent to prison for continuing to preach where and how he could. When the Declaration of Indulgence made things a little easier, he managed to obtain a licence to preach once again, and he wrote that it was through his wife that this came about.

> "She first fisht out of me in what place I most desired more preaching. I told her in St Martin's Parish, where are said to be forty thousand more than can come into the Church. . . . When she once heard this, without any knowledge she sets one to seek after some big room there; and none was found, except over the market-house at St James and she took that."

But, as was not unusual in those days, the building was old and unsafe and one day while Baxter was preaching there, there was an ominous crack. Margaret, hearing it, ran down the stairs and into the street and stopped the first man that she met to ask for help. By a miracle he was a carpenter.

> "Saith she, 'Can you immediately put a prop under a beam' . . . the man dwelt close by, had a prop ready and put it under which all we above knew nothing of it."

Such prompt presence of mind says much for Margaret's practical efficiency but it is just as characteristic of her that, though she had probably saved many lives, she was haunted by the thought that it was she who had chosen the place and that if the floor had given way, close on eight hundred people would have been buried in the ruins. She therefore kept the day every year as a special thanksgiving day to God and determined to build another room with her own money. This she did, but an end had come to the Indulgence and Baxter was prevented from using it.

Margaret also started a school for teaching poor children to read and to give employment to an indigent teacher who had been a minister. She tried to save Baxter's beloved library for him, hiding some books and sending some to New England. She followed him to prison and loved him the more for his intrepid spirit and refusal of all wordly advancement. She had a good brain, knew her classics and helped to educate her husband's nephew. Baxter says that she possessed great tact and was the more practical of the two and

> "except in cases that require learning and skill in theological difficulties, she was better at resolving a case of conscience than most divines that ever I knew in all my life . . . insomuch that of late years, I confess that I used to put all, save secret cases, to her and hear what she could say."

Marriage dispersed all her melancholy and fears of damnation but her highly-strung temperament sometimes showed in other ways. "She was exceedingly impatient with my nonconforming ministers who shrunk for fear of suffering," and "she could not bear a disputing contradiction." She was distressed too by delays and disappointments. It was probably a merciful thing that she was spared the infamous trial of her husband by Judge Jefferies.

Her enthusiasm and her labours wore out her frail body and she died at the age of forty after a short distressing illness, during

which her mind gave way. She had always been haunted by fear
of madness. Baxter, "under the power of melting grief", wrote a
brief but moving biography of his wife. It was for her also that
he composed one of his best known and loved hymns:

> "Lord it belongs not to my care
> Whether I die or live,
> To love and serve Thee is my share
> And this Thy grace must give.
>
> Christ leads me through no darker door
> Than he went through before.
> He that in to God's Kingdom comes
> Must enter by this door.
>
> My knowledge of that life is small
> The eye of faith is dim,
> But 'tis enough that Christ knows all
> And I shall be with him."

The Christianity of these seventeenth-century women was an
intensely personal affair. While their husbands fought on the
battlefield or disputed from the pulpit, they retired into their
closets to pray and to meditate. The best attributes of Puritanism
were common to both Anglicans and Nonconformists — a sincere,
disciplined and ardent dedication to what they believed to be the
pearl of greatest price. They lived during the last period of English history when faith was unquestioned, though the form it
should take was hotly debated. Doubt of God and of his Son never
entered into these women's minds, only doubt of their own worthi-
ness. Except for Margaret Baxter — and even she plainly possessed
a mind and a will of her own — they do not seem to have been
much influenced by their husbands or by any man. The Protestant
sense of individual responsibility was strong in them. It may be
thought that they were too much concerned with the state of their
own souls, but it is obvious that their piety did not stop there
but that they were much occupied in the care of their servants, the
poor and everyone who might come to them for help. It was an
age in which organised charity hardly existed and when private
personal caring was almost always actuated by religious fervour.
These women led busy lives in troublesome times, yet spent longer
with their Bibles and on their knees than is conceivable to us.

The seventeenth century produced our greatest religious literature. There is a power and a purity about it, due possibly to the fact that in this period men had not lost the vision of their fathers but at the same time were conscious of wider horizons ahead. The Age of Reason did not yet threaten the Age of Faith, but both reason and faith combined to light the "Candle of the Lord".

Bunyan's *Pilgrim's Progress*, appearing in 1677, was immensely popular with women as well as men, with young as well as old. Bunyan had no book learning other than the Bible and the inevitable Foxe, but the impact of his original genius was irresistible. In 1684, the second part of Bunyan's great work appeared, and this was written especially for women. Bunyan, like Milton, undoubtedly looked upon them as weaker vessels, but there is neither fear nor contempt in his attitude, only compassion. Christiana and Mercy and their children have a much easier time of it than Christian and Faithful. They are provided with Mr Greatheart to fight their battles for them and to guide them throughout their pilgrimage. Mr Ready-to-Halt and Master Feeble-Mind are of their company but neither they nor the women are ever represented as foolish or contemptible in any way. On the contrary, there are certain valuable qualities which they alone possess and which aid them in their Pilgrimage. The Valley of Humiliation, where Christian met with Apollyon, held no such terrors for the humble of heart. Instead they perceived "how green was the valley and how beautiful with lillies" and Mercy exclaims: "I think I am as well in this valley as I have been anywhere else in all our journey. I love to be in such a place where there is no rattling of coaches or rumbling with wheels." Lady Warwick would have agreed with her.

Christiana, like Mr Fearing, but unlike her husband, was untroubled by the Hill of Difficulty, by the Lions or by Vanity Fair, but feared only her own unworthiness to reach the Celestial City and this "made her knock the louder" for forgiveness and help. Margaret Baxter would have understood how she felt.

Christian would have been quite overcome by Giant Despair had it not been for his companion, but the little band of the women and disabled were neither frightened nor cast down when they came to Doubting Castle but cheerfully trusted in Greatheart and the boys to protect them, and when these returned in triumph

110

with the giant's head upon a pole and the rescued prisoners, Despondence and his daughter Much-Afraid, it was the women who converted a crude battle scene into the grace and joy of a new hope.

> "Now Christiana, if need was, could play upon the viol, and her daughter Mercy upon the lute; . . . so she played them a lesson and Ready-to-Halt would dance. So he took Despondency's daughter, Much-Afraid, by the hand, and so dancing they went in the road."

This second part of Bunyan's great book is suffused with poetry and a gentleness which is quite lacking in the first part. Puritan though he was, he is not afraid of beauty:

> "And when Christiana and Mercy were returned out of the garden, the Interpreter took them and looked upon them and said 'Fair as the moon'."

Flowers and trees and birds are mentioned and the air seems often to be filled with sweet sound.

"Hark," says Mercy on entering the House Beautiful, "don't you hear a noise?" and Christiana answers, "Yes, it is as I believe a noise of music for joy that we are here." Mercy cries: "Wonderful! Music in the home, music in the heart, and music also in heaven for joy that we are here!" It is as if Bunyan realised that the "weaker vessels" brought out the graciousness of Christianity and that they alone could do this.

Christiana and Mercy are no allegorical puppets but real women, and Bunyan struck a true note when he stresses their personal approach to religion. Christiana had been unconvinced by Christian's arguments and had refused to go with him. What ultimately sends her forth on her pilgrimage is no heaven-sent evangelist and no fear of destruction, but the simple longing to see her husband again and to be with him, while Mercy goes with her out of the natural kindness of her heart to keep her company and help look after the children. Love was the reason of their going and Love was the end of their journey. When at length the company are awaiting their summons to the Celestial City, a messenger arrives "with a token that was come to bid her make haste to be gone. The token was an arrow with a point sharpened with love". At her departure her children wept. But Mr Greatheart and Mr Valiant

111

played upon the well-tuned cymbal and harp for joy. To how many humble Christianas must these words have brought comfort and hope. Bunyan's book was in the succeeding century more popular with the less aristocratic and highly educated sections of society, and with Nonconformists rather than Anglicans. Mrs Elizabeth Montague, the famous bluestocking, dismisses it as "one of those classics of the artificers in leather", but it was undoubtedly, next to the Bible, the most widely read and best loved devotional work among women for the next two hundred years, and thousands of God-fearing housewives saw to it that, to their children, Christian and Christiana, Faithful and Greatheart, Apollyon and Doubting Castle, the Delectable Mountains and the Celestial City were as real and as vivid as the scenes and the characters that they met every day.

8
The Quakers

There was one notable exception to the general view of women among the Puritans of the seventeenth century. The Quakers, founded by George Fox in 1647, preached the equality of the sexes from the very first: "There can be no male and female, for ye are all one man in Jesus Christ." But their aim was not merely to proclaim women's spiritual equality in the eyes of God but to develop their powers in the cause of humanity as the complement rather than a poor copy of man. As the Quaker historian Rufus Jones writes in *The Later Periods of Quakerism*: "What Fox was concerned with was to give women their place, their right place . . . to liberate for the service of the Church the gifts of government which lay dormant and barren both in men and women. The venture, in the case of women, was a daring one and taxed seventeenth-century feminine capacity to the utmost but this only adds to its significance."

The Quakers had at first sight much in common with many of the extreme sects that flourished in England at this time, offshoots of the Anabaptists. What distinguished them, however, almost from the first, was George Fox's emphasis on practical and thorough organisation. This emphasis was strengthened by his friendship with Judge Fell and his wife Margaret, an educated and influential couple, exercising much local power in Westmorland where their home at Swarthmore Hall became a famous Quaker stronghold. Although Judge Fell himself never actually joined the sect he was friendly towards them, while his wife Margaret devoted all the energy of an unusually intelligent, determined and capable personality to the new movement. Some time after Judge Fell's death she and Fox married, however their spiritual partnership began long before and was an even closer and more fruitful one than that of St Clare and St Francis or St Teresa and St John of the Cross. They dedicated their great talents to shaping and fostering this new force and at the time of Fox's death in 1691 the

Quakers were the largest body of nonconformists in the country numbering one in every hundred of the population and this in spite of (or possibly because of) intense and prolonged persecution.

This persecution was the reason for the formation of the first "Women's Meeting" in 1660. Very soon there were two separate Women's Meetings, the first to give moral support and advice, the second to provide material assistance to all who were suffering from imprisonment and loss of livelihood, thus carrying out the aim which has always been characteristic of the Quakers of keeping the balance between the spiritual and the practical, a balance which owes much to an equal status and contribution of male and female elements. The second meeting among Quakers was nicknamed "the Box", from the box which received the charitable gifts. It still functions and has an unbroken record from 1671.

All women in the Society of Friends, the name by which the Quakers prefer to be called, were encouraged "to come into God's Service that they may be serviceable in their generation and in the Creation. . . . Let the Creation have its liberty." The Women's Meetings were run on the same lines as the men's with a presiding Clerk (or Chairman), and seemed to be particularly concerned with any personal problems that might arise. One minute of a London Women's Meeting opens with the words "Truth is that which is pure" and continues with a resolution that "all backbiting and whispering must be stopped", advising that this should be the task of the older women and concluding wisely "but when anything is once condemned and judged, let it not be raised up again, but keep it in ye grave, and raise not up ye dead out of ye grave any more."

One group of Friends that somewhat surprisingly seems to have been the special responsibility of the Women's Meetings was that of travellers, "seamen, merchants, masters of ships and passengers out and home", and if information was lodged against any of these that "they had in anyways dishonoured the Word of God or brought an evil report in either their trading or lives or conversation" they were summoned before a committee of women whose duty was "to search into the bottom" of the matter. Emigrants of both sexes were also the special concern of London's Women's Meeting and all intended marriages within the Society had to be publicly announced first before the Women's Meeting and then the Men's. Eventually the women's and men's business meetings were merged for purposes of convenience. But during the whole of this early and most famous chapter of Quaker history the influence of women and most of all of Margaret Fell is of the utmost importance.

Margaret had supreme self-confidence in herself and in her faith. Her tactics were those of a direct personal approach to authority. She had no hesitation in advising and admonishing both Cromwell and Charles II. Cromwell she pressed to grant religious toleration to all, accusing him of hypocrisy in talking about liberty of conscience while Quakers were being persecuted. But probably Cromwell was unable to control his more bigoted followers. He seems however to have protected the Friends to some extent during his rule. In 1660 Fox himself was imprisoned and Margaret travelled to London to try and obtain both his release and that of hundreds of other fellow sufferers. She was no humble suppliant. She wrote to every member of the Royal Family and protested vehemently against the paying of tithes and the taking of oaths. "Methinks I hear the Bishops mutter, murmur and contemn . . . therefore I do hereby give them my Reason and Cause." She actually got an order for the release of Quaker prisoners signed by the King and Council but then, tragically, the "Fifth Monarchy" Plot against the King was discovered, panic ensued and the Quakers, who were suspect because of their habit of holding private meetings, were persecuted worse even than before. Margaret remained undaunted in London seeking constantly to plead with the King. At last "the ayre was cleered and the darknesse layde" and Charles ordered the release of all suspected Quakers. It is to be feared that this favour was granted in the spirit of the unjust judge to the importunate widow rather than from any sincere conviction for it was merely a temporary relief and Margaret was soon herself to suffer imprisonment at Lancaster for refusing to take the oath of allegiance, though she declared her complete loyalty to the King. She explained that, like all the Friends, she must abide by the command: "Swear not at all." But this plea was rarely if ever accepted and she was led away crying, "Although I am out of the King's protection, I am not out of the protection of the Almighty God." She received a life sentence though had only to serve four and a half years during which period she wrote persistent addresses to her fellow Quaker prisoners throughout the land, to the magistrates and to the king. Her approach to him was that of a disappointed friend and of a sad and solemn counsellor:

> "What do you think will become of this Nation if you continue to go on and take so many thousands of poor Husbands and Tradesmen from their Husbandry and Calling, now in this season of the Year, when they should Plow and Sow their Ground to maintain their Families."

She told him not to listen to the bishops who "were the Ruine of thy father", she declared that the visitation of the Great Plague was a sign of God's displeasure, and she reminded him that he "must beware how thou rulest in this Nation for the people of this Nation was a brittle People generally". And why, she asks, and for what offence "hast thou kept me in Prison three long Winters, in a place not fit for People to lie in: some time for Wind and Storm and Rain and sometime for Smoke: so that it is much that I am alive, but that the Power and Goodness of God hath been with me." It would have taken more than these hardships, however, to quell Margaret and at last her protestations were effectual and she was set free and without the loss of her property. She at once started on a series of journeys to visit other Friends in prison and again to appeal to the King for them, but Charles was in the last year of his life and did not respond. At James II's accession he proclaimed a pardon for all Quaker prisoners and a Meeting House was built on part of Margaret's property at Swarthmore. She lived to be eighty-six and to the last was an active influence in the Society. She continued her habit of corresponding with the head of the State and wrote to King William thanking him for his moderation and mercy.

Margaret Fell was a most attractive character. She was a complete person, a much loved and loving wife to two notable husbands, a good mother to seven children, an able and energetic worker in both the spiritual and practical fields of her chosen faith but no bigot. We find her in her old age pleading for greater tolerance for youth, reacting somewhat against the stricter Quakers and rejoicing in the beauty of nature.

The equal part that women played in the ministry of the Society of Friends may be gauged by the equality of the persecution meted out to them. No allowances were made for their sex and none expected. They were beaten till the blood ran, set in stocks for hours on end in torturing positions, driven out of their homes in the depths of winter, imprisoned in revolting conditions but nothing could bend or break them. Besides the special duties of ministering to the suffering, resolving quarrels and looking after the good conduct of travellers they were the chief means of distributing Quaker pamphlets and they also numbered among them some of the most notable of Quaker missionaries.

Barbara Blangdone, like Margaret Fell, was both well connected and well educated. She was not converted until middle age and confesses that after conversion she still hankered for good food and soft clothes. To punish herself she abstained from all meat for a year and drank nothing but water. This was typical of a fanatical streak (lacking in Margaret) that even rejoiced in her sufferings. When she was imprisoned at Bristol she went on hunger strike for two weeks "as a witness against that dark professing people", and when she was whipped she sang aloud: "And the Beadle said, 'Do ye sing? I shall make ye cry by and by' and with that he laid more stripes and laid them on very hard and I shall never forget the large experience of Love and Power of God which I had (then)." No one ever made Barbara cry. At Bridgwater she testified in the church or Steeple House as the Quakers called it (the true Church being Christ's people and not a building) and for this she was driven out of the town. It was winter and very cold but she found "a Pig-stye swept very clean, and the Trough turned up and never a pig in it. And I sate me down on the Trough and that was my lodging all that night." The personal approach to Authority seems always to have been the chosen method of women Friends and they believed in making straight for the man in authority. So Barbara, when she felt called to Ireland in 1656, sought out Henry Cromwell, who had been appointed by his father to command the forces out there and to act as Deputy. The Quakers had been establishing themselves in the towns amongst the English settlers and in spite of imprisonments were becoming a nuisance to Henry by preaching pacifism to the troops. He wrote home that they seemed to him "to be the most considerable enemy" so stricter measures were taken against them and this it was that sent Barbara to expostulate with him. Characteristically she was not put off by a first denial of an audience, nor by a trick played upon her when at last permission to see the Deputy was granted. A priest entered the room and impersonated Henry but Barbara saw through the disguise and refused to speak until the real Deputy appeared. She then let him off easily laying the blame for the treatment of the Quakers upon "the evil magistrates and bad priests" who were acting in his name. Henry was impressed by her sincerity and by her appeal to his well-known love of justice and "was so sad and melancholy after she had been with him that he could not go to the bowls or any other pastime". But for all that, probably upon orders from home, he did little to protect the Quakers and Barbara left for England after a few months.

However, in the winter of that same year she was back again. Both voyages, incidentally, were hazardous and on this second occasion she was actually shipwrecked and had to swim for the shore. As usual she wasted no time on subordinates but began at once to preach to the judges sitting in the Court of Justice in Dublin. For this she was immediately imprisoned and "suffered much". She became involved in a secular case of murder for which she believed a fellow prisoner, an innkeeper, to have been wrongly condemned. The trial was an obviously trumped-up affair and on the uncertain witness of one man the poor innkeeper and his whole family were hung. "A heavy day it was," said Barbara, "and I bore and suffered much that day." She also determined that the Judge should suffer and she told him that it was a terrible thing to run the risk so lightly of condemning the innocent and prophesied that "the day of his death drew nigh wherein he must give an account of his actions". She had friends in Dublin who pressed for her release to which the judge agreed at last with great reluctance and not without reason, as she went at once to the church which he habitually attended "to testify against him" and whether by coincidence or whether from a heart attack brought on by anger and fear, he died that very night. The result was to enhance Barbara's notoriety to an unfortunate extent. She was imprisoned three more times and finally banished from the country. Needless to say, her homeward journey too was disastrously dramatic. She was attacked by pirates and robbed of all her goods and even of the coat she was wearing, upon which she "began to

118

consider whether there was any service for me to do among those rude people — but I found little to them."

So much for Ireland. At home she continued upon the familiar round of preaching and prison and we hear of her writing to James II in 1686 protesting that in spite of his recent proclamation, there were still Quakers languishing in Bristol prisons. Barbara was certainly no meek Quakeress. She was incredibly tough and in spite of all her imprisonments, floggings, hunger strikes, shipwrecks and privations she lived to be ninety-five. She had much of the Old Testament prophetess about her, stern, unyielding and absolutely sure that "the Lord God Himself was with her".

Another intrepid Quaker missionary, but in all else a complete contrast to Barbara, was Mary Fisher. She was of humble origin and had been a servant but was probably taught to read and write in prison by a fellow prisoner, Elizabeth Hooton, who was Fox's first convert and woman preacher. Elizabeth had come from the Cambidgeshire Fens and on Mary's release she decided to go with another Friend, Elizabeth Williams, to preach Quakerism at Cambridge. The university was at this time the centre of Puritan learning. For two poor working-class women to lecture on religion to Cambridge students was from every point of view extraordinary. Nor did they mince their words:

> "The Women, observing the Froth and levity of their Behaviour, told them they were Antichrists, and that their college was a Cage of Unclean Birds and the Synagogue of Satan."

Not surprisingly the undergraduates hauled them before the mayor who asked them their names: "They replied that their names were written in the Book of Life." He then asked them their husbands' names: "They told him they had no husband but Jesus Christ." The mayor then perhaps understandably lost his temper but his subsequent treatment of them was savage. He ordered them to be beaten unmercifully at the Market Cross and to be thrust out of the town but the Cambridge justices afterwards repudiated the mayor's sentence.

Two other young Quaker women, following Mary and Elizabeth's example, set forth to convert Oxford. Here they were treated worse by the undergraduates but a great deal better by the mayor, who defended them and gave them food and clothes and offered to lend them money. But in spite of him they were committed to a whipping though this seems to have been carried out unwillingly and with much less severity than at Cambridge.

Mary Fisher, three years later, set out for America with an older companion. On arrival at Boston the two women were shipped back to Barbados but not before suffering the indignity of being stripped and examined for the devil's marks on their bodies. The Puritans of Boston were witch-hunters and though no marks were found the two Quaker women were thrust into prison and would have starved there had it not been for one brave old compassionate man who bribed the jailer weekly to give them food. Five weeks passed before they were allowed to take ship again but in Barbados they had some success in their missionary work and left "many people convinced of the Truth which meet together in silence".

On returning to England, Mary Fisher decided to go to Turkey to convert the Sultan! She was not the first Quaker to attempt this extraordinary enterprise but she was the only one to reach her journey's end, if not to accomplish her aim. The Sultan was the great symbol of heathendom, magnificent in his titles: "Son of God, thrice known as the renowned Emperor of Turks, King of all the inhabitants of the Earth, Lord of the Tree of Life." Nothing perhaps illustrates the confidence born of perfect faith than these small bands of Quakers setting out to confront the mighty Prince of Paganism himself surrounded by the barbarous splendours of his court in an unimaginably distant and mysterious country. They were not allowed to get far. Embarrassed and hostile ambassadors and consuls relentlessly turned them back. Mary Fisher, however, managed with three men and two other women Friends to get to Smyrna where once again the English consul intervened and dispatched them home via Venice. Mary Fisher, the servant girl, outwitted him none the less and contrived to get herself left behind on the coast of Morea from which she calmly set out to walk six hundred miles through Greece and Macedonia to Adrianople with no knowledge of country, people or language. Cities were dangerous, but far from so-called civilisation, the peasant population, though extremely poor, were friendly to strangers and as they probably considered Mary mad, they treated her as sacred.

At any rate she arrived safely at Adrianople where the young Sultan was temporarily encamped in great style. Considering the utterly inferior status of Turkish women it seems amazing that Mary was even granted an audience with him. It would hardly be possible to imagine a greater contrast than between the humble, middle-aged Quaker woman in her plain grey travel-worn dress and the Eastern potentate among his scarlet and gold seraglio with "their feathers, their jewels and their bows and arrows". Mary was neither shy nor troubled. She stood there in silence waiting for the Inner Voice for "she knew it would be given her in this hour, what she should speak". The Sultan thought from her silence that she was overawed and courteously offered to withdraw to a less magnificent and crowded inner court but she refused and at last "spoke what was in her mind". All listened gravely and when she had finished the Sultan asked her if she had more to say but she said no if he had understood her. "He assured her, 'Yes, every word,' and further that what she had spoken was truth. Then he desired her to stay in that country, saying that they could not but respect such a one, as should take so much pains to come to them so far . . . with a message from the Lord God. He also offered her a guard to bring her into Constantinople, whither she intended, as it was dangerous travelling." But Mary would have none of this guard. She was then asked the ticklish question of what she thought of Mahomet. She was equal even to this and answered that

> "she knew him not, but Christ was the true Prophet . . . and Him she knew. And concerning Mahomet she said that they might judge of him to be true or false according to the words and prophecies he spoke, saying further: 'If the word that a prophet speak all come to pass, then shall ye know that the Lord have sent that prophet' and having performed her message departed from the camp to Constantinople without a guard, whither she came without the least hurt or scoff."[15]

From Constantinople she came home and there testified to her fellow Quakers in favour of the Turks. "They are more near truth than many Nations, there is a love begot in me towards them which is endless but this is my hope concerning them, yet He who hath raised me to love them more than many others, will also raise His seed in them unto which my love is." But, alas, it would have taken more than Mary Fisher's love to have effected a reconciliation between Christian and Turk in the seventeenth century. She herself made a late but happy marriage with a master mariner, a Quaker preacher, and like Barbara Blangdone and Margaret Fell lived to a ripe old age being known always as "that Mary Fisher who spake to the Great Turk".

It was natural that the only sect of the Reformed Church to allot an equal part in ministry to both sexes should have attracted a number of women of unusual abilities. Certain it is that there were many influential women in the forefront of the Quaker movement and this may have accounted for that healthy mixture of practical service with spiritual fervour, of concern for the individual with sound business-like administration which distinguished the Society. When the decline set in with the deaths of Fox and Margaret and the cessation of persecution, it was notable that Women's Meetings maintained more vigour and inspiration than the men's. An old Quaker woman writing towards the close of the century complains that "too much love of this world stains our pristine glory" but asserts that "the women's meetings are accompanied with the power and presence of the Lord as ever". It seems that the men, no longer suffering active persecution but still debarred with other non-conformists from the Universities and the professions, turned their attention to business and through the honesty and thoroughness of their dealings began to grow prosperous and respectable. The women, however, were still actively engaged in the work for which their meetings were initially established — that of relieving suffering, of which there was still enough to keep them busy.

But gradually in the succeeding century the Friends turned in upon themselves and became less and less concerned with outward affairs: their peculiar dress, assumed first as a protest against the extravagance of Restoration fashions and felt as a real sacrifice of vanity by the well-connected members of the Society, took on undue significance. Margaret Fell had foreseen the danger of a strict adherence to inessentials when she had pleaded for more colour and latitude for younger Friends. What had begun as a spiritual testimony could in many directions easily degenerate into mere outward conformity. To a certain extent this happened and in the eighteenth century the torch of inspiration passed to the Methodists. But the influence of women among the Quakers continued to be considerable especially in the social sphere. An amusing illustration of their ideas upon equality of the sexes occurs in Boswell when a certain Mrs Knowles, "the fair Quaker well known for her various talents", dared to assert to the great Dr Johnson himself that men were not entitled to their assumed superiority. She was of course immediately set upon for such an outrageous sentiment. But she went down fighting. "I hope, at least," she said, "that in another world the sexes will be allowed to be equal." To which Boswell replied, "That is being too ambitious, madam. *We*, men, might as well desire to be equal with the angels."

It remained however for a woman, Elizabeth Fry, to put Quakerism once more in the forefront of Christian social endeavour after its decline during most of the eighteenth century.

9
The Age of Reason and Methodism

When the inspired dreamer John Bunyan was released from his second imprisonment, he found "Vanity Fair" in full swing but no longer were the faggots piled high for Faithful and Christian, and by the end of the century the vision of the Celestial City, too, had grown less distinct. The Delectable Mountains had been somewhat levelled and the Valleys of Humiliation filled up. The struggles of the preceding age were played out and men and women in England settled down to less troubled times. Somehow it was singularly fitting that the plump prosaic figure of Queen Anne "who sometimes counsel took and sometimes tea" should occupy the throne at this time, instead of a tragic Mary or a magnificent Elizabeth. Not that Anne had no contribution to make as a Christian monarch, but again it was a suitable one. She was a sincere and firm supporter of the Anglican Church, who took her duties seriously as its Supreme Head, and she insisted on her right to appoint its bishops. More important for posterity, she determined to set right a wrong committed by the Crown at the Reformation, when the taxes, formerly paid by the clergy to the Pope, were appropriated by the King. She set aside a fund for the augmentation of poor livings which was named after her — Queen Anne's Bounty — and was a memorial to her practical piety. This was an augur of the new era in which the spirit of Christianity, in women especially, was to express itself in social philanthropy rather than in private devotion. This was the age of Newton, of "natural" religion and of a degree of secularisation comparable in part with the present day.

It was a social age: "The proper study of mankind is man", wrote Pope, and he meant man in relation to his fellows. His readers would hardly have thought it worth while to include women in their studies but, in fact, certain women played no inconsiderable part in the growth of the social conscience which gradually emerged during the century.

A less pleasing change was that, for the first time, religion in England became class conscious. During the Middle Ages, and indeed up to the mid-seventeenth century, there was little or none of this. The lady of the manor, the merchant's wife and the peasant woman all worshipped in the same church and all served the same ceremonies. At the Reformation, Catholics and Protestants were separated by doctrine but not by rank. Later still Cavaliers and Parliamentarians, Anglicans and Independents could, and often did, belong to one family. But after the Restoration, the stringent laws against Dissenters, excluding them from all high office and from the universities, gradually had their effect in equating the Anglican Church with gentlefolk. Its livings became the recognised provision for the younger sons of the county families, who were often in possession of private means, whereas dissenting ministers had nothing but their often low stipends to depend upon. Finally, when the Wesleyan movement took firmest root among the new industrial poor, it was inevitably confounded with radicalism. This made for difficulties unforeseen by its founders. Nevertheless Methodism was the most important antidote to the prevailing scepticism and deadness and it spread like fire among dry stubble.

Susannah Wesley has been called the Mother of the Movement and that she was so, both in the physical and spiritual sense, is undeniable. She was the daughter, wife and mother of clergymen, receiving, nurturing and transmitting the "Sacred Seed".

The history of the Wesley family illustrates the unimportance of sectarian differences compared with an attitude and way of life. Then doctrinal allegiance swung from dissent to conformity and again from conformity to dissent, but their commitment remains through three generations, fundamentally Puritan in the highest sense of the word. Susannah's father Dr Samuel Annesly was a close friend of Richard Baxter. He was a Presbyterian minister who suffered under the Act of Uniformity, but his generous spirit had no use for bitterness or intolerance. Defoe described him in telling lines:

"Strange were the charms of his sincerity
Which made his actions and his words agree
At such a constant and exact a rate
As made a Harmony we wondered at."

This harmony was not apparently disturbed at the resolve of his youngest and favourite daughter, when she had reached the mature age of twelve, to join the Church which had persecuted her father. Long after, she wrote down for the benefit of her sons her reason for taking this step, which she never regretted or retracted. But the paper was destroyed in the famous fire at Epworth Rectory which nearly destroyed the little John Wesley as well. So we can only guess at her arguments. It was certainly not revolt against a revered and much loved father, nor escape from her family. She upheld the family as of vital importance to a Christian community. This conception that piety begins in the family, which ought to be "a little gathered Church" was as deeply held by Puritan Anglican Nicholas Ferrar or William Law as by Puritan dissenting John Bunyan or Richard Baxter. Perhaps Susannah's strong personality, the youngest of many children, felt the need to find for itself a separate identity. Perhaps, a lover of order and discipline, she was drawn to a more exacting, objective and definite spiritual ruling than that of her father, whose influence none the less was felt by her all her life and through her was transmitted to his grandsons. Without it a nature like hers might have become intolerant. As it was, his spirit did not desert her and she could say with her best loved sister Elizabeth "that the image of Christ is the same lovely thing, whether formed in a church or a meeting". Her husband, the Reverend Samuel Wesley, was not so inclined. Ironically, he prided himself on having imbued all his children with "a steady opposition and confederacy against any who were not staunchly for High Church and for inviolable passive obedience". But it was Susannah and not he who was the formative influence in their family.

She has often been criticised for excessive severity in her ideas upon the upbringing of children. Certainly by modern standards her advice, that "when turned a year old they should be brought to fear the rod" and that "the first thing to be done is to conquer a child's will", seems shocking and destructive. But to her contemporaries these precepts were almost platitudinous and on the other hand what *was* unusual were the injunctions never to punish a confessed offence, never to punish for the same thing twice, "never to correct your children to satisfy your passions . . . and to be careful to let the measure of correction be proportionable to the fault". She advised that great allowances should be made for their age and immaturity and that patience and encouragement should overrule all.

She herself had infinite patience, which her husband, who was short-tempered, would often wonder at. "You have told that child twenty times the same thing." "It was the twentieth time that crowned it," she replied. Her insistence on early obedience was founded upon the belief that the younger the child was in grasping the fundamental reality of other people's rights and reasons, the easier it would be to learn self-discipline and that good habits were also far less painful to acquire then than later. It is arguable that the feeling of responsibility Susannah had for the total welfare of each of her children which led her "never to spare them through foolish fondness" might not show more real creative love than an indulgence which is too often another word for laziness.

Susannah's severity was all part of a carefully reasoned "method" — the word is her own choice and probably influenced her son Charles's famous use of it when he formed his first little group of "Methodists" at Cambridge. With ten lively masterful children (she actually bore nineteen) whom she had to feed and clothe and educate on a very low income, some method was necessary if they were to be brought up at all. "Tell me, Mrs Wesley," said the Archbishop of York to her one day, "whether you ever really wanted bread?"

" 'My Lord,' said I, 'I will freely own to Your Grace that, strictly speaking, I never did want bread. But then, I had so much care to get it before it was eat, and to pay for it after, as has often made it very unpleasant to me.' "

The children were early taught to help with the household jobs and the elder ones to mind the babies, but regular time was also set apart for book work and for play with plenty of sleep and plain fare. With such a crowd the mother saw plainly that it was advisable to make opportunities for individual contact so: "On Monday I talk with Molly; on Tuesday with Hetty; Wednesday with Nancy, Thursday with Jacky, Friday with Patty, Saturday with Charles, and with Emily and Sukey together on Sundays." Years later, when he was a Fellow of Lincoln College, Oxford, John, who still sought his mother's advice, wrote:

"If you can spare me only that little part of Thursday evening which you formerly bestowed on me in another manner, I doubt but it would be as useful now for correcting my heart as it was then for forming my judgment."

Thus the vindication of Susannah's ideas on the early training of her children lies in the subsequent lives and their affection and reliance upon their mother. No one can accuse John and Charles and Samuel and Patty of leading a cowed and repressed life. That her severity was always tempered by love is clear yet again from the testimony of Charles, who in one of his hymns for parents writes:

"We would *persuade* their hearts today
With mildest zeal proceed
And never take the harsher way
When love will do the deed.

To watch their will, to sense inclined
Withhold their hurtful good;
And gently bend their tender mind
And draw their souls to God."

The training of her children was Susannah's priority but as a clergyman's wife she had many other duties. They were made more difficult by her husband's temperament. Courageous and clever, he was also improvident and fiery-tempered. There was mutual love and respect but as Susannah confessed to John: "Your father and I seldom think alike." One serious difference was political. Susannah was a Jacobin in her sympathies and refused to pray for King William: "I do not believe him to be King," she stated. "If that be the case," said her husband, "you and I must part; for if we have two Kings, we must have two beds." Susannah would not give way, so off he went to London declaring that he would do anything rather than live with a person "that is the declared enemy of his country". Susannah was not to be cowed though she was desperately unhappy. Eventually after several months, through the opportune death of King William and the interventions of friends, a reconciliation was brought about. The child of their reunion was John Wesley. Samuel was hopeless about money matters and was once imprisoned for debt. He sought the help of the Archbishop of York, writing: "My wife bears it with that courage which becomes her and which I expected of her." On this occasion her strength of mind, which had caused havoc over the sad matter of King William, stood him in good stead. On other occasions also; whenever, as seemed to happen frequently, he had to be from home, Susannah carried on the business of the parish with the hindrance of a curate who objected to her authority, to her holding classes at the vicarage and above all to her reading a sermon to the congregation. Samuel was too conscious of her value to forbid this, though he agreed with some reluctance. It had important repercussions for when the question of lay readers and preachers of both sexes came up with regard to the ministry of her sons, Susannah's influence and experience swung the balance in their favour. A young lay helper had begun to preach, unauthorised by John who heard of it with disapproval. But Susannah was at hand with quiet words of advice:

> "John, you know what my sentiments have been. You cannot suspect me of favouring readily anything of this kind. But take care what you do with respect to that young man, for he is as surely called of God to preach as you are. Examine what have been the fruit of his preaching and hear him also yourself."

The result of her counsel was the beginning of the famous evangelistic work of the Methodist lay preachers.

From the early years women had been appointed within the movement as band and class leaders, but gradually they began also to be accepted as preachers. Sarah Crosly and Mary Bosanquet were among the first. There is a letter from John to the latter in which he vindicates his consent to her preaching as regards the bugbear of St Paul's stricture:

> "My dear sister – I think the strength of the case rests there, on your having an extraordinary call. So I am persuaded has every one of our lay Preachers. Otherwise I could not countenance his preaching at all. . . . St Paul's ordinary rule was 'I permit not of women to speak in the congregation.' Yet, in extraordinary cases he made a few exceptions — at Corinth in particular."

The extraordinary cases appeared not to be so extraordinary after all, for the number of women lay preachers quickly increased and made their mark, though the general opinion of the public was probably even more unfavourably prejudiced than Dr Johnson's:

"Sir, a woman's preaching is like a dog's walking on his hinder legs. It is not done well, but you are surprised to find it done at all."

There is no doubt that these Methodist women lay preachers were wholly committed and indefatigable. Sarah Crosly travelled 960 miles and held 120 public services and 600 class meetings in one year. She is probably "the blessed woman" who was a friend of Dinah Morris in *Adam Bede*. There is an unforgettable description of Dinah herself preaching on the village green which conjures up a vivid and true picture of the Methodist woman preacher at her best. Dinah is founded on the personality and vocation of George Eliot's aunt, Elizabeth Evans. Patty Wesley was a preacher and is described by Boswell as "lean and lank, the sister of the Rev. Mr John Wesley and resembling him, as I thought, in figure and manner".

Altogether, as teachers, visitors to the poor and sick, class leaders and certainly not seldom as preachers, women played an important part in this great religious revival of the eighteenth century. As in the case of the Quakers, this was a cause of calumny and of persecution and the Methodists were accused not only of radicalism but also of sexual immorality. After Wesley's death women preachers were discouraged and finally, in 1835, the practice was formally discontinued. That they were ever accepted was chiefly due to the influence of "the Mother of Methodism".

Susannah herself did not fully adopt the faith and doctrine held by her sons until her old age. She belonged by temperament more to the discipline of an earlier time — to the conscious fostering of virtue rather than the sudden salvation by grace. In fact she distrusted the doctrine of conversion by grace alone and she feared too many innovations. She was also critical of the subjectivity of Methodism: "I wish they could talk less of themselves and more of God." Like Dr Johnson, a man of deep but humble piety, she was unable to feel a triumphant assurance of forgiveness. But this assurance seems to have come to her in her old age. Charles, always more emotional and extreme than his brother, commemorates the event in a hymn:

"She knew and felt her sins forgiven
And found the earnest of her heaven."

130

Less graciously the following verse speaks of "her legal night of seventy years". But the fact that Susannah was enabled to find the meeting point between faith and reason so that, while not deserting her heritage of discipline, she could also understand the joy of "hearts aflame with God" certainly rendered her last years happier and full of peace and praise.

There were two other offshoots of Evangelism in the eighteenth century — the Calvinist followers of George Whitefield and, much later, the movement fully within the Anglican community, of which the Clapham group were the outstanding representatives.

Wesleyan Methodism denied the concept of election. Many of the hymns which they made so popular declared this anti-Calvinist doctrine:

> "Thy *undistinguishing* regard
> Was cast on Adam's fallen race,
> *For all* Thou hast in Christ prepared
> Sufficient, sovereign, saving grace."

In spite of the New Testament teaching it seems easier for the rich to believe themselves the elect, and whereas the Wesleys' brand of evangelism appealed chiefly to the poor and outcast, George Whitefield's mission was mainly successful among the fashionable world. Foremost of his supporters was the Countess of Huntingdon. Born in 1707 (four years after John Wesley), she grew from a serious little girl into a serious young woman, though her marriage to the ninth Earl of Huntingdon brought her into a worldly and aristocratic circle. A severe illness and the loss of two sons and her husband in a comparatively short period turned her thoughts towards Methodism. It needed some courage in the fashionable world to confess to any such leanings. Lady Anne Cumley, a friend of Lady Huntingdon, was turned out of her home by her husband for such depravity and died, as it was believed, from the results eight months later. Lady Huntingdon, none the less, openly declared her admiration for George Whitefield and decided it was her particular mission to convert her acquaintances. She took them with her to hear the great preacher, much as she might make up a party for the opera. In fact Whitefield's was a highly dramatic performance and like most Calvinists, his sermons were shot through with livid flashes of damnation. Lady Rockingham retired on one occasion in hysterics believing herself to have been personally insulted from the pulpit. But such incidents only added to the attractions. Lady Buckingham, an illegitimate daughter of James II, wrote a letter which well illustrates both the odium which Methodism aroused among the aristocracy and the entertainment value of its popular preachers:

"I thank your Ladyship for information concerning the Methodist preaching; their doctrines are most repulsive and strongly tinctured with impertinence . . . as it is monstrous to be told that you have a heart as sinful as the common wretches that crawl on the earth. This is highly offensive and insulting and I cannot but wonder that your Ladyship should relish any sentiments so much at variance with high rank and good breeding.

"Your Ladyship does me infinite honour by your obliging enquiries after my health. I shall be most happy to accept your kind offer of accompanying me to hear your favourite preacher and shall await your arrival. . . . The Duchess of Queensberry insists on my patronising her on the occasion, consequently she will be an addition to our party."

Two other letters, very different in tone, from the famous Sarah, Duchess of Marlborough, who, whatever faults she may have had, was incapable of insincerity, bear witness to some success on Lady Huntingdon's part in her efforts for her friends:

"My dear Lady Huntingdon is always so very good to me and I really do feel so very sensibly all your kindness and attention, that I must accept your very obliging invitation to accompany you to hear Mr Whitefield, though I am still suffering from the effects of a severe cold. Your concern for my improvement and religious knowledge is very obliging and I do hope that I shall be better for all your excellent advice.

"God knows we all need mending and none more than myself . . . women of wit, beauty and quality cannot bear too many humiliating truths — they shock our pride — but we must die, we must converse with earth and worms."

And again:

"In truth I always feel more happy and more contented after an hour's conversation with you then after a whole week's round of amusement. When alone, my reflections and recollections

132

almost kill me and I am forced to fly to the Society of those I detest and abhor. Now there is Lady Frances Sanderson's great rout to-morrow night . . . I do hate that woman . . . but I must go if for no other purpose than to mortify her and spite her.

"This is very wicked I know, but I confess all my little pecadillos to you, for I know your goodness will lead you to be mild and forgiving and perhaps my wicked heart may get some good from you in the end."

These moving letters are a testimony needed by Lady Huntingdon, as she had many detractors. John Wesley himself disliked her as an arrogant and despotic woman and Horace Walpole, who always spoke affectionately of Hannah More, scoffed at the Countess and her works: "The Queen of the Methodists got her daughter named for Lady of the Bedchamber to the Princess, but it is all off again as she will not let her play cards on Sundays."

Walpole's comments on Wesleyan Methodism, by the way, were little less contemptuous and he was certainly typical of the general attitude of the polite world:

"I have been at one opera, Mrs Wesley's. They have boys and girls with charming voices that sing hymns so long that one would think they were already in eternity; except for a few, from curiosity like myself, and some honourable women, the congregation was very mean. There was a Scotch Countess, who is carrying a pure rosy vulgar face to heaven."

The hymn-singing referred to by Walpole was one of the most famous of Methodist innovations and was reviled by their opponents, both for vulgarity and also because it "distracted the labourer from the field, and his wife and children from the wheel".

Lady Huntingdon's endeavours then to involve the Upper Classes with evangelism was no easy task, but that she was successful at least to some extent is to her credit. Lady Chesterfield was a convert. "I know who chose that sober gown for you," remarked George III to her, "it was Mr Whitefield and I hear you have attended on him this year and a half." The countess, however, did not confine her attentions to her friends at Court. She founded a college in Wales to train Methodist students which was afterwards moved to Hertfordshire. She even wrote to George Washington about a mission to North American Indians. But her chief memorial remains in the many elegant little eighteenth-century chapels scattered throughout the country and especially charming in those once fashionable resorts of Brighton, Bath, Tunbridge Wells and Cheltenham. Upon these she lavished her wealth, even selling some of her jewels to build and to found them, and they were known as the Chapels of Lady Huntingdon's Connection.

10
Women and the Evangelical Movement

Methodism gave greater scope to women in the eighteenth century for public ministry than they had previously enjoyed except within the Society of Friends. Incidentally Methodist women workers were sometimes confused with Quakers, partly because they favoured sober fashions of dress. Dinah Morris in *Adam Bede* is described as wearing a Quaker bonnet and black or grey gowns. Lady Huntingdon had made Whitefield's brand of Methodism fashionable among a few of her aristocratic friends, but the Wesleys had been turned out of the orthodox church and the Methodist movement was suspect among the comfortably off, both because of its radicalism, its popularity among the working classes and also for its "enthusiasm" — a dirty word in the eighteenth century. "Sir," said Bishop Butler, "the pretending to extraordinary gifts of the Holy Ghost is a horrid thing — a very horrid thing." It was left to the Evangelicals within the Anglican community to try to make evangelicalism acceptable to the Establishment, and one of the foremost influences in this movement again came from a woman.

Hannah More's life reflects in a fascinating manner the general pattern that is observable in the society of the age — a change from the secular to the serious. This change was actually brought about by the influence of Methodism which re-vitalised the Church which disowned it.

In Hannah's youth she was accepted as one of the fashionable blue-stocking set but also, owing to her great friendship with the Garricks, she was in close touch with the world of the theatre, and was herself for a time a successful playwright. She was ambitious, elegant and something of a flirt. However, she had her roots far away from London and the fashionable world.

She was the youngest but one and the cleverest of a family of five intelligent good-natured girls, whose affection for one another evoked Dr Johnson's admiration and wonder. As a child, her father was worried at her precocity, and, believing with the rest of his contemporaries (but in a curiously complete retrogression from the Renaissance attitude) that women were physically incapable of absorbing much learning, he refused to teach her mathematics. She was, though, as a special privilege, allowed Latin. Her sisters were also unusually well-educated for the time, and together they started a school at Bristol which became greatly sought after. Obviously, unlike the poor Brontës with their similar but utterly abortive efforts, the More sisters liked and understood children and were born teachers. Little Marianne Thornton (who became E. M. Forster's great aunt) and little Tom Macaulay (who became the great historian) both adored Hannah. "I always felt that in her I had a companion of just mine own age," said Marianne. She gives in her journal a seductive description of the whole More household,

> "with its roses and haycocks and strawberries and syllabub and huge brown home-baked loaves, its warm welcome for visiting children, its two cats called 'Non-resistance' and 'Passive Obedience' whom we fed all day long. And all these cheerful delights interspersed with wonderful stories from the Old Testament 'of the adventures of the children of Israel', told by Hannah with such eloquence and force that I fancied she must have lived amongst them herself."

In old age Marianne still remembered, too, the exhortations made by Hannah and Patty to the village children in the newly set up Sunday school, full of vivid simple anecdotes and practical advice. "Surely there never was such a household so full of intellect and piety and active benevolence." These adjectives exactly suited the best brand of eighteenth- and early nineteenth-century evangelism.

When Hannah turned away from the theatre, after Garrick's death, because it appeared to her to "elevate passion, jealousy, hatred, pride and revenge to the rank of virtue, and because it formed a dazzling system of worldly morality in direct opposition to the Christian religion", she became increasingly drawn into the evangelical sphere and absorbed in active charity among the poor. At first sight, then, it appears that her life was dramatically divided into two, but this was not really so. It is true that the influence of friends such as Wilberforce and Newton (the one-time slave trader and later famous as a preacher and hymn-writer) directed her energies into specifically religious channels, but she was always a moralist and a teacher by temperament, and teach she endeavoured to do with clarity and decision, both young and old, both friends and strangers, both rich and poor.

As has been said, the age was notable for the polite paganism of the fashionable world. When Sir Joshua Reynolds exhibited his picture of the infant Samuel, he was grieved to learn how many of those who went to view it were totally ignorant of the subject. At the same time the rude paganism of the peasants was beginning to make itself uncomfortably felt and feared. Hannah attacked on both fronts. Her *Thoughts on the Importance of the Manners of the Great in General Society* (1788) and *An Estimate of the Religion of the Fashionable World* (1790) were published anonymously, but their authorship was soon guessed and far from bringing upon her the reproaches she expected, they achieved immediate popularity, seven editions were brought out in a few months, and though Horace Walpole wrote, "Good Hannah More is labouring to amend our religion and has just published a book. It is prettily written but her enthusiasm increases," there is no evidence that anyone took offence. Newton wrote with approbation: "There is a circle by which what you write will be read and which will hardly read anything of a religious kind that is not written by you." It was certainly the authorship and not their contents which accounted for the success of these rather trivial books. They are interesting, however, for the light they throw on the climate of thought at the time. They attack the prevalent scepticism, the licentious living and the substitution of a little pecuniary relief for true Christian charity. The sentiments they express were sincere but mild. They could not by any stretch be condemned as revolutionary, for Hannah believed in authority and, as far as government, and especially church government was concerned, held that "whatever is, is right".

Far more influential and successful was her attack on the paganism of the poor. This, from small beginnings, led to really important repercussions. One day Wilberforce, who had, like Hannah, belonged to London high society and, also under Newton's influence, had felt the call to life of notable service, came to stay with the More sisters at their country retreat in the Mendips. Hannah took him to see the famous caves at Cheddar, but besides the caves he also saw the appalling conditions under which the neighbouring villagers lived. "Miss More," said Wilberforce, "something must be done about Cheddar," and it was. The earliest of the famous More village schools was started there in a cottage, at first only on Sundays, to teach the Bible and the catechism. Then it was extended to cover instruction in some simple crafts. The work of enlightenment prospered in spite of determined opposition and this was because, united to Hannah's inborn desire to improve and far stronger than her somewhat priggish impulse to reform her own equals, was a real forceful compassion. While pursuing her village educational efforts, she wrote: "I believe that I see more misery in a week than some people believe exists in the whole world."

The hostility to her plans came chiefly from the farmers. One begged her "not to think of bringing any religion into the country, it was the worst thing in the world for the poor for it made them lazy and useless". We find a telling confirmation of this attitude in George Eliot's *Scenes from Clerical Life*. The rich miller of provincial Milby is reviling the efforts of the evangelical clergyman to educate the working classes and especially the women:

> "I know well enough what your Sunday evening lectures are good for — for wenches to meet their sweethearts and brew mischief. There's work enough with the servant maids as it is — such as I never heard the like of in my mother's time, and it's all along o' your schooling and newfangled plans."

In one district the farmers refused to ask for a resident clergyman, in case their tithes should be raised. "In one village there had been no resident clergyman for 100 years and no Bible except one used to prop up a flower pot." In another, the incumbent was intoxicated six times in a week and was often prevented from officiating on Sundays by two black eyes. Such clergy as these united with the farmers in trying to thwart Hannah and her sisters, holding that "the poor were intended by God to be servants and slaves". They were also outraged and jealous of interference by women and described the sisters' Sunday School picnics and little rewards of gingerbread and pennies as immoral. Hannah was also accused of revolutionary sympathies and of praying for the French. But the Mores continued their fight against ignorance and poverty both staunchly and sensibly, tackling the worst centres, such as the Nailsen glassworkers, with courage. Hannah has left an account of her first visit there. They were accompanied by a gentleman who,

> "fearful of these wild savages, left us to pursue our own devices, which we did by entering and haranguing every separate family. We were in our usual luck regarding the personal civility which we received even from the worst of these creatures."

For her civilising agent she relied first of all upon the influence of the Bible expounded in a clear and simple fashion: "I have given away annually nearly 200 Bibles, Prayer Books and Testaments." Then, too, she appealed to the parents' love and ambition for their children. This was to be almost exactly the same approach as Elizabeth Fry used to tame the Newgate criminals. It entailed teaching both parents and children to read, though Hannah did not consider writing necessary. Then it struck her practical mind that much could also be taught the women in the way of simple household crafts which would make the lives of their families healthier and happier. She also started welfare clubs.

> "Finding the wants and distresses of these poor people uncommonly great (for their wages are but one shilling per day) and fearing to abuse the bounty of my friends by a too indiscriminate liberality, it occurred to me that I could make what I had to bestow go much farther by instituting societies for the women as is done for men in other places, and these benefit Societies proved a great relief to the sick and lying-in, especially in the late seasons of scarcity."

As the most oppressed and deprived section of society, women undoubtedly benefited most by evangelistic philanthropy. George Eliot again in her country stories illustrates the new hope and interest and dawning independence which it brought into their lives.

Under the constant supervision of Hannah and her sisters, especially of Patty More, the village schools flourished. For the most part the teachers chosen by them were suitable and popular. In August 1793 there appeared in the *Bath Chronicle* an enthusiastic report of the Annual School Feast in which nearly a thousand children from nine neighbouring Sunday schools picnicked in an old Roman Camp: "A more captivating sight cannot be conceived than of this infant cavalcade marching to sound of a band of rustick musicians." Nothing could have better pleased the respectable benevolent patriotic piety of the age. The children sang "their favourite song of God Save the King", arrived at a magnificent laurel arch and "burst into hymns of praise to their Maker and then partook of beef, bread pudding and cyder".

The *Chronicle*'s account reads today as both complaisant, condescending and paternalistic. Yet any other attitude in those times would have been unthinkable and hymns and beef and Bibles and bands were surely better than the darkness and dereliction that Wilberforce had found at Cheddar. As it was the Mores were considered by many, besides the farmers, to be dangerously methodistical and revolutionary. As fear of radicalism and of France grew, so did distrust of all efforts to teach the poor. The Establishment took alarm and the Evangelical party of the Anglican Church to which Hannah belonged was criticised as being too much tinged with Methodism. Her schools were attacked and it was recommended by some fanatics that her moral tracts for the poor should be burned by the hangman. In 1800 what became known as the Blagdon Controversy blew up which took the form of a virulent attack on Hannah, the "She Bishop", as she was scornfully called — that a woman should be nicknamed a "Bishop in Petticoats" was naturally an insult to both sexes in one! The quarrel was over the dismissal by the resident curate of a Methodist schoolmaster appointed by Hannah at Blagdon.

The fact that ten years earlier on the publication of her *Estimation of the Religion of the Fashionable World*, Westminster School boys had burned her effigy on a bonfire, had troubled neither her nor anyone else, for it was generally felt that no harm by anyone was meant; but to teach the poor and encourage Methodism was a different story. The Blagdon affair preyed upon Hannah's mind for she was not in sympathy either temperamentally or theologically with the more extreme Methodists:

"I do not vindicate enthusiasm; I dread it. But can the possibility that a few should become enthusiastic be justly pleaded as an argument for giving them *all* up to actual vice and barbarism."

Hannah, like a good many practical women, had not much use

for doctrinal differences. The division between Calvinists and their opponents which had rent the Methodists also divided the ranks of Anglican Evangelism. "How I hate the little narrowing names of Calvinism and Armenianism", Hannah once exclaimed and she could not see either why she should not have friends among the Dissenters. Her own faith was simple. She clung to a definable and precise creed and belief in redemption through Christ, in punishment for those who turned away from this, and in the Bible as a constant and sure guide. Hers was not a deeply spiritual nature and she sometimes grieved that she found contemplation difficult, but wisely concentrated on the work for which she felt herself called. It is ironic that Hannah with her respect for authority and common sense should have been accused of fanaticism and revolutionary tendencies. Nothing could have been further from the truth. Her aim was to make the poor happier and healthier and therefore more content in that station of life to which she firmly believed that God had called them; but she did not believe that God had called them to misery and ignorance. To extend her work beyond the confines of her locality she began to write her famous tracts. She was not the pioneer of the Sunday School movement, that had been set on foot by her friends Mr Raikes and Mrs Trimmer, but the authorship of the series of cheap, simple, readable moral tales was peculiarly her own, and the project was a huge success. Hannah went about the task with her usual practical thoroughness, collecting a number of popular chapbooks to find out their general make-up and their appeal. She used the same methods for her very different aims and subject matter, but the presentation with entertaining woodcuts and bold lettering was similar and *The Story of Sinful Sally, The History of Idle Jack Brown, The Two Shoe Makers* and many others proved as acceptable as the histories of murderers and thieves. They were indeed much more successful than her polite exhortations to the rich to stop gambling and to become more charitable. The best of them grew out of her real love and knowledge of country life and the hero of her most loved tract, *The Shepherd of Salisbury Plain,* was founded on an actual character as were some of her stories of destitute children whose lives had been changed by the benevolent Clapham Village schoolmistress — Rebecca Wilkinson. The Bishop of London begged her to explain to the uneducated what

141

the dangerous terms "liberty and equality" really meant, in other words what they could safely be made to mean to the British working classes in 1792. Hannah's answer was a tract, *Village Politics,* in which Will Chip, the village carpenter, proves that "Old England has the best laws and the best religion in the world if men would only observe both properly"!

Hannah's tracts show both her ability and her limitations. She was too much of a Tory not to think it dangerous to aim at anything but the simplest scheme of education for the poor; to teach history or science was asking for trouble, besides, adds this practical woman: "supposing they had money to buy such books, where would they find time to read them without the neglect of all business and the violation of all duty". The schoolmasters and schoolmistresses she chose were selected for their sound piety, good sense and competent knowledge and these were the qualities most admired in her age. It is the usual fate of the balanced personality to be attacked by both sides and Hannah More was abused on the one hand for being revolutionary and methodistical and on the other for lacking spiritual fervour. Her life does present a certain ambivalence, not only between her youthful comparatively worldly and fashionable phase and her later dedicated moral and religious work, but also in her subsequent reputation. She suffered here again from extremes. Her first biographer portrayed her as an angel which she certainly was not, and later critics tended to undervalue her personality as arid and her attitude as reactionary. But those who knew her well, and her own letters and the best of her writings, testify to her warmth of heart and humour and splendid commonsense. As to her achievements, she was so successful in publicising her charitable work that in spite of herself (for her Tory prejudice would have distrusted and disowned this) she might be said to have revolutionised the whole attitude towards elementary education.

Hannah was always in close contact with the Clapham Sect, or the Saints, as they were nicknamed. These were a remarkable group of families — Thorntons, Wilberforces, Macaulays, Venns, Stephens, Grants and Teignmouths, all of whom lived, at least for a time, round Clapham Common. They were renowned for evangelical piety and good works, for a high level of intelligence and for ample means (they were responsible for financing

Hannah's popular series of moral tales). They left their mark in many different quarters, literary, educational, political and religious. Venn was founder of the Church Missionary Society. Thornton, Wilberforce and Zachary Macaulay (father of the historian) were prominent in the anti-slavery campaign, Teignmouth was the first president of the British and Foreign Bible Society. All these men married wives who entered fully into their interests and several had notable daughters. The Family, "that little gathered Church" so dear to the heart of Mrs Wesley, was certainly of the utmost significance in the history of the Clapham Sect and the girls seem to have enjoyed more freedom and a better education than most of their contemporaries. Henry Thornton's "method" followed Susannah Wesley's in some respects, but from principle only and certainly not from necessity, for there were plenty of servants in the household. But the children were assigned useful tasks from their earliest years and enjoyed feeling themselves of use, though Marianne, the eldest and the darling of Hannah More, remarks: "I believe my governesses were not a little surprised by what they considered the menial occupations that were given me." She was also trained to act as her father's secretary, "to copy his MS instead of writing copies", to read the papers to her parents and to take an interest in public affairs.

Another intelligent lively Clapham daughter was Emilia Venn, who grew up to a partnership with her brother in working for the poor in his parish at Hereford, with starting allotments for them, and getting up missionary exhibitions and lectures and prayer meetings and teas, combining, as E. M. Forster says, "their peculiar virulent evangelicalism with jollification and joy".

The same atmosphere pervades the Wilberforce family. Marianne Thornton describes family prayers in the household:

"There is a bell which rings when Mr W. finishes dressing, upon which the Tutor begins to play a hymn and by degrees the family come down to the hall — first one joins in and then another; Lizzy calling out, 'Don't go near dear Mama, she sings so dreadfully out of tune,' and William, 'Don't look at Papa, he does make such dreadful faces.' So he does, waving his arms about, and occasionally pulling the leaves off the geraniums and smelling them, singing out louder and louder in a tone of hilarity, 'Trust Him, praise Him, trust Him, praise Him, ever more.' Then we all adjourn to his room where he reads a chapter, and has a thoro' talk over it; it's very entertaining and though it lasts $\frac{3}{4}$ of an hour, I never was a bit tired which is more than I could say of any other Bible exposition."[16]

The great events of the year for the Clapham Saints were the May Meetings of all the newly formed societies, where the wives and daughters of the sect were carried away on waves of enthusiasm for foreign missions and the anti-slavery movement — for, truth to tell, the Clapham Saints were more aware of the needs of the poor Africans than of the new industrial poor of their own country. Missionary zeal could not be accused of radicalism and the slaves of the plantations were more romantic than the slaves of the factories and mines. The foundation of those societies which so excited Marianne Thornton and her friends was significant of the change that had begun, channelling private and personal philanthropy into official and public charity, which at this stage provided a less satisfactory outlet for the Christian woman worker, who was still perforce an amateur. Even teaching, the commonest form of service, in the Sunday Schools or classes for older boys and girls, was a haphazard affair. The parson or squire's wife and daughters were *ex officio* mostly responsible. In Marianne Thornton's long life we can trace the development from the small beginnings, each teacher free as air, to the beginning of regimentation and the often resented visits of inspectors.

Anything outside the family, other than teaching, as the Christian "works" that should accompany "grace", was only achieved by a miracle, for time, money, training and health were all hard to come by, especially for the married woman who usually had a large family to rear. Families indeed were now more numerous than at any other time, for far fewer children died than in preceding centuries and any effective method of birth control was unknown. As for training or money, the first was unobtainable and the second entirely dependent on the goodwill of a father or husband. But miracles did occur and one such was the prison reform accomplished by Elizabeth Fry, the Quaker.

The Society of Friends had declined in membership and influence during the eighteenth century and they were now divided into Plain Friends, who kept up the strict rules of their founders, and those who, without breaking away altogether, allowed themselves latitude in the way of dress and worldly amusements. Both groups tended to be prosperous. The professions having been denied to them, they went into trade and proved the truth of the maxim that honesty is the best policy. Amelia Opie, the artist's wife, wrote: "In all Quaker homes there is a most comfortable appearance of neatness, comfort and affluence." Elizabeth Gurny's family did not belong to the Plain Friends. Her beautiful and cheerful home at Earlham had much in common with the prosperous evangelistic homes of the Clapham sect. The Gurnys were just such a family as the Thorntons and Elizabeth was the smartest and gayest of the sisters, taking pleasure in her boots of purple leather laced with scarlet and fidgeting through Sunday meeting in no very devotional mood. She was however drawn towards a more serious frame of mind in her late teens and with a good deal of heart-searching she eventually married a Plain Friend, Joseph Fry. Her in-laws regarded her with disfavour as worldly, though she made efforts enough to conform so that her own relatives complained of her dreary new puritanical ways. Poor Elizabeth then proceeded to produce eight children, with a good deal of pain and difficulty. Yet she found time and energy somehow to take up the inevitable teaching among the poor, including gipsies, who were encamped near her country home, and, in London where her husband ran a banking house, she founded a school for girls. All this however did not satisfy her and she wrote in her diary: "I fear that my life is slipping away to little purpose."

But then, in the same sort of simple way in which Hannah More's work also began, she was taken one day in 1813 by a visiting American Quaker to Newgate, where she found appalling conditions among the women prisoners which she could not forget. Her labours for them are well-known. Fearless as the More sisters among the Nailsen glassworkers, she insisted on braving worse and more hopeless savagery without protection. Both women trusted in the appeal of the love of the mothers for their children, and both succeeded in an amazing way in drawing out an immediate response from these poor creatures. As Elizabeth's was the harder task, so hers was the finer and more spiritual nature, but she was as practical as Hannah. Who but a woman would have attended so to detail in the provision of decent clothes and above all to restoring self-respect in providing employment in many simple ways and by teaching the girls and women to teach the children themselves. The wretches who were to be transported, had been treated like cattle on the convict ships and those who survived the voyage were unloaded on the strange shores with no provision whatever for maintaining life. Elizabeth, as soon as she realised this and heard of the desperate riots that went on during the journeys from the prison to the docks, whipped around her friends for wool and knitting pins and cloth and in no time provided knitting and dressmaking materials to employ the women in making garments which they could sell on landing to keep them from starvation, and she used to go with them to the ship to help them conquer panic and despair. She organised them into little groups with a leader to act as a sort of mother and this she did for every convict ship that sailed from London for about twenty years, until she died. Such practical "aftercare" was full of commonsense as well as Christian charity.

Maria Edgeworth, that lovable, humorous and highly intelligent writer, has left a contemporary picture of Elizabeth Fry which is probably a more faithful portrait of her than later adulations. She visited Newgate in 1822:

> "We went through dreary but clean passages, till we came to a room where rows of benches confronted a table on which lay a large Bible. Enter Mrs Fry in a drab-coloured silk cloak and plain Quaker cap. Her first smile I can never forget. The prisoners came in and in an orderly manner ranged themselves on the benches. All quite clean, faces, hair, cap and hands. On a very low bench in front little children were *settled* by their mothers.
>
> Mrs Fry opened the Bible and read in the most sweetly solemn sedate voice I ever heard, slowly and distinctly without anything in the manner that could distract attention from the matter. Sometimes she paused to explain, addressing the convicts, 'We (*not you*) have felt . . .', 'We are convinced . . .'. The women were perfectly silent, with their eyes fixed upon her . . . and the children sat quite still the whole time."

These were the same women whom the jailer had tried to prevent her from meeting, saying that the least to be expected was that she would have her clothes torn off — the place was the same, Newgate, in which "the foulness of the air" had been described as "insupportable", where three hundred women with children had all been crowded into a space not more than fourteen yards square, and where many had no coverings and lay ill on the bare floor and the transformation was effected by the energies of a woman doing what had to be done, but what had *not* been done through years of misery.

Prison reform was the chief, but by no means Elizabeth Fry's only, work of mercy. Wherever she went, whether it was to Brighton, to recover from an illness, or abroad to investigate prisons, or in the English countryside, she became aware of small, or not so small needs which she made it her business to attend to. The coastguards and sailors, and shepherds, had too many lonely empty hours and must be provided with books. There were no Sisters of Charity in England like those she saw at work in Germany and France, so she set about planning for an Institute for training Englishwomen "without distinction of class" for nursing the poor. ("Miss Fry's Establishment" anticipating the work of Florence Nightingale, was finally opened in London in 1840.)

All this was accomplished against a background of none too easy a family life. Three more children were born after she had begun her prison work, bringing her total to eleven. Her husband, an upright but not an inspiring character, had the misfortune to fail in his banking business through no fault of his own. But bankruptcy was held to be a disgrace among Quakers and he was expelled from the Society, and this was deeply felt by both husband and wife. In time, too, the very success of Elizabeth's work led inevitably to the usual drawbacks of publicity. There was the strain of frequent journeys and meetings abroad and at home, and she had never been strong. But when she died at sixty-five, she certainly could not say as she had once feared that "her life had slipped away to little purpose".

It is interesting to compare Elizabeth Fry's methods with that of that other great pioneer in prison reform, John Howard. He bent all his energies to getting laws passed to put an end to certain universal abuses and on imposing rules from without to ensure measures of elementary hygiene and order. *His* reforms were general and accomplished through official channels, *hers* were particular and personal. Both were appallingly necessary.

147

11
The Victorian Age

During the Victorian age the patriarchal family unit assumed greater social importance than ever before. As wife, mother, daughter and sister many women undoubtedly found creative satisfaction within the family circle, but many others were stifled by and sacrificed to its demands. The education of girls had sunk to a low level. The Industrial Revolution produced on the one hand a mass of female labour exploited to its limit, and on the other the ignorant, parasitical "lady". Yet from this unpromising social pattern emerged in due course the demand for better education and a wider sphere of service. This demand had its early foundations in Christian charity and the emphasis shifts more and more to a fulfilment for the Martha and Mary within a vocational training, though the very opportunity for this training had itself to be created out of faith and courage.

The vitality of the age was not to be denied. In defiance of oppression and opposition, towering personalities, a Florence Nightingale, a Priscilla Sellon, a Catherine Booth, a Josephine Butler, thrust themselves to the forefront and managed to influence the shape of things to come. They had their complements across the Atlantic. But these women, possessed though they were of strongly individual personalities, no longer worked in isolation as they might have done of old, but in association with organisations and societies, some of which they themselves helped to found, and which were necessary to an age that was becoming more and more complicated and interdependent. "The Spirit bloweth where it listeth", and it seems a law of nature that it must constantly change its direction. The evangelical movement had by now lost its impetus — Mark Pattison could write in 1830 "that it was effete". This was an exaggeration, for Methodism continued to be a powerful influence especially in the great industrial centres, but it is true that inspiration now seemed to flow most freshly and invigoratingly in the direction of High Anglicanism

148

and one of the developments of this movement was the foundation of Anglican orders for women of sisterhoods and deaconesses. A small group of High Churchmen, among whom was Mr Gladstone, founded the first sisterhood community in 1845 at Park Village West. But previous to this Dr Pusey had thought that such a foundation "might serve to give holy employment to many ladies who yearn for something of the sort". He sent for the rules of the Sisters of the Order of St Augustine and of St Vincent de Paul from Paris and, influenced by the death of a young daughter who had longed for a dedicated religious life, and also by his friendship with the redoubtable Miss Sellon, he sponsored a second community at Devonport, under her supervision.

These sisterhoods had at first to walk very warily for their likeness to the old pre-reformation orders was a focus of attack. The High Church movement had to balance on a tightrope from which descent into the clutches of Rome was not infrequent, the most dramatic being that of Newman and Manning. Pusey managed to keep his balance but was greatly hated by the Low Churchmen and Nonconformists. The Sisters were forced to discipline themselves as regards the use of symbols and at a third community, that at Wantage, the nun's dress was not adopted for many years. Scandals occurred. Sister Charlotte White of Park Village became a fanatic convert to Roman Catholicism and attempted to abduct another sister, Clara Powell, and a tragicomedy followed. Sister Clara was waylaid in the street and tried to flee, but her escape was blocked by Sister Charlotte waving a crucifix and "whichever way she turned, Miss White with great agility managed to place the crucifix in her path". A cab drew up and Sister Clara leapt into it but the cab was in the plot and took her to a Roman Catholic convent where she was finally tracked down by a distracted parent and her Mother Superior, and after another abortive attempt at kidnapping by Sister Charlotte, she was sent, on the advice of Dr Pusey, to Devonport. Pusey himself defended the sisterhoods as likely "to direct zeal which might otherwise go over to Rome". His Devonport community was less austere in its rules than Park Village. The sisters were divided into three groups, the black sisters, who were active in good works among the poor, such as teaching, nursing, and so on; the white sisters, who were contemplatives;

and the grey sisters who took no vows and did not actually live in the community. Miss Sellon might be said to be the abbess and Pusey the patron saint of Devonport. Priscilla Sellon was a remarkable woman. Not only was she responsible for the Devonport sisterhood, but she ran a college for sailor boys, an orphanage, an industrial school for girls, and a lodging house for destitute women. No doubt having had eight younger brothers helped! Such experiences could only make or mar an elder sister, but she must, however, have possessed other qualities besides those of a disciplinarian and superb organiser, for people loved her. One of her sisters wrote of the community:

"Hard work, love and obedience were all in all. The household was the happiest, busiest, merriest and least constrained and most united that I was ever in."

Pusey's argument "Why should not God call women as well as men to a life of devotion?" seems unanswerable, and in the light of history an unnecessary query, but the second line of attack on the sisterhoods came from those who saw in such foundations a threat to family life. An appeal was launched to all true Englishmen to have these orders suppressed. Bishop Tait solemnly pronounced "the first of all duties are those which we owe to our family — these are imposed by God".

The Victorian middle- and upper-class woman may indeed have been regarded as the "Angel in the House" but she was often a sadly exploited angel, if married, entirely dependent upon her husband financially, legally entitled to no property whatever of her own, and for the most part dedicated to constant childbearing and rearing, and if single, expected to care in turn for younger brothers and sisters, nieces and nephews, and ageing parent. But the sisterhoods offered no easy option and the novice who sought them out merely as an escape from family duties seldom stayed the course as she needed to have a true vocation for the life of the community. This was of course only for those of gentle birth (Elizabeth Fry's Nursing Institute was unique in being open to all classes). There was a curious but widely and strongly held view that, as Archdeacon Harris stated it at the Church Congress of 1866:

"Christianity in its highest form was manifest in the highly educated devout English women – surely there is no higher form."

Though this debatable maxim was accepted in theory, it did not affect the male view that the work of these pattern Christians should be strictly confined to the feminine roles of nursing, teaching and of rescuing their fallen sisters. This last was considered to be particularly suitable to ladies of gentle birth and in fact to them only for, as Bishop Butler put it,

"they must be such as the penitents know to be in every possible way so superior to themselves, living among them apart from their friends, apart from all ordinary pleasures and enjoyments of life, for the sole purpose of guiding them into the way of peace."

Belief in the moral and religious influence of the "pure" gentlewoman was not confined to the sisterhoods, nor to its effect on outcasts from society. In no other age have Christian women been held to be so spiritually superior yet so mentally inferior to men. This view appears over and over again in the literature of the period from Dickens and Trollope to Coventry Patmore and Tennyson. It is observably *not* present in the great women novelists of the period, but it does appear in popular lesser works. Charlotte Yonge, an exceptionally popular and prolific influence, pays homage to the innate superiority of men's judgement, though her heroines are never silly. Some women writers indeed, among whom was sensible Mrs Jameson, used the argument that as the elevating influence of women on society was acknowledged, so they ought to be better educated and trained in order that they could improve it further. It is to the credit of the sisterhoods that they did aim at a proper training in the three great services of teaching, nursing and social work and after they had proved their worth in the serious cholera epidemic of 1854, they increased rapidly in numbers and influence.

The orders of deaconesses were to a much greater extent under the direct control of men. The Greek meaning of the word "deacon", i.e. helpful service, sums up their role. They conformed more easily to the Victorian male conception. Two pronouncements on the institution of deaconesses illustrate this. The Bishop of Winchester as late as 1885 emphasised the need for their supervision because "women need more support than men", and Cotton on discussing their education said it should be moral "of the heart and not of the head because there was where the particular attributes of women lay".

Generally speaking the establishment of these orders, sisterhoods and deaconesses provided a stepping stone to a wider and more professional training for women. Florence Nightingale's attitude towards them is significant. She went to study the Deaconesses Institute at Kaiserwich in 1845, just as the Park Village Community was starting, and wrote home in a letter:

> "Well, I do not much like talking about it, but I thought something like a Protestant Sisterhood without vows, for women of educated feelings might be established."

The idea terrified her mother and Florence herself later thought the English sisterhoods were too much connected with the High Church party, though she acknowledged their usefulness. They must have made her work easier, as a contemporary writer observed,

> "Sisterhoods were the first to show that the work of nursing the sick is a high and holy one to which Christian women of gentle and noble families may be glad to dedicate themselves."[17]

Florence Nightingale's achievements are too well-known for more than a mention here, but though her fame as a superb administrator in so many fields is probably unequalled by any other woman, it is not so generally acknowledged that she was a Mary as well as a Martha. Her practical ability was fed and balanced by a deeply mystical nature, which was not bound within the confines of any church party or doctrine. She writes:

> "Where shall I find God? In myself. That is the true Mystical Doctrine. But then I myself must be in a state for Him to come and dwell in me. This is the whole aim of the Mystical life; and all Mystical Rules in all time and countries have been laid down for putting the soul into such a state . . ."

She was in the direct line from the medieval mystics whom she studied, but her genius, deeply rooted though it was in devotion, could never be satisfied until that devotion was translated into action. As a mystic she is closest perhaps of all to St Teresa of

Avila who might well have used Miss Nightingale's own words in describing the mystical state as

> "the essence of commonsense for the ecstatic state is unreal and should not be at all . . . we can only act and speak and think through Him; and what we need is to discover such laws of His as will enable us to be always acting and thinking in *conscious* concert with Him."

It thus must clearly be recognised that the first impetus towards vocational training for women in nursing and pioneer medical work, in teaching and in social service in the Victorian age sprang from their faith. Elizabeth Blackwell, the first woman to qualify as a doctor in the face of enormous difficulties, might be speaking for all when she wrote:

> "A deep conviction came to me that my life was accepted by God, that I should be helped and guided. A peace, as to the righteousness of my course, settled down upon my mind that was never afterwards destroyed."

The same sense of dedication is to be found in many of the women writers of the Victorian age. Authorship was a more respectable occupation for women than those for which training was required and it also had the great merit that it could be carried on within the home. Yet still in many cases women found it better to adopt a male pseudonym and any income from a wife's work belonged by law to her husband. None the less, like everything else in this abundant age, books of all kinds by women proliferated and the majority were diffused with religion and morality. Samuel Rogers remarked to Crabb Robinson that "where we men are modestly content to amuse by our writings, the aim of women is invariably didactic".

It is difficult to choose from what has suddenly grown into such a mass of Christian material, but Charlotte Yonge's extremely popular novels probably give a better picture of the contemporary lives of girls and of women than those of a writer of greater genius. Also, independent of her fame as a novelist, she stands in direct succession to Hannah More for her many able books for use in schools of all kinds were of real value in the task of educating a nation. She published more than fifty for both children and teachers on history, nature study, the classics, poetry and

153

civic studies, and above all on the Bible, the Catechism and church history. She is in advance of Hannah More in her ideas upon educating the working classes, but is still cautious, and though she welcomes Gladstone's great Education Act, she is apprehensive about the damage which may be caused by divorcing secular from moral and religious training. In fact she would have preferred all schools and colleges, had it been possible, to have been closely allied to the Church. Miss Yonge was also representative of her particular period in being inspired by the High Anglican movement, her spiritual guides being Keble and Pusey.

She is very critical of Hannah More's evangelicanism and remarks that she does not seem to understand the Church Ordinances or the Sacraments as means of grace. She herself thought of joining the Wantage sisterhood but luckily realised that she was not suited to the life and could better serve God by her writings. In the novels we get glimpses of the work of the sisterhoods, especially during the cholera epidemic and many a sidelight on the influence of the High Church movement, the restoration and rededication of ancient abbeys (though the division between the Anglican and Roman persuasion is clearly maintained) and the enormous stress laid upon Confirmation and the Eucharist. In perhaps her best known book, *The Daisy Chain*, the chief preoccupation of the lovable heroine Ethel May is the building of a church and the establishment of a Sunday School in a poor industrial district. We are persuaded to believe that all this piety was an accepted characteristic of the middle-class "nice" girl of the period and what convinces us is that Miss Yonge's fictional characters are alive for she possessed the power of creating personality in the round, and what is unusual, even in writers of greater genius, she could make goodness attractive, for her piety is hardly ever touched by sentimentality and she gives what is perhaps the best and most subtle study in Angela Underwood of the over-romantic, temperamentally unhealthy, religious adolescent. Also, her books would never have achieved their popularity had not the actual Victorian girl, avidly identifying herself with Miss Yonge's heroines, felt with them that the highest romance of the age was to be found in the restored Gothic architectury with its nineteenth-century medievalism, that the knights of the Arthurian chivalry now wore clerical collars and that the controversially surpliced choirs and splendid new organ were very close indeed to the Heavenly Hosts on high.

But Charlotte Yonge's vision goes deeper than any pictistic fashion. She perceives with an almost childlike simplicity and clarity the creative nature of a true relationship between man, woman and God. God's importance alone gives significance to the individual, but every individual has access to this. In no modern sense of the word was Miss Yonge a feminist, yet in the light of this knowledge she gives equal weight to the humble as to the influential, the wife and mother as to the husband and father, the sister as to the brother.

Once again it is in the realm of human relationship that the contribution of the Christian woman becomes explicit; there were many other women writers of the nineteenth century, far more than in any previous age, and all apparently endued with a strong personal faith.

Hymns were made popular by Watts and the Wesleys, and following in their wake came a whole host of nineteenth-century hymn-writers among whom women were responsible for some of the best loved. Charlotte Elliot gave us "Just as I am without one plea", "Christian, seek not yet repose" and "My God and Father, while I stray"; Harriet Auber "Our blest Redeemer, ere he breathed his tender last farewell"; Dorothy Gurney "O perfect Love, all human thoughts transcending"; Mrs Adams "Nearer my God to Thee"; Frances Havigal "Take my life and let it be, consecrated, Lord, to Thee"; Mrs Maude "Thine for ever God of Love", and Catherine Winkworth successfully translated several splendid German hymns including "Now thank we all our God". But foremost among the women hymnists must come Mrs Alexander (1823-95). She was the author of "Jesus calls us o'er the tumult" and "The roseate hues of early dawn", and she also translated the beautiful "Breastplate of St Patrick", but her claim to fame rests on her skill in writing hymns for children. "We are but little children weak" and "Do no sinful action", once so popular, at least with Sunday School teachers, are now understandably outdated, but "All things bright and beautiful" continues a favourite, while "Once in Royal David's city" and "There is a green hill far away" are immortal. She managed here to express profundities with an inspired simplicity suitable for a musical setting, and though meant originally for children, they have reached the hearts of thousands, irrespective of age. No Christmas service is complete without the one, no Easter without the other.

The "green hill" that she pictured so vividly was actually not far away but near her Irish home, and somehow she brings nearer to us also our own particular hill of sorrow and redemption, as we sing her simple words, while in the children's hymn which has become the traditional processional carol for the King's College Choir Christmas service, she manages to convey in the first lines majesty and humility, time and eternity: "Once in Royal David's city stood a lowly cattle stall".

Besides women hymn-writers, the Victorians produced a religious poet of the first rank in Christina Rossetti and one of the greatest religious poems ever written — Emily Brontë's "No coward soul is mine". This poem, however, is not specifically Christian, it is stoicism illuminated by faith in God.

Emily and Christina have points in common — both were passionate, strong personalities (the popular image of Christina as a serene stained-glass-window saint is a mistaken one as any serious study of her life and work will show). Both were outstanding in an abnormally gifted family and both appeared to become ill when parted from that family. Both, moreover, seem from their poetry to have experienced the heights and depths of passionate love, if only through the power of imaginative genius, for with Emily, the evidence of the actual experience is totally lacking, and with Christina it certainly remains a mystery for neither of her suitors seem to have inspired in her more than a mild affection. (Lorna Mosk Packer makes out a good case for Scott Bell as the "onlie begettor" of the love poems but it remains largely supposition.)

But here the likeness ceases, for whereas Emily is always fearless and free, "an undaunted daughter of desire", Christina is a divided spirit, torn between guilt and glory. Emily cannot be called a religious poet (her sister Anne was so, but *her* gifts were not equal to her piety). Christina, however, like Donne, is as renowned for her devotional as for her love lyrics. The guilt and glory are as much present in the one as in the other. Edith Sitwell thought that "sweetness and charm were the blood and sap of her poetry" but that "she had not the irradiation and fire of the saints" and that her religion "cast a cold clay upon her".[18] It is not possible to agree. True, "sweetness and charm" are there but these are as apparent in many of the religious poems as in the secular lyrics. More characteristic though of both is intensity of emotion: despair and exultation, joy and mourning, are each present in turn and there is often a sense of fierce tension between the two extremes. Even the popular fairy tale "Goblin Market" is deeply symbolic of the conflict between temptation and redemptive love. There were always the two sides to Christina's personality, a warm sensuousness that is reflected in the pre-Raphaelite richness of the texture and imagery of her verse, and the spiritual and sacrificial. It is therefore impossible to isolate the one from the other, for her poetry is the outcome of both. The same poignant struggle in different terms is present in both Donne and Herbert, and with the latter Christina has a certain affinity. Both wrote poems which read like "a dialogue of the soul with God". Her "I will accept" might have been Herbert's.

> "I will accept thy will to do and be,
> Thy hatred and intolerance of sin,
> Thy will at least to love, that burns within
> And thirsteth after Me."

> "I cannot will."

> "Does not thou will, poor soul? Yet I receive
> The inner unseen longings of the soul.
> If thou desire, it yet shall come to pass
> That thou but wish indeed to choose My love;
> For I have power in earth and heaven above—"

> "I cannot wish, alas!"

> "What, neither choose nor wish to choose? and yet
> I still must strive to win thee and constrain:
> For thee I hung upon the cross in pain.
> How then can I forget?
> If thou, as yet dost neither love nor hate
> Nor choose, nor wish — resign thyself, be still,
> Till I infuse love, hatred, longing, will."

> "I do not deprecate."

Christina's intensely personal religious verse is often shot through with an earthly passion and the love lyrics with a heavenly aspiration. In the poem "After Death" both meet. The soul, love bound to this world, lingers on its passage heavenwards:

"I did not hear the birds about the eaves
Nor hear the reapers talk among the sheaves,
Only my soul kept watch from day to day.
....
At length there came a step upon the stair,
Upon the lock the old familiar hand.
Then first, my spirit seemed to scent the air
Of Paradise, then first, the tardy sand
Of Time ran golden, and my soul expand."

Sometimes the longing for the earthly love, which seems to have abandoned her, drives her to a passionate need for the heavenly love:

"None other Lamb, none other Name,
None other Hope in heaven or earth or sea,
None other Hiding Place from guilt and shame,
None beside Thee.

My faith burns low, my hope burns low,
Only my heart's desire cries out in me,
By the deep thunder of its want and woe
Cries out to Thee."

Again in the strangely beautiful "Marvel of Marvels" with its tolling bell of intricate monotonous rhyme, the two elements of earthly and heavenly love are mixed:

"Marvels of marvels, if I myself shall behold
With mine own eyes, my King in his city of Gold
....
Where the dimmest head beyond a moon is aureoled.
O Saints, my beloved, now mouldering to mould in the mould,
Shall I see you lift your heads, see your cerements unroll'd,
See with these very eyes? who now in darkness and cold
Tremble for the midnight cry, the rapture, the tale untold,
The Bridegroom cometh, cometh, His Bride to enfold!
Cold it is, my beloved, since your funeral bell was toll'd,
Cold it is, O my King, how cold alone in the world!'

Perhaps undue emphasis has been laid on the sadness of Christina's poems. Although classing her with the few great religious poets, David Cecil, for instance, says "she has faith and charity but not hope". True, the sense of guilt and self disgust is often present, but there is also sometimes magnificent adoration and triumph: "Stroke a flint and there is nothing to admire, strike a flint and forthwith flash out sparks of fire." Her "sparks of fire" cannot be denied and towards the end of a life, frustrated in all but the exercise of her poetic genius, the divided heart at last became one. She was dying of cancer when she wrote one of the most triumphant and unified of her poems:

"Voices from above and beneath,
Voices of creation near and far,
Voices out of life and out of death,
Out of measureless space,
Sun, moon, star,
In oneness of contentment offering praise.

Heaven and earth and sea jubilant,
Jubilant all things that dwell therein,
Filled to fullest overflow thy chant,
Still roll onward, swell,
Still begin,
Never flagging, praise interminable.

Thou, who must fall silent in a while,
Chant thy sweetest, gladdest, best at once,
Sun thyself today, keep peace and smile.
By love upward send
On sins
Accounting love thy lot and love thine end."

Surely there is plenty of hope and "irradiation" here.

Christina Rossetti was, of course, not the only woman of her age to write good religious poetry. Anne Brontë at her best is sometimes poignantly moving, Emily's one great poem shines alone in meteoric glory, Dora Greenwood, a friend of Christina's and a fine Christian character, wrote simply but well, Mrs Hemans, Jean Ingelow and Mrs Browning produced some religious poems worth remembering, but there is no one to match Christina for quality and quantity, and her influence was important in affecting even such original writers as Gerard Manley Hopkins, who much admired her. What has she especially to contribute as a woman? First perhaps the intimacy and tenderness of her approach. Christ is the baby in his mother's arms:

"Enough for Him, whom Cherubim
Worship night and day,
A breastful of milk
And a mangerful of hay."

He is also the lover:

"Yet what I can, I give Him,
Give my heart."

Then, her poems emphasise the significance of all small and helpless creatures and there is a general awareness of detail which is more often found among women than among men. There is also a natural understanding of women and their special problems. She was not a recluse, though perhaps she was tempted to be one, but though she was almost as unhappy and unsuccessful a governess as the Brontës, she worked satisfactorily for ten years at the St Mary Magdalen Home for Prostitutes at Highgate, and her experience there found expression in poems such as "Under the rose" and "From sunset to rise star". There is evidence also in her prose writings of a strong sympathy and interest in women's role in life. There is an interesting comment of hers on the Exodus account of how Pharaoh ordered the sons of the Israelites to be destroyed and the daughters saved. She says:

"There seems to be a sense in which, from the Fall downwards, the penalty of death has been laid on man and of life on woman. To Eve, 'I will greatly multiply thy sorrow and thy conception; in sorrow thou shalt bring forth children' — to Adam, 'Unto dust shalt thou return.' The mere name, Eve, was 'the mother of all living' or it may be 'of the Living One.' "

She goes on to imply that this conception of a dead Adam made the Virgin birth a necessity — only a living God in conjunction with a mother could create between them a uniquely living Son. She might have added that whereas a woman gave life to the Son, man sent Him to His death. No woman had any part in the Crucifixion, nor did they forsake Him and it was to a woman that the ever-living risen Christ first revealed Himself. Finally, she points out that both in nature and in the history of man, the male is the combatant, the female the prize.

> "Under human dominion, too, the male half of domestic breeds is maimed and consumed, the female, far more largely at least, preserved and made much of. . . . In wars . . . the men are many times exterminated, the women spared."

This symbolic conception of Eve as Life and Adam as Death turns the tables on the age-old degradation of women derived from the Old Testament story and it is surely ironic that such a revolutionary point of view should be advanced by one whose popular image was that of the self-effacing, meek, ministering presence of a Victorian home. An exceptional piety was in the air, varying from the movingly sincere to the morbid and sentimental. We find it no less in the factual world of biography as in the world of the novel or of poetry. The life and letters of Maria Hare, collected and edited by her adopted son, are typical. The Victorian era was the greatest age of the vicarage and the manse and from their burgeoning families came many a famous son and daughter.

Maria was a clergyman's daughter, wife and widow, and fulfilled each role with exemplary and characteristic devotion. She was connected with the Stanleys of Alderley and with the Spencers and numbered among her friends Bishop Heber, Cardinal Manning (before he went over to Rome) and the liberal-minded F. D. Maurice. Her father belonged to the earlier more worldly minded wealthy Anglican clergy and her first engagement to Heber's assistant was frowned upon. The sad little story ended in wistful vows, separation and the early death of the curate in India. His college friend, Augustus Hare, then succeeded him in Maria's affections, but, once again, the now not so young daughter was made to wait three years before Augustus's prospects satisfied the father. Filial piety thus robbed Maria of precious time, for her married life was only to last for five years altogether. This period, which she looked back upon as Paradise throughout the rest of a long life, was spent in a tiny Wiltshire parish, where she found perfect satisfaction in the duties of a country parson's wife: teaching the villlage girls, visiting the old and sick and cherishing her husband. The parishioners were simple, ignorant and amenable and were treated by Maria with all the loving, self-sacrificing care

161

that a good mother gives her children. They were in fact her family (for she was childless) and all was bliss until consumption carried off her adored Augustus.

Widowhood in Victorian times was almost a profession in itself. Anniversaries were kept with reverent fervour and every memory, every relic, every saying treasured and shared with friends and relations. Nothing that could be said on the subject of bereavement was left unsaid. The Victorians could be as boring about death as we are these days about sex and their attitude was as far from the matter-of-fact acceptances of earlier ages as it is from the repressions of today. To the Middle Ages death was a commonplace, to the Victorians it was an occasion, to us it is an irrelevance.

In one volume alone of Maria Hare's life, forty-six pages are devoted to detailed accounts of deathbeds. She herself fulfilled an almost archetypal role by providing her family and friends with three. In 1865, her adopted son writes:

> "She is indeed, I can no longer conceal from myself, fast fading away. . . . My darling has been sitting up in bed listening to sweet voices — but they were no earthly voices . . . the nurse went away saying all *must* be over in three hours."

On and on he writes — the parting hymn is chosen by both to be sung as a sign that life is ending. Yet three months later she is enjoying all the delights of Biarritz. The second deathbed scene is described at even greater length. This time her doctors had declared recovery to be impossible.

> "We all knelt round her bed feeling that every instant must be the last. 'It is the Valley of the Shadow of Death,' she said, 'it has come at last. I have always tried to be ready for it.' "

But she was mistaken. She recovered to endure, without succumbing, a severe fall and to drive about Rome on farewell excursions before revelling "in the luxuriance of the Euganean hills". The third and final occasion, as dramatic and as well attended as the two former, was not until 1870.

Perhaps the gulf between the attitude of the Victorians and ourselves on this subject is brought out most clearly where children are concerned. When Maria's adopted son (who was also her nephew and godchild) was nine years old she wrote to him about the death of a young friend:

"Mrs Bunsen took me up to her room where she lay in the still sleep of death. . . . I should much like you to have been with me and to have seen her. . . . She looked so peaceful. . . . She was dressed in white with roses on her head. . . . Yesterday at four o'clock was the funeral. Uncle Jule chose the spot close under the great yew tree. . . . In just such a narrow bed, dearest child, shall we someday be laid and then whether it is a happy rest or a state of misery must depend on whether we have lived in this life for our own pleasure, or to please and obey God."

The religious education of children was generally the responsibility of the mother and many a Victorian child was nurtured in fears of Hell and hopes of Heaven and familiarised with all the appurtenances of death and burial.

Besides the sacred duty of keeping green the memory of "the sainted departed" there was the special task of social welfare to which the Christian, and more especially the clerical widow was the more dedicated because the less tied. The poor were always to be with us and to have a manageable number of these around one was as much of a necessity as a comfortable house or a pleasing prospect. Maria Hare's sister-in-law writes of a Cornish village:

"There is here just all we miss at home — the poor people, the wild flowers and copses and perfect retirement in the country. This would be the ideal home for the widow. The poor alone would make it so and the power of being useful."

Maria, after the death of her husband, moved to the Sussex parish of her brother-in-law Julius, to whom she soon became indispensable. Her approach to village people was always intimate and loving: "each village girl saw in her one who was as necessary a part of her life as her own family". The time spent on visiting and teaching were regular and frequent, and often the duties she undertook were arduous and unpleasant. True, she never had to lift a finger at home in house or garden, but was always devotedly served by domestics, but Julius Hare certainly spoke no more than the truth when he named her in a dedication of a book of his sermons as one "whose love for the poor of my parish, since she became a widow, has been their blessing and mine". The poor were to be patient and obedient in that state of life to which God had called them, but they were also to be made as comfortable in mind, body and spirit as possible, at the expense of much time, thought, prayer and above all of personal caring. And it was not only the poor who were to be patient and obedient. The conquest of self and the complete submission to God's will is the ever-recurring theme of Maria's private meditations. Her spirit hovers between the misery of self-condemnation — "the crushing sense of one's own littleness and vileness" and the joy which freedom from self and the love of her God always brought. One source of reproach was that she loved her husband, family and friends too much — more than she loved God, and she was haunted by the fear that therefore she might, for her own good, be deprived of them. There is much of what we call morbid introspection in Maria's religion, but this is typical of Victorian Christianity, especially among women. When Julius Hare argues that as a tutor at Cambridge he is doing as much, or more, good as he would as a country clergyman, he exclaims:

> "Your womankind won't understand or sympathise with me in this; but they are no authority on such matters. Women are too purely heavenly-minded — that is to say, when they are so at all, religion is to them everything; and they cannot see religion in anything but religion. Science, philosophy, state craft, they know nothing about and therefore of course cannot care about."

Like the poverty of the working classes, this state of ignorance apparently seemed divinely ordained, to Julius and to his male contemporaries. But though Maria's outlook may have been restricted and obsessional, it was not without perception and even occasionally an ironic turn. "So closely does self-love cling to us," she observes, "that we are still continually tempted to look through a false medium and see ourselves with the partial eyes of others — *this being one of the rare cases in which we are willing to esteem their judgement superior to our own.*" Or again, she quotes with approval from a sermon:

> "If a messenger from heaven should come down and ask what we are doing here in England in the year of our Lord, 1843, what would be the answer? Quarrelling whether we should preach in a black gown or a white."

And:

> "We are sad lovers of variety that even goodness and religion should be recommended under various forms in order not to clog."

What, however, gave Maria and many of her contemporary "womenkind" courage and ultimate peace was their unquestioning faith in an omnipotent, all-loving God, whose will was to be discerned, trusted and obeyed in every detail of their lives.

The Victorian vicarage and the Scottish manse continued to provide throughout the century a continuous supply of intellectual and social vigour, much of which depended upon the parson's or minister's wife, whose life was often a miracle of quiet heroism. Canon Anson, in his book *Looking Forward*, describes his mother's struggle with continual child-bearing which

> "she often felt to be an intolerable burden, but she faced it with a high courage, offering each child solemnly to the service of God, awaiting the birth of each, as she used to say, 'like a man going into battle.'"

But in addition to this, she, and many another like her, had to run the huge household, to provide simple remedies for the poor, sick and aged in the village and to encourage and inspire their husbands in *their* work. Some of them even managed to produce literary work of their own, to cultivate their minds and to educate their children. Mrs Anson was fluent in three languages, Mrs Gatty, herself brought up in a Yorkshire vicarage, had eight children, wrote many books and made a scientific study of seaweed, was an etcher and calligrapher and a pioneer in the care of sick children and the use of chloroform. She was the mother of Mrs Ewing, outstanding for beautifully written children's classics such as *Six to Sixteen*, *A Flat Iron for a Farthing*, *Jackanapes* and many more which, without the obtrusive piety of earlier religious and moral tales for the young, breathe a much more fundamental and effective atmosphere of goodness, such as provided a security and satisfaction for hundreds of children as well as incidentally giving them a fine sense of the English language at its best.

The manse was famous for the number of its children sent to the university on a very small income. An average of £90 to £150 per annum and a four-roomed house with attics and outhouses would often have to provide for a large family. Mrs Grant, for instance, had twelve children and also had to run a dairy and supply the needs of shepherds and farm men. But families and parishes were not the boundaries for the work of the parson's wife. At home what was to become an international society started in a Hampshire village parish in 1876 at a vicarage drawing-room meeting called by the vicar's wife, Mary Sumner. Her object was "to raise the moral and religious life of the country through the home". Soon it concentrated on religious training for motherhood and became known as the Mothers' Union. The movement did much to help married women to learn and to exercise leadership. (It was confined to the Anglican Church and was first a diocesan, then a national and lastly an international movement. It is now half a million strong but like most societies founded in the nineteenth century is going through a difficult process of adaptation to the modern world.) The parsonage and the manse also sent out many of their children to missionary service abroad.

12
Women in Missions Abroad and at Home

The Victorian era was the great age for foreign missions. It was the period of rapid expansion of British rule and, together with much that was power seeking, went a sincere, if paternalistic and narrow "caring" for the spiritual and physical well-being of the native races. With this sense of responsibility there was also tremendous romantic appeal. The imagination of the young (always, in every age, looking for causes to which to dedicate themselves and through which to find themselves) was fired by visions of "Greenland's icy mountains" and "India's coral strand". Stirring hymns with grand tunes urged them "For my sake and the Gospels go and spread redemption's story," and for the majority it was unthinkable that Christianity was not the only possible religion nor that eventually "the earth shall be filled with the Glory of God as the waters cover the sea". Bazaars in aid of missions and lectures, illustrated later in the period by the wonderful magic lantern, were immensely popular and were often the only respectable form of entertainment available in country towns and villages. They were a source of wonder and inspiration and in many a home throughout the British Isles the cherished ambition was to send forth a son to the missionfield in far-off "heathen" lands. Daughters were rather a different matter. Besides the accepted fact that their first duty was to look after parents and other relatives at home, single women, unless they were nuns, found it difficult to achieve the desirable training or to muster the necessary funds for mission work abroad. By far the greater number of women in the missionfield went out as missionaries' wives and led heroic lives of self-sacrifice and humble service. In *The Complete Letter Writer for Ladies and Gentlemen*, by Mr Beeton (husband of Mrs Beeton of cookery book fame), there is a pattern letter for a lady accepting a missionary's proposal of marriage and it is notable in relation to the immense appeal of the missionary field that this is the only specific profession dealt with in this section of the book. As a period piece it is perhaps worth quoting the whole:

"My dear Sir, Our friendship, if I may use the word, has not had a long existence, but short though it has been, I have learned to appreciate it more than you can imagine. Indeed, were it not so, I should shrink from replying frankly to the question you ask. You ask me will I consent to accompany you to Africa and share the trials of a missionary's life there, and I answer that I will, believing it my duty to join in so noble an undertaking as the wife of one whom I esteem. I cannot, as your wife, aid you as I would like, and to the work I cannot bring more than a willing heart, but perhaps the Almighty will strengthen both my heart and my hands and enable me to be useful as your helpmate in your distant home.

The day of your departure is, as you say, drawing nigh, but however near it may be, I can be ready. The sorest part of the preparation will be saying goodbye to those I love, and they are many. They will, however, I feel, not tax my strength too far when they know in whose care I shall go. You will tell me what to do.

      And believe me
         my dear Sir
           Yours sincerely."

There is also included a pattern refusal on the grounds of health — the only conceivable reason apparently for a denial in the face of such a sacred call: "I feel myself that I would only be an incumbrance even were I spared and at a missionary station there should be no incumbrance." She was right there; missionary wives were required to work as amateur teachers, nurses and often, too, as doctors and not for them the luxury of the sahib's women. The conditions they faced were often primitive and unhealthy. Indeed, early widowhood, or their own premature death, was an all too common fate awaiting them. Worst of all was the necessary separation from their children who had to be sent home generally before they were six because of the climate. This entailed a parting of five to ten years and when furlough at last came, not only had they missed the most formative years but they met their children again as strangers and seldom could ever hope to catch up on the relationships. Sometimes the children had no suitable homes in Britain to which they could be sent and good boarding-school fees were often beyond the parents' reach, for in spite of popularity, the missions were never wealthy and stipends were small. To meet a great need the first school for the daughters of missionaries was founded in 1838 at Walthamstow (then a village) by a Mrs Foulger, whose husband was a director of the London Missionary Society. (It was undenominational until the Church Missionary Society opened their own school a few years later.)

The first object of this foundation was that it should be a home as well as a school and though the girls could spend holidays with relatives or guardians, many actually stayed there throughout the year. (A similar school for boys was established ten years later.) How far it carried out its purpose of providing a substitute home varied with the ladies in charge, but on the whole it was a happy place, though *of course* the children suffered from the parting with their parents for so large a part of their formative years. The education naturally had a predominantly Christian bias, but it was from the first in some ways in advance of its times, for Latin was taught as well as good plain sewing, history and geography, as well as music "as tending to enliven domestic worship". Such broad-mindedness, however, was offset with strict rules in accordance with the prudery of the day, for as a school report pronounced "the female character expands best in the shade". Nevertheless, by the 'seventies professors were engaged to teach mathematics, literature and the classics, and the academic standards of the school always remained high.

The existence of this school must have been a tremendous boon to the missionary parents. The fees were kept low, for stipends in the mission field were not in proportion to the work achieved or the hazards accompanying it. Towards the end of the century the girls' school, rapidly expanding, moved to Kent and became the flourishing day secondary school of the neighbourhood, though retaining its missionary boarding nucleus, and its tradition of Christian service. Its success in this field may be measured by the number of pupils who followed in their parents' footsteps, many of whom in their turn sent their children to their old school.

Besides the mute, inglorious, but often heroic missionary wives, there were those few outstanding single women who achieved notoriety in the mission field. Of these, Mary Slessor illustrates perhaps most vividly the romance and the power of this particular

Christian calling in the nineteenth century and also the peculiar gifts which the woman missionary had to offer in virtue of her sex.

The prospects for Mary Slessor becoming a missionary or even of surviving at all were pretty poor. She was born in 1848, one of the seven children of a Scottish shoemaker, a confirmed drunkard, who was incapable of holding down a job. The mother, indomitable, pious and poetic, kept the family going on her earnings as a weaver. Mary herself started work at eleven, alternating school with her textile mill. From fourteen she was working full time and attending evening classes. All Sundays were given up to worship. "We would as soon have thought of going to the moon as of being absent from a service." Interestingly enough she confesses to being "converted" through fear of the Calvinistic hell that was preached from her Presbyterian pulpit, but conversion accomplished, she repudiated the idea of Hell for the rest of her life. The father's timely death released the family from their worst trials. The mother's only entertainment had been local missionary meetings in Dundee and her dream was to equip Robert, her eldest, for service in Africa. He died while still in his teens (none in the family were strong and all the boys died young) but Mary's ambition had been fired and as soon as she could she became a mission teacher and then, inspired by Livingstone's death in 1874, she determined to offer herself for service in West Africa, and was accepted at a salary of £60 a year to join the mission at Calabar, one of the most unhealthy spots in the whole continent for which, as Mary Kingsley remarked "no return tickets were issued". Yet Mary was to find other women established there, described by the Mission Board as "economical and effective", which indeed they had to be to survive at all. "I tell you true," an old African chief is reported to have said, "them women be best man for mission."

Mary Slessor never took kindly to working under another's discipline and the mission was strictly disciplined. Her gifts lay in pioneer work and she rejoiced when an opportunity arose for exploring inland towards more remote regions. She seems to have been born without the faculty of fear and neither wild men nor wild animals could deter her. Where the latter were concerned, "I prayed 'O God of Daniel, shut their mouths' and He did." As to the former, she would attack any bully or braggart chieftain with

170

completely disarming courage. The fight against alcohol, to which she had been used since she was a baby, pursued her here also, as it was one of the chief evils to which the natives succumbed. A girl who has had to defend small sisters and brothers from a drunken bully of a father and who has looked to her mother for all the comforts and necessities of life, will be likely to be particularly sensitive to women's sufferings. Mary Slessor, though she had many devoted friends among the men of the African tribes with whom she lived, devoted herself first and foremost to trying to better the sad and frightened lives of the native women. The lot of any woman who was unfortunate enough to bear twins was frightful. The babies were killed as a matter of course but their mother was accursed and shunned more rigorously than if she had been a leper. Even to use the same path as she had once trod was forbidden. The British unavailingly tried by law to put an end to this horror. Mary fought it by every possible means and collected a large family of deserted twin children around her — one little girl became a most beloved adopted daughter whom she brought to England on her rare furloughs and who was a great draw at missionary meetings. She also brought the despised and outcast widows under her protection and helped them to support themselves. Her earliest independent exploring mission was to Okoyong inhabited by a fierce Bantu race. Conditions in the women's quarters where she first lived were primitive beyond belief — "a bed of dirty sticks and a litter of cornshucks with plenty of rats and mice shared with three native women and a 3-day old baby . . . but I had such a comfortable quiet night in my own heart." She was beyond law, beyond companionship, but she rejoiced in her freedom. The middle-class Victorian social conventions of the mission station had irked the working-class Scottish lassie. She entered on her fight with cruelty and ignorance in a district considered only fit for armed intervention with the utmost faith in her belief that a woman and *only* a woman working on her own could disarm opposition and suspicion. Her trust was justified. She created a bond among the women of the tribe and was given secret support by the wife of the most influential chieftain. She was lucky in treating successfully the wife of another chieftain with her simple remedies. She built a house and a humble mission centre by her own efforts aided after a while by the

171

wondering natives. But she had enough common sense to see that patience was necessary, perhaps for a long while, before much could be expected in the way of results. She realised that conventional methods and Western ways of thought could make absolutely no headway in such a society and disregarding the official advisers, she concentrated on making friends with the natives and trying to show by her own behaviour what is meant by reverence for individual life (which should always be the core of Christian teaching). In such small apparently unimportant ways as tending sick and dying babies with loving care and by burying them decently after death, she began to influence the mothers. Unlike most lady missionaries, she discarded the inhibiting European women's clothes and wore no hat, no shoes and a sort of one-piece cotton chemise. The young administrators who visited the station at Okoyong from time to time with their escorts and their elaborate health and safety equipment were confronted with this extraordinary woman who went striding about the forests, bare-headed and barefooted, often with no companionship but a native baby or two and who lived in a mud hut eating African food. They were dumbfounded. On one of her infrequent visits home she became engaged to a romantic young man, Charles Morrison, eighteen years younger than herself and far less tough. He was a missionary, of course, engaged in training young men at Duke Town. Mary had no idea of submitting herself to the subordinate position of missionary wife and refused to leave Okoyong: "If God does not send him up here, then he must do his work and I must do mine." God, in the shape of the Duke Town Mission authorities, did *not* send Charles up-country and Mary, without much sign of regret, continued her work alone. Poor Charles suffered the all too common fate of broken health and an early death, but Mary went on from strength to strength. She wished to develop industry among the Africans as well as to convert them and her growing reputation as a mediator between the tribes and the Protectorate resulted in her being allowed to hold court and transact government business in the district.

In 1892 the "Great White Ma" became the first Vice-Consul. As such she carried out justice guided by her personal knowledge and opinions rather than by the law. For instance, a thorough rascal of a native brought to court an honest neighbour who owed him a small sum of money. Mary, who knew the characters of both men, ordered the one to pay the sum owing but allowed him to thrash the other before paying. She changed customs she thought bad whenever she could but was against doctrinaire, unsuitable Christian procedure, and this made her unpopular with the more conservative missionaries.

One person who definitely did not disapprove of Mary's attitudes towards the native customs was another remarkable, if very different woman, Mary Kingsley, the naturalist and explorer. She was no missionary and indeed held very unorthodox religious views in spite of her upbringing (she was the niece of Charles Kingsley) but she had the greatest admiration for Mary Slessor. "This very wonderful lady," she wrote after their meeting in 1895, "whose great abilities, both physical and intellectual, have given her a unique position among the savage tribes. . . . Her knowledge of the native, his language, his ways of thought, his diseases, his difficulties, is extraordinary and the amount of good she has done no man can fully estimate."

Mary never ceased to champion women, to fight for mothers of twins and for alleged witches. It was said that her court was the only one ever where no woman ever lost a case! Her success was phenomenal — a report states "for fully a year there has been no violence . . . it would be impossible apart from belief in God's particular and personal providence in answer to prayer to account for the ready obedience and submission to judgement . . . there seems to have dawned on them that life is worth saving even at the risk of one's own."

In 1900 a military force was sent to subdue the Africans who were carrying on their traditional slave trade internally. Mary was employed to draw up terms after the expedition and this fired her with the determination to establish a mission among these fierce people and their oppressed neighbours. Without official backing, she left for the Cross River Region together with her seven adopted native children. "Whether I shall find God's place for me up river or whether I shall come back again to my own people I do not know. He knows and that is enough!" She felt that had she been able to come earlier the punitive expedition might not have been necessary — that a woman should always be first on the scene. "Ma, we don't want a man", seemed the universal cry.

Her ambition was to establish a new centre and next to get a hospital built and to rescue the weakest among those who had been exploited by their warlike neighbours. She received no authority to do this but she managed to get on well with the English civil servants who were engaged in opening up the district by road making. Though adapted to African living, Mary was quick to make use of any benevolent Western inventions. She learned to ride a bicycle and welcomed the gift of a phonograph which could relay hymns to the enchanted natives. At length the Mary Slessor Hospital became a reality and by this time she had two splendid woman collaborators, Janet Wright and Mina Amiss. Her leave of absence from her original station was up but she refused to return. "Whether the Church permits it or not, I feel I must stay here, and even go on further as the roads are made." The authorities were helpless but tried to save their face by declaring that "the Woman's Foreign Mission should not lead but follow in future". There was not much chance of Mary agreeing to that! There was a plan afoot which she supported for a women's settlement to train the native woman in basic skills, but when it was proposed that she should stay there to organise the scheme, she was not pleased. Exploration, not organisation, was here forte. She was "the feet of the Church" marching ahead. Ill health never stopped her — wrapped in blankets in canoes, her fevers subdued by laudanum, she would set out to brave head-hunters, swamps and mosquitoes ("how I wish they were as tired as I am!"). She made a great friend of one of the finest of our District Commissioners, Charles Partridge, who became to her "my dear old Boss" and her advice to him on taking office was worth noting: "If you can discriminate between fear and stubbornness in those with whom you have to deal, you have won half the battle." She never ceased to ask for more women to be accepted for the expansion of missions because they were most successful in the spade work and she never ceased also to express her views with determination but to temper them with disarming humour. "O dear Miss Slessor," she wrote, "you are on the war path again and God does not work that way, and it is quite possible that other people may be right — and you not far from wrong."

She died in 1915 where she would have chosen, among her African friends, and it was significant that her last prayer, "O

God relieve me", was spoken in the native dialect. Twenty years later when a magic lantern show at the Mary Slessor Hospital reproduced her portrait, an old chief afterwards asked if he might have the cloth that had been used for the show because "I liked that woman too much". She is still a legend but would she consider her lifework wasted today? No, for the Christian belief that each individual living here, in time, has value in eternity must contain the justification for such work as hers, even though her hospital is in ruins, together with much else for which she had striven and hoped. But she had freed many during her life from terror and pain and, moreover, the lot of the African women in the regions where she worked was improved for all time.

A similar compassion for wretchedly oppressed women, this time for the aborigines in Australia, was the concern of Daisy Bates, another remarkable pioneer. She stands mid-way between the dedicated missionary and the purely scientific or administrative traveller such as Mary Kingsley or Gertrude Bell. Actually, she was a journalist sent in 1899 to Western Australia to investigate charges of cruelty to the natives, but she began her work while staying at a mission station run by Trappist monks and though, like Mary Slessor, her innate common sense early recognised the mistakes made by the conventional missionary attitudes towards such primitive peoples, she managed to convey to them the Christian message of love through the example of her own lifelong devotion to their service. Daisy wrote of a dying woman, tended for eight weeks through an agonising illness, who was nearing her end:

> "I sat beside her holding her hand. Suddenly she sat up in the firelight searching my face with troubled eyes. 'Where am I going?' she cried in fear. . . . 'My Father is sitting down where you are going, Jeera' I told her, 'and as soon as I let go your hand, my Father will catch hold of it. He will take care of you until I come.' 'Your Father? Then I shall be safe' she said and settled down to sleep. I did not know she was dead until her hand grew cold in mine."

It was through such well-earned trust that she, like Mary Slessor, taught the natives something of the brotherhood of man and the love of God:

"I could have taught them prayers easily enough but I did not want parrot repetition. . . . I tried to give them the only Christianity I knew they understood which was nothing but loving kindness and an unfailing trust and example, example always."

Daisy Bates saw so clearly what many of the good and self-sacrificing *men* who were trying to convert the natives by more conventional methods failed to see — that "there is no hope of protecting the Stone Age from the 20th century". Bishop Salvada tried to educate them and selecting a band of "promising young aboriginal boys took them to Rome to study for the priesthood". All died except one who returned home, fled to the bush, "flung away his habit and died there". There was another bishop who insisted on making confirmed Christians of all the natives in the district, who were merely completely mystified at the whole business. The same bishop, worn out with his labour, was making the voyage back to the mission station in company with an old native "naked and unashamed". "Go and put your clothes on!" called the bishop to the poor old fellow, who had neither clothes nor need of them in his rough life on the seas.

The same sort of unimaginative approach on a greater and disastrous scale was made by the government in trying, at much expense, to establish an isolation hospital for the aborigines on two islands. "Regardless of tribe and custom and county and relationship" they were rounded up and brought to these islands to be cured. Many of them died in terror at seeing the sea for the first time — others at being separated from their tribes — "some cried day and night and others stood silently for hours on a head-land" straining their hopeless eyes towards home. All the benefits of civilisation were worse than useless to them. Daisy Bates alone seems to have realised that there was "nothing you can give them but freedom and their own fires" and she, with her sympathetic understanding, became the one comfort of those who survived and was christened by them "Kabbaili" (Grandmother). But so many died from fear and homesickness that the costly experiment was abandoned. If she had been consulted beforehand it would never have been undertaken. Not that she passively accepted all the evils of these primitive peoples. She fought cannibalism which was rife, though she did not allow herself to be openly revolted by it; she fought disease through tending her patients in their own environment; she fought the dangers of inter-family quarrels though "certain duels, among brothers, I allowed, always standing by the duellists". She fought cruelty towards women as much as lay in her powers and, being a woman herself and having made herself respected by the tribes*men*, her example and her reprimands carried much weight.

For thirty-five years Daisy Bates devoted her life to these dying peoples and put on record before it was too late their customs and their myths. She loved not only the people but the country and its flora and fauna. "My reptilian friends were many, they too gave me joyous hours!" Yet unlike Mary Slessor in this, she retained meticulous standards of dress and personal fastiduousness and amid all the savagery of climate and conditions, appeared an utterly incongruous Victorian spinster-like figure, a "Miss Prism" in stiff collar, white blouse and long voluminous skirt, carrying an umbrella and a reticule. Actually she had had a husband but he died early and seems to have counted for little in her life in comparison with her beloved aborigines whom she looked upon as her children. For undoubtedly the most successful among these independent women missionaries were strongly maternal and it is not uncommon to find united with this instinct a dominating temperament and a disregard, especially where their children are concerned, of personal ease or danger. Yet both Mary Slessor and Daisy Bates found that their sex protected them against fear and hostility that the white male aroused among primitive peoples. They repaid trust by trust and above all showed a truly Christian respect for the individual, however different in culture or tradition, while their practical common sense saved them from expecting too much conformity with Western thought. Had there been more women like them in positions of responsibility, perhaps the racial situation today would have been happier. Though numbers decreased, the commitment of Christian women to foreign missions continued, of course, in the twentieth century, becoming more informed and more definitely aimed at an ultimate transference of responsibility to the native population. Sister Dorothy Raphael, for instance, founded in Johannesburg "The House of Peace Making", which, during the twenties and thirties became responsible for three churches, seven schools and three nursery schools, for expanding the mission hospital and for building the first swimming baths open to natives. In *The Times* of 28 January 1977, the Bishop of Stepney wrote: "I have no doubt whatever that the existence of an African Church, strong and vigorous as it is in the turmoil of Soweto today, bearing its witness against all the odds, to reconciliation and justice owes much to 'The House of Peace Making' [Ekutuleni] and the ideals it stood for."

Towards the end of the nineteenth century a great missionary movement was started at home "in darkest England" (to borrow the title of General Booth's famous book), and the joint founder of this movement was a woman — Catherine Booth. About forty years after Mark Pattison had declared evangelicanism effete, the Salvation Army, perhaps the best known of all evangelical missions, was inaugurated to rescue the most wretched of the victims of the new urban industrialised society. Just as John Wesley had been repudiated by his church, so William Booth was forced to leave the Methodist ministry because of "extreme" views. But it proved as impossible to muzzle a Booth as a Wesley. Many demanded his reordination but difficulties arose and, chiefly due to the determination and courage of his wife, the Booths determined upon total independence.

> "William is afraid. He thinks of me and the children . . . but I tell him that God will provide. . . . It is strange that I who always shrink from the sacrifice should be the first to make it."

If Susannah Wesley was the mother of Methodism, so Catherine Booth came to be known as the mother of the Salvation Army. It was she who first had the idea that the outcasts they were seeking to help would never be found in the Methodist chapels but must be sought out in their own hovels. Of course both the evangelists and the high church sisterhoods had visited the poor and the sick, but with the support of their church behind them and with the final aim of drawing them into church membership. When the Booths decided to concentrate on the worst slums of London, they determined to do without any backing at all. They had no private means, poor health and a growing family. But one night William had come home, overcome with the desperate plight of London's "East Enders". Catherine tells of this evening of crisis in their lives:

"After a pause for thought and prayer, I said to him, 'We have trusted the Lord before for our support, we can trust Him again.' "

The question to be decided was would they devote their energies wholly to these outcasts. Hitherto they had maintained their work and themselves by itinerant ministry in which they could rely on collections made among the better off of their congregations, but from these poor creatures they could hope for nothing. Catherine continues:

"There was not in our minds at the time we came to this decision the remotest idea of the marvellous work which has since sprung into existence."

Help came in spite of the opposition of all the churches. At this period Catherine became the better known of the two for she was a practised speaker, natural, eloquent and firm, and the novelty of a woman preacher, as in the early days of Methodism before it was forbidden, drew many to listen when she pleaded the cause. "Come and hear a woman preach" proclaimed the handbills, and they came in crowds. Some were wealthy and some proved sympathetic, and it was Catherine who by the full use of her gift managed to obtain the necessary funds. "I am glad you had so good a meeting," wrote her husband, "I have no doubt about your adaptation for that sphere, or for almost any sphere, and I could never stand in your way." Nor did he, for both realised it was a joint venture. Catherine had the better intellect and the more sustained courage and William was often guided and always upheld by her but, if the first germ of the Army originated with her, it was William who developed the system of getting converts actively and immediately to become involved in the work of converting others, an idea which he actually derived from Wesley's "Instructed Saints". It was William, too, who perceived the lure of creating an Army of Salvation with its uniform, its flags, its bands and its discipline.

Besides the established churches (though many members of these came to sympathise) there was fierce hostility from the publicans because of the Booths' uncompromising fight against drink, which they knew to be perhaps the chief enemy of the poor. From these and the mobs they incited to violence, the Army had to endure real persecution, women suffering equally with the men and both showing so much courage that literally many who came to jeer stayed to pray.

Another cause of unpopularity was Catherine's special concern for prostitutes, and especially for the notorious traffic in young girls. This was such an inflammable and hateful subject that even William was frightened to tackle it. Catherine appealed to Queen Victoria to have the age of consent raised from twelve to sixteen. The Queen, however, could do no more than sympathise. Mrs Booth next approached Gladstone, but it took the combined efforts of many, including W. T. Stead, Mrs Butler and Catherine's eldest son Bramwell, to get this measure passed in 1885. Catherine and Bramwell were here acting independently of William who feared repercussions on his wife and son. Bramwell in fact was put on trial, together with Stead, after the notorious *Pall Mall Gazette* exposures, but he was acquitted.

Catherine Booth died of cancer at the age of sixty-one after a long and painful illness which was exploited to the uttermost in the cause. There is no other word for it. Once again the dramatic appeal of a deathbed proved irresistible to the Victorians. Sometimes Catherine co-operated, sometimes it was too much even for her. She complained that her house was become a hotel for all those who wished to visit her in her illness, many of them total strangers. As in the case of Maria Hare, there were several rehearsals for the final parting, at which "with streaming eyes and faltering voices the gathered family sang again and again her favourite choruses with irrepressible emotion".

We, with our "strong silent" repressions upon the subject of death and our terror of sentiment, may question the sincerity of these manifestations of grief. We should be wrong to do so. William endured agonies during his wife's illness and her sufferings proved the greatest trial to his faith in a loving Father, but also he undoubtedly found relief in behaving as showman and believed that in acting thus he was doing God's work. July 1890 was the twenty-fifth anniversary of the founding of the Army. Here was a marvellous opportunity for the dramatic presentation of Catherine's last message which, printed on a broadsheet of calico, was slowly unrolled across the full width of the dais above the orchestra in the presence of more than fifty thousand spectators gathered together at the Crystal Palace. To the discreet but impressive accompaniment of an organ it was declaimed to the sorrowing multitude.

> "My dear Children and Friends. My place is empty but my heart is with you. You are my joy and crown. Your battles, sufferings and victories have been the chief interest of my life these twenty years. . . . Live holy lives. Be true to the Army. God is your strength. Love and seek the lost; bring them to the Blood."

And the message ends:

> "I am dying under the Army flag, it is yours to live and fight under. . . . I send you my love and blessing.
> Catherine Booth."

It was not until ten months later that the actual death took place and then followed a tremendous funeral at which all the Army wore white and all the trumpets sounded for the triumph of her life and joy at her release. Catherine was well named the mother of the Army, and not only because she helped to originate it but because she cared for it like a huge family. Where William thought more of his glorious band going forth to war, a great force against evil, she was concerned to bring each lost soul through redemption to Christ. She had great love, great courage and great faith, and she had beside a sense of humour which sometimes saved her, though not always, from the excesses of evangelicanism. For instance, her last illness was not all agonies and ecstasies. She could still joke — even about heaven:

> "I don't believe I shall be fastened up in a corner playing a harp. I shall let the folks do it who like it but I shall travel about if I can."

Josephine Butler, the woman connected with Mrs Booth and even more with her daughter (a second Catherine Booth) in their work for prostitutes, was a very different personality with a very different background. Her family was a younger branch of Lord Grey's (of Reform Bill fame) and she was one of a large, happy, clever family with every advantage of birth and breeding. It was not surprising therefore that she was highly intelligent, witty and even beautiful, inheriting looks and brains from both parents, but sainthood, like genius, is not determined by such factors and

Josephine was a born saint. She possessed from a child a perfectly natural relationship with her God, a sort of direct line of communication which never seems to have left her. In later life she wrote:

> "Now the things which I believe, I had learned direct from God. I never sat at the feet of any man; I never sought light or guidance even from any saint . . . though I dearly loved some such whom I had known — nor on Churches and creeds had I ever leaned."

Then she, the privileged and sheltered, had also always that vivid identification with the sufferings of others which leads inevitably to a life of dedication. At the threshold of a brilliant youth, she would creep away into the woods of her father's estate and pray with almost uncontrollable grief for those in trouble, and as an old lady, very near to death, when met at a railway station by members of an adoring family, she was too full of the massacre of the Armenians to talk of anything else. "We felt," wrote her grandson, "that we should be singing Milton's 'Avenge, O Lord, Thy slaughtered Saints' rather than fetching her baggage and shawl."

Josephine's sainthood, then, consisted in her inborn gift for prayer and in her overpowering concern for others, but the particular direction which this took was determined by circumstances. She was always to be the champion of the exploited and as such she early became an active supporter of any movement to better the lot of women generally. In this period all such movements were interrelated, and as Josephine married into the teaching profession, her first efforts were towards improving girls' education. She found the intellectual society of Oxford, where her early married life was spent, stimulating but "oppressively male". Then her husband, George Butler, became headmaster of Cheltenham College and after some years at Cheltenham, it was a little daughter's death by a tragic accident that decided the parents to move to Liverpool, where Butler had been offered the principalship of Liverpool College. Here Josephine came into contact with that class of women who were the most degraded in their own and in others' eyes, and who therefore were the most in need of help.

182

It is difficult for us to realise how emotive the whole question of prostitution was to the Victorians. Once again, no other age had so separated their women into the pure and the impure, nor felt such horror at the contamination that any contact between the two groups might cause. One only has to read Dickens or almost any contemporary novelist to be continually amazed at this phenomenon. Members of sisterhoods by virtue of their vows were allowed to help to a limited degree and the Salvation Army (though against severe opposition) included prostitutes among the lost souls they were striving to save, but Josephine's position as a married woman whose husband held an important official post was radically different. More significant still was her attitude She identified herself with these women, she was not shocked by them, she took them into her own home. She passionately set herself against the double standards by which the men who had used them went free and protected, while their victims were treated as outcasts of society.

"Those who wish to do good must do it in minute particulars," wrote Blake. Josephine began with individuals. One girl prostitute dying in her house said to her, "God has given me to you that you may never despair of any." So she always emphasised that these women "were as varied as our excellent and virtuous selves", and to class them together as beyond hope "is to be guilty of blasphemy". In a letter to a friend she expands this conviction:

"Now look at Jesus. He never talked about love of souls, and never judged people as a class. He always took the man, the woman, or the child as a *person*; and he loved the whole being of that person."

In another letter she expressed her gratitude to Christ for His attitude towards women:

"You remember how sweet and lovely Jesu always was to *women*, and how He helped their *women's* diseases, and how respectful He was to them, and loved them and forgave the sins of the most sinful. And He was born of a woman — a woman only — no man had any hand in that!"

Decline in the belief of a Virgin Birth today is not indeed a very obvious anti-feminist factor, but one can see Josephine's point.

From championing individual prostitutes and working for them as a group in Liverpool, she went on to a long and arduous campaign for the repeal of the Contagious Diseases Act. Her opposition to the Act was founded upon two passionately held convictions: first that the licensed brothels were for the protection of men at the expense of women, and secondly, that they outraged the dignity of the individual woman as a human being. Later, in conjunction with Stead and others, she proved that in all countries where such acts had become law the traffic in young girls was rife.

Her opponents were active and bitter. There were the brothel keepers and all those who made money from the trade, and there were also those who honestly believed that the Act was the lesser of two evils and was for the benefit of the country as a whole. But Josephine Butler gradually won through, helped, it should be emphasised, by the support of many men, and her husband most of all. Bishop Moberley, Cardinal Manning, James Stuart and James Stansfield all upheld and strengthened her and the patient work through official channels of Stansfield in particular was essential to her success (as was Herbert's similar help to Florence Nightingale). But, as happens not seldom, the inspiration is supplied by the woman, for without Josephine's personal appeal, the nation would never have been roused to action.

She herself attributed victory to prayer. Prior to the parliamentary debate, she organised prayer meetings, both public and private, throughout the country. These were advertised in all the leading papers and all denominations, including of course the Salvation Army, took part. A band of women including rich and poor, and even some of the prostitutes themselves, interceded with God for twelve hours on end near the Houses of Parliament, which embarrassed some members. It was said even by her bitterest opponents "Mrs Butler is absolutely invincible," but she of course would have answered "it is God who is invincible".

She next turned her attention to Europe. Germany's whole attitude towards women aroused her indignation and, at a time when Prussia was much admired by many Englishmen, she denigrated their reliance on oppression. "They see but one gleam of hope when faced with problems of violence and vice and that is to double the stringency of the system!" She believed that nothing effectual could be achieved "except by moral and social influences of a very different nature, born of Christianity and simple charity of thought among men." In Switzerland she found licensed brothels supported even by State Councillors and pastors "for the protection of their *sons*". This enraged her but here the abolitionists were heavily defeated and she and Catherine Booth, the second (founder of the French branch of the Salvation Army), were actively persecuted. Catherine was told to leave the country because she and her followers "might endanger the safety of the State"! Josephine and Catherine became close friends and Josephine wrote a book upon the work of the Salvation Army in Switzerland.

Like Florence Nightingale, Josephine Butler cared little for the differences between Christian churches in faith and worship. She had friends in every denomination, but the "propriety and deadness" of some of the churches were sometimes "an agony" to her. One of her maxims was that "Truth has often to be rescued from orthodoxy". She loved the old saints and especially St Teresa of Avila, though she herself was no mystic. She had most in common perhaps with the early Apostolic Church: a direct simple and personal approach to God. She believed in spiritual healing of the sick and had a great faith in the Pentecostal promise and the power of the Holy Spirit. "Our Christ has been saying to His poor deaf Church, 'I am here, I am with you *now*. You have forgotten my promise to come in the Person and fullness of the Holy Ghost'."

Mrs Butler held strong political views. She was deeply patriotic and believed in the mission of England to save the world. She offended some of her Liberal friends by her support of the Boer War, explaining this by her conviction that the Boers were more oppressive than the English towards the natives, "to whom if anyone the country belongs". Her courage on behalf of others never failed her; on behalf of herself it sometimes did. Like all saints worth listening to, she knew the dark night of the soul.

> "There is no need for anyone to press upon me the reality of Hell, as the early Calvinists did with stoney hearts, for I have been in Hell, but having been there myself, I am driven to believe that there is Love below all."

185

Above all else, Josephine Butler should be remembered not only for the work she did for women, but the spirit in which she did it, seeing and proclaiming the blasphemy of generalisation.

The phenomenon of Angela, Baroness Burdett Coutts, refuses to be ignored, though she does not fit into the pattern of representative devout Christian women of the nineteenth century. She is far from representative because she possessed vast financial resources, inherited from her grandfather, at her own disposal, unusual for any age, but miraculous for a Victorian woman. She kept her power because she kept her head and did not marry until she was sixty-seven, and then chose a man forty years younger than herself. She died in her ninety-second year and thirty thousand Londoners filed past her lying-in-state in her own home. Why did they come? Because she had made philanthropy her first concern in life and as she was shrewd, kind, strong-minded and personally involved, her charities were on the whole beneficial as well as immense. As a woman, she put child welfare high on her list. She was a great supporter of the Ragged School Movement and was one of the joint founders of the London Royal Society for the Prevention of Cruelty to Animals. Another founder was Hesba Stretton, one of the popular Victorian evangelical women writers of sob stories about poor children; "Jessica's First Prayer" aroused almost as much emotion at the time as Dickens's studies of child neglect.

Public libraries, swimming baths, soup kitchens, African exploration, hospital equipment for the Zulu wars, emigration projects, famine relief in Ireland, fisherman schools for poor boys, all received from the Baroness not only largesse but love — love expressed in personal expenditure of time and energy. Every day the post would bring from three to four hundred letters and all these she would try to read herself. Of course she had many helpers in her philanthropic labours, Charles Dickens above all others, but she kept her vast benevolence under personal management. She had one passion which in its splendid self-confidence and display was typical, not only of her own nature but of the age. She was an impassioned builder. She erected four huge Gothic blocks surmounted by a clocktower at Bethnal Green. Nova Scotia Gardens were to house 183 poor families including costermongers, often discriminated against by other landlords, and for whom the Baroness founded a Costermongers' Club and was presented by the members with a silver donkey in gratitude.

But, as a devout churchwoman (she founded and endowed the colonial bishoprics of Cape Town, Adelaide and British Columbia), she delighted first and foremost in the building of churches. She built St Stephen's Church, Vicarage and Schools at Westminster, a church in a poor district of Carlisle, and she gave Bishop Blomfield £15,000 towards church building in his London diocese. It was said that had she so served the Catholic Church, she would undoubtedly have been canonised St Angela. These large Victorian Gothic buildings, of excellent workmanship, remain today as a distinctly encumbering monument to the Baroness's devotion to Anglicanism and to architecture. But she will go down in history as a woman who, though not remarkable for personal piety, was certainly so for personal philanthropy.

In assessing these Victorians who, in greater or lesser degree, are representative of the developing scope of Christian women in the community, it is difficult to prevent their achievements from canonising them to a certain extent but, of course, each possessed their individual failings. Elizabeth Fry and Catherine Booth were neither of them very wise mothers; Florence Nightingale and Mary Slessor were martinets; Charlotte Yonge was rigid and narrow in her Anglicanism and in her conception of filial duty; Maria Hare and Christina Rossetti were morbidly introspective and Christina found it hard to control her temper, as anyone can deduce from the frequency with which prayers for patience and tolerance occur in the collection of her private devotions; Daisy Bates had no mean opinion of herself; Angela Burdett Coutts loved power and display. Even Josephine Butler indulged in an extreme patriotism which was almost jingoistic. They certainly were *not* saints but they *were* marvels and, though they and the many other women who dedicated themselves to Christian service, often despite harsh opposition and the continual ailments which were then the common lot of most women, they never gave in, because their lives were founded upon a rock.

The age of personal philanthropy, however, was drawing to a close. For some time the indiscriminate character of a great many overlapping private charities had been causing disquiet as encouraging pauperism. The Victorians had looked upon poverty as an individual calamity brought about sometimes by misfortune, but more often in the popular view by some moral weakness. Now, at the turn of the century, a change of attitude was beginning to evolve. The lifework of Mrs Barnett was a force in the development of organisational Christian charity but she also lived to appreciate the dangers of the pendulum swinging too far in the direction of institutionalism.

She and her husband, Canon Barnett, are another example of the successful partnership of a woman and a man (such as we have seen in the case of Hannah More, Catherine Booth and others), although significantly, the Canon used to say that he was only the mouthpiece of his wife and had the courage of *her* convictions. He was a feminist. He wrote:

> "Have you ever noticed how much women's influence has been wanting in history? It is hard to mark the mighty work it doubtless has done because it works secretly, but in a great many characters we may see the want of it. . . . Unity of life surely means that all human relations must be part of one whole."

None the less he praised Jane Adams, a famous American follower of Mrs Barnett, as "the greatest man in America". Commented his wife wryly, "So like men to appraise her as a *man!*"

Mrs Barnett was associated with Octavia Hill in the formation of the Charity Organisation Society to combat the degrading custom of issuing dole tickets and to oppose, in general, indiscriminate charity. The Society and the Institute of Lady Rent Collectors aimed at respect for the poor rather than patronage but, later, Mrs Barnett saw that though the abolition of outdoor relief in its old indiscriminate form was necessary, there was a danger of a too rigid attitude on the part of the C.O.s. She describes a dream she once had that she, herself, was a poor woman who had offended in some way but "had a passionate desire to do well in the future", if given a chance. She was waiting in the Whitechapel Infirmary when a door opened and a lady came in. "Then came the paralysing fear — 'Oh, she may be a "C.O.'s" lady and I am not a deserving case'." This dream should dispose of the view that Mrs Barnett was merely a tyrannical "do gooder", bossing the private lives of the poor. Naturally she was influenced by the paternalist attitude of her age but she did have imagination and sympathy and she realised that warmth of heart was more important than rules and regulations especially when dealing with children:

> "I think now that with their mother, even in a poor house, children are best reared and the decision given almost without exception to a widow, that the Guardians would take most of her children away seemed to me a cruel policy. I used to argue that women were paid to rear the children of the poor and what women could be so suitable as their mothers! Pharaoh's daughter had found that out."

The same loving caring was active in Mrs Barnett's work for workhouse women:

> "Never did I so realise the cruel kindness of the poor law system than when I helped twenty-two old ladies out of the break which had brought them from the Whitechapel workhouse to my door. Ugly clothing, sterile and forbidding faces . . . suspicious manners, silent and antagonistic attitude to each other — but who can wonder, if love flags among those who are herded together without individual interests? . . . We shove them all together out of sight into barrack wards — why? Oh, because rents are so dear."

It is interesting to read a contemporary article on housing management which looks back with nostalgia to the work of the Charity Organisational Society under Octavia Hill. "This great lady," says the article (which is entitled "People versus Computers"), "embodied the view of personal contact in her work in the poor areas of St Marylebone."[19]

Mrs Barnett started the Children's Country Holiday Fund because, as she confesses, she got tired of inviting children to her own country cottage. She disliked the big Sunday School outings such as were described with such enthusiasm by Hannah More. These were a welcome innovation in the past century but "a healthy charity exists to destroy itself". Mrs Barnett thought the children should be given time to learn something about the country and its way of life. (We seem now to have reverted to outings for town children, poor or otherwise, and to viewing the countryside from the windows of a closed car.)

189

The idea of friendship with "down-and-outs", though not pursued to the extent it is today, had developed a new idea in the formation of settlements of young men and women, mostly from the universities, actually to live and work in some of the poorest districts of London. The Barnetts were interested in this experiment and, at an inaugural meeting for the founding of Toynbee Hall, Canon Barnett had remarked that the women involved in the movement as a whole were out of proportion to the men. Mrs Barnett's later comment is significant. "It must not be forgotten," she said, "that at that time men, young men, intellectual men, had but recently joined the ranks of the philanthropists, the care of the poor, the children and the handicapped had hitherto been left to women."

Jane Adams, the American disciple of Mrs Barnett, is an example of the cross-current of inspiration which flourished between the Christian women of the two continents. She founded a successful settlement, Hull House, where men and women lived and worked together, perhaps the most fruitful form of community service.

13
Christian Women in Nineteenth-Century America

The tide of women's growing participation in social work, especially for the outcasts of their own sex, flowed even more strongly in nineteenth-century America than in England and drew its inspiration from the same Christian concern for the individual. It is possible to find fairly close parallels — in prison reform, in the education of the underprivileged, in medicine and nursing. America had its Elizabeth Fry and Florence Nightingale, its Josephine Butler. It had also its popular women authors and in Mary Baker Eddy it possessed the only woman to found a religious sect and a successful newspaper both of which, moreover, are creatively active to this day.

Dorothy Dix (1802-71), like Elizabeth Fry, made it her special mission to reform prisons and this led her on to work for the insane, whom she found treated worse than criminals. This concern brought her into contact with the pioneer treatment done by the Quakers in York, at the Retreat, and on a visit to England the Quaker family of Rathbone befriended her, so forging another link with Elizabeth Fry. But, unlike Elizabeth, she began life as a poor, unhappy and delicate child, her ill-health pursued her to the end. She, like so many women, had to begin in a tiny way, studying and teaching herself, chiefly from the Bible, and then trying to give to others what she had learned by starting a small class for poor girls. She was asked to find some older women to take a Bible class among women prisoners in a Massachusetts jail, but not able to hear of anyone suitable, she offered, in spite of her youth, to lead the class herself. She was appalled by the conditions she found there and especially with the brutality with which women suspected of being insane were treated. Her ultimate aim was to reform the law and in 1843 she addressed the members of the legislature thus:

> "I proceed, gentlemen, briefly to call your attention to the present state of insane persons confined within the Common-

wealth, in cages, closets, cellars, stalls, pens, chained, naked, beaten with rods and lashed into obedience."

Two points are specially worth noting in the history of Dorothy Dix's struggle. First that, seemingly like all Christian women reformers, she was especially aware of the importance of "minute particulars". She made it a practice to give little personal presents to the shattered personalities for whom she was working. This had been the way Elizabeth Fry went about humanising her prisoners. Secondly, being a woman, she was unable to act directly to change rules and customs and to finance new projects, and she had always to find a man through whom she could effect her reforms. Sometimes she was successful in this but often she became unutterably weary at the opposition of apathy and fear. The outbreak of the Civil War changed the direction of her work and an Elizabeth Fry gave place to a Florence Nightingale. She was growing old and worn out but the hopeless inefficiency and inadequacy of the field hospitals goaded her into the same dogged fight against red tape, medical etiquette and general male hostility to save the lives which, as in the Crimean War, were being destroyed by disease far more than by death in battle. She seems to have had less support than Florence but she possessed the same force and the same faith. By the time war was over, the worst abuses had been overcome. She returned to her concern for the insane and in her old age she had the satisfaction of seeing nurses specially trained in her own established hospitals to care for those whom in her youth she had seen treated with utter ignorance and brutality.

The relentless impact of the climate, the harsh conflicts between nature and men, the huge expanses of the New World, emphasising the need for sharp definition, all these perhaps tended to heighten light and deepen shadows. For instance, if the difficulties and opposition to Hannah More's pioneering efforts to educate the children of the poor are multiplied and brutalised, some idea may be formed of the enmity Prudence Crandell aroused when, according to her Quaker principles, she decided that God meant her to educate black girls as well as white in her highly respected and successful school in Canterbury, Connecticut. It was 1831 and slaves had been freed in Connecticut State but they were denied the rights of full citizenship. The same arguments against educating the working classes which had been used in late eighteenth-and early nineteenth-century England were used again here with greater vehemence. Negroes, like the English poor, had been created by divine ordinance to serve their betters, and it was both dangerous and wicked to educate them above their station.

Prudence Crandell preached a more daring equality than Hannah More for she wished to give black girls the same education as the white. This could not be borne and the inclusion of even one coloured pupil spelled ruin for her school. She decided to close the school to all but black children and William Lloyd Garrison (editor of the anti-slavery paper *The Liberator*) warned her that "all the forces of darkness will try to stamp you out if you knock away one of the strongest props of slavery, but the cause of freedom everywhere demands that you accept the challenge".

She did accept it and opened the school again with twenty coloured girls. Now the town, once so friendly and respectful, became savage with hatred. Manure was thrown into the school well to poison the water, tradesmen refused to serve it, the girls taken out for a walk were pelted with stones and garbage was heaped up before the door. Both girls and teachers endured this with courage and dignity, and Prudence's family and Quaker friends supplied food and water. Finally the State Legislature made it illegal for anyone to run a school against the will of the town and Prudence was arrested. Her twenty-four hours' imprisonment, however, did much for her cause, and so did her subsequent trial at which she was found guilty but appealed. While awaiting the second trial, the school buildings were actually set on fire and she herself was accused of arson. The second trial widened the whole issue to the question of allowing free Negroes the full citizenship which would include education. The judges backed out of a positive decision on a legal technicality and soon after the school buildings were again attacked and partly wrecked.

Prudence gave in, not because of fear, but because she recognised that hate for her assailants had invaded her own soul. It was a local defeat but a long-term victory, for her struggle resulted in much greater pressure to alter the law in favour of black citizenship. She herself opened another school for coloured girls in Illinois.

In 1851, a former slave, Sojourner Truth, attended a Women's

Rights Convention at Akron, Ohio, and made a momentous speech. The audience were predominantly hostile to women's rights and that a woman, and a slave at that, should be heard with attention was in itself something of a miracle but her simple passionate eloquence moved even that audience:

> "Look at me! Look at my arm. . . . I have ploughed and planted and gathered into barns and no man could head me, and ain't I a woman? I have borne thirteen children and seen most of them sold into slavery and when I cried out in my mother's grief none but Jesus heard me! And ain't I a woman? . . . That little man . . . he says that women won't have as much rights as men, 'cause Christ wasn't a woman! Where did your Christ come from? From God and a woman! Man had nothing to do with him!"[20]

Both as a woman and a slave Sojourner Truth turned to Christ as her one defence against injustice and despair, and in so doing repeated the cry that has echoed down the ages since the Magnificat — "For he hath exalted the humble and the meek." That the Christianity of the New Testament lifts up rather than debases women is a truth declared by such divergent voices as St Bernard, Julian of Norwich, George Fox, Susannah Wesley, Florence Nightingale and Christina Rossetti and is here given a simpler but not less effective utterance.

Women's emancipation in the USA was ahead of Britain, and Elizabeth Blackwell was able to qualify as the first woman doctor sixteen years before Elizabeth Garrett Anderson. She visited London in 1859, on which occasion *Punch* celebrated the occasion in the following verses:

> "Young ladies all, of every clime
> Especially of Britain,
> Who chiefly occupy your time
> In novels or in knitting

> Whose highest skill is but to play,
> Sing, dance or French to clack well,
> Reflect on the example, prey,
> Of excellent Miss Blackwell."

Elizabeth Garrett Anderson *did* reflect on this example to the benefit of all concerned. But although Elizabeth Blackwell was, through sheer determination, able to blaze the trail for English women, when she first announced her decision to become a doctor she had been told it was not possible for a Christian girl to dream of such a vocation. She was terrified of defeat, but then a mystical experience came to her and the strength which it brought carried her through all subsequent difficulties:

> "A brilliant light of hope and peace filled my soul. At once, I knew not how, the terror fled away. . . . A deep conviction came to me that my life was accepted by God. . . . This unusual experience at the outset of my medical career has had a lasting and marked effect on my whole life. To me it was a revealed experience of Truth, a direct vision of the great reality of spiritual existence, as irresistible as it is incommunicable. I shall be grateful to the last day of my life for this great gift of faith."

Elizabeth Blackwell was the most outstandingly religious of the early women medical pioneers. She devoted her life to work among the poorest of women and children in New York. After a great deal of opposition she opened a hospital for training women medical students. At first she and two other women were the only staff, and in seven months they treated nearly a thousand cases. Inspiration flowed to and fro across the Atlantic, for Elizabeth Blackwell's hospital was planned to open on Florence Nightingale's birthday and its existence was a direct encouragement to Elizabeth Garrett Anderson in the founding of *her* hospital.

Mary Baker Eddy has no parallel in England. Perhaps the nearest was Catherine Booth, but here again the situation in the New World is more dramatic, more sharply defined. Where Mrs Booth was joint founder with her husband of what might be termed a fresh brand of evangelical Methodism, Mrs Eddy was the sole creator of a quite new Christian sect.

She had a Calvinistic upbringing against which she revolted, refusing to make the outward confession required from Calvinist children at the age of twelve. She suffered physically and mentally as a girl and young woman. She married young and her husband died of malaria, leaving her pregnant with their first child and destitute except for the ownership of three slaves, whom she immediately freed. She returned home but became ill, and when her mother died Mary was unable to cope with her baby son who was sent to be reared elsewhere and with whom, to her sorrow, she subsequently had little to do.

195

She married again and unsuccessfully. Then she took up the study of homeopathy, spiritualism and mesmerism, in order to combat suffering which she refused to believe came from God. It could be said that personal suffering was the specialised education needed for her subsequent career for all her studies led her to the conclusion that mind was more powerful than matter. She became for a time associated with a faith healer, but there was a significant difference in their methods — he sought to control matter by personal magnetism, Mary to understand the healing power of spirit.

Then came the next step in her education — a severe accident causing concussion and spine injury. She and her friends were told that she might die or, if she recovered, be a helpless invalid. She remained unconscious for three days, then she asked to be left alone and turned to Matthew's account of Jesus healing the palsied man. She then prayed, got up from her bed and walked into the next room completely cured. Her friends were frightened — the experience was beyond them — but for Mary it was the culmination through personal experience of the doctrinal theory that "mind is all and matter naught", which became the cornerstone of her new "Christian Science" of healing: "Spirit alone created all and called it good. Therefore evil being contrary to God cannot be the product of God." True healing has to be wholly spiritual — no matter could come into it, not even the laying on of hands. She produced her book *Science & Health*, which was privately printed and circulated. Bronson Alcott, the father of Louisa and one of the Transcendentalists, read it and wrote to her:

> "I hail with joy your voice, speaking an assured word for God and Immortality, and my joy is heightened that these words are *women's* divinings."

He called her work "a reaffirmation of the Christian revelation". In 1876 the Christian Science Association was formed. By this time her second marriage had broken up and now Asa Gilbert Eddy, who had been cured by her of a long illness, became one of her disciples and was the first to call himself a Christian Scientist and Practitioner. In him she found the male partner so often essential to a woman to carry out the official side of their visionary enterprise and they were married in 1877.

196

Of course there was violent opposition, including an unsuccessful charge of murder, but once again persecution resulted in strengthening rather than weakening the movement. As it grew so, inevitably, the Christian Scientists had to become more officially organised, and eventually to form their own church. Mary Eddy was granted a charter for this church and for a college. All seemed to be going well when Gilbert Eddy suddenly died. Mary blamed herself for her preoccupation with public work which she felt had prevented her being with him and curing him. It was a great test of her faith but she emerged triumphant: "For I do believe in God's supremacy over evil and this gives me peace."

The orthodox churches, the medical profession and above all, perhaps, the sensationalists, were her chief enemies, and of course she was also attacked simply for being a woman. In answer to her opponents she made a confession of faith which included a definition of God as being both Mother and Father, and then, on an ascending plane of thought, Divine Principle or Mind. In time she acquired influential friends, William James and Mark Twain and even a popular clergyman, Edward Everett Hale of Boston. A Mother Church was built at Boston and the rules which the Society had evolved over the years were co-ordinated by Mrs Eddy and published as the *Christian Science Church Manual*.

In 1883 she had founded the *Christian Science Journal*, which spread her teaching beyond the confines of the United States. By 1900 Mark Twain wrote "a new Christian Science Church is appearing every four days!" Her last project at the age of eighty-seven was to establish a daily paper, probably as the result of press hostility to the new Sect. It was *The Christian Science Monitor* and has become an international force.

14
From the Edwardian Era to the Present Day

Side by side with the growing institutionalism of Christian philanthropy in the pre-1914 era and, perhaps as an antidote to it, there sprang up a sudden fresh interest in mysticism and in contemplation which was adopted with enthusiasm, especially by women who may have turned to it in relief after the strenuous cultivation of social work in the preceding age.

The pioneer in the research and popularisation of the lives and writings of the early mystics, till then known only to a very few scholars, was actually a woman, Evelyn Underhill who, in 1911, published *Mysticism, a study of the nature and development of man's spiritual consciousness.* Her attitude was essentially that of a romantic and not of a historian. She writes as a woman, that is to say her approach, though scholarly, is intensely personal and she interprets philosophy and metaphysics in human and often emotional terms. But later, under the influence of Von Hügel, she modifies her strongly individual treatment of the subject and, in subsequent editions and in her other writings she acknowledges the value of an impersonal framework: "Divorced from all institutional expression mysticism tends to become strange, vague or merely sentimental." She never, however, gave so much importance to the historical setting as to the emotional quality of the mystical experience.

In 1912 her edition of *The Cloud of Unknowing* appeared and she also edited or introduced many other medieval texts for the public, including those of Ruysbroeck, Walter Hilton, Boehme, Richard Rolle and Julian of Norwich. As religious editor of the then widely read *Spectator* she published a series of articles from writers of all shades of opinions and sects from Bertrand Russell and Bernal to William Temple, Chesterton and T. S. Eliot.

Her last work was a formidable *History of Christian Worship* of which Christopher Armstrong, her latest biographer, writes:

"Such a sympathetic rearticulation of the past for the enlightenment of the present has long been the glory of women writers."

Evelyn Underhill instituted and led retreats at Plashy and elsewhere and she was surrounded by a group of disciples, mostly
women. It is perhaps significant that in one of her earliest works,
a novel entitled *The Ivory Tower*, Truth is represented as a woman
who proclaims: "I am older than God." She is in fact Sophia,
that ancient mythical female figure referred to mysteriously in
Proverbs. But, like many another outstanding woman, she needed
the balance of a more detatched and institutional approach and
this she found in her men friends, though she remained free and
independent. She learned to emphasise the importance of training
and discipline in the mystic way and that contemplation must lead
on to action. The pendulum swung again with the cataclysm of
war and Evelyn's reputation waned, but she remains *the* pioneer
in mystical history and the same spirit that sent her adventuring
into the past also reached out into the yet undiscovered: "The
coming of the Kingdom is perpetual — the real Christian is always
a revolutionary — God is with the future."

Another woman pioneer in the rediscovery of our spiritual
heritage, though in a different media, was Dame Laurentia
McLachlan, Abbess of the Benedictine nuns at Stanbrook. She
was responsible for the great liturgical revival in England. While
choir mistress at Stanbrook, she carried out research into the
Gregorian chant and the English tradition of its use, and in 1915
published *The Grammar of Plain Song* which became the standard
work on the subject and has a great effect on the sacred music of
the present age. Her fine and scholarly musicianship brought her
many unusual friends outside the community who were first
attracted by her work and then by her personality. Sydney
Cockerell, the famous bibliophile, wrote of her:

> "Indeed I regard you as a beacon from whom spread shafts of
> all the virtues to lighten those who sit in darkness — or as a
> piece of radium which can heal and strengthen those who falter,
> without losing any of its own substance."

He introduced her to Shaw who wrote her delightful letters, sign-
ing himself "Brother Bernard", which reveal him in a totally new
light. The most moving and interesting of these letters is a long

account of his visit to the Holy Land. As a souvenir of this visit he says:

> "I picked up a little stone (at Bethlehem), a scrap of limestone rock which certainly existed when the feet of Jesus pattered about on it . . . in fact I picked up two little stones, one to be thrown blindfold among the others in Stanbrook garden so that there may always be a stone from Bethlehem there and the other for your own self."

The stone for Dame Laurentia he had set for her in a model of a medieval reliquary. She was greatly pleased and wrote asking him to supply a suitable inscription including his own name as donor. His answer, so unlike the Shaw most people know, in its humility and reverence and yet so like in its wit and wisdom:

> "What the devil — sorry your cloth — could we put on it ? . . We couldn't put our names on it — could we? It seems to me something perfectly awful. 'An inscription explaining its purpose'! If we could explain its purpose we could explain the universe. . . . Dear Sister: our fingerprints are on it and Heaven knows whose footprints may be on the stone. Isn't that enough!"

What may be termed the new religious romanticism of the Edwardian period in which Evelyn Underhill and Dame Laurentia rediscovered and popularised the mystics and the music of an earlier age was also apparent in the work of Dorothy Kevin who established the first Faith Healing Homes in England. She was miraculously cured of tubercular peritonitis as a girl, a cure more startling and sudden than that of Mrs Eddy's, for she was lying unconscious in the coma that precedes death when in her own words "the living Lord laid His Hand upon my life and restored me to perfect health and wholeness in the twinkling of an eye". She had seen a great light and heard a voice telling her to get up and go about her usual business. As a child she had seen visions and she retained the simple unquestioning beliefs of a child all her life. Her story indeed seems to belong more to the world of Margery Kempe than to our own century for it was a world in which miracles often occurred and did not surprise her. The account of her life reads rather like that of one of the medieval saints, with the same mixture of the trivial and the tremendous and often it appears she possessed more piety than wisdom though she certainly exerted a strange power over both animals and human beings and money poured in for her Homes while her cures were attested by doctors from far and wide.

Beatrice Hankey also travelled back in time for the inspiration of her Arthurian Fellowship of Knights of a spiritual Round Table. Her aim was to band together young women from the leisured classes as disciples in the service of Christ — to give personal service, personal friendship and personal dedication. In time the fellowship widened to take in men and more than justified itself in wartime and in the depression that followed and in refugee work of all kinds until the present day. Canon Raven wrote of Miss Hankey: "She was far more a bishop, a mother in God, than any ordained or consecrated Christian."

The cataclysm of the 1914 war brought about change in every sphere of life. In many directions women achieved greater political and social influence and in their struggle for entry into Parliament and the professions, for legal rights and for equal pay, committed Christians were of course involved, sometimes trying to connect more definitely and effectively faith and practice.

At the Christian Conference on Politics, Economics and Citizenship (COPEK) held in 1924, for instance, this was strikingly obvious. As Raven wrote:

> "The genius of the whole movement was Lucy Gardner. Certainly she mothered and sustained our whole community but she had also gathered and organised it. I do not believe that any man could have shown such ruthless and untiring efficiency without losing the human touch. . . . Politics were for her always secondary to human relationships."

There were, however, certain new developments which affected women in a fresh way: the pacifist movement which had come into being during the 1914 war, the invention of radio which enabled women speakers on religious and moral subjects to be widely heard and accepted and, leading out of this as well as from many other activities, the steady progress towards ordination.

A pacifist of the Second World War, Kathleen Lonsdale, has put the case for the natural support any Peace Movement ought to have from women:

"There are two very good reasons why women ought to be particularly effective in working for peace and freedom. In the first place they are able not only to teach children with words, but also to demonstrate to them and to the world generally, that sheer physical strength is not so important as the moral strength that all can possess. In the second place, women are used to the fact that a price has to be paid for anything that is worth having. Neither peace nor freedom can be had without working for them."

To work for peace during the 1914-18 war meant paying the price of active hostility, except perhaps for the Quakers, whose peace testimony was of such long and tried standing. Among Quaker women who gave unstintingly of their time and energy for peace and war relief work was Ruth Fry, one of a famous band of sisters. She became Secretary to the Friends War Victims Relief Committee and carried out such valiant and demanding work that her health never recovered from the strain. But there were others who braved unpopularity and even violence for their pacifist opinions. Among these was Maude Royden, the famous Congregationalist preacher. She had much to do with the foundation of the interdenominational Christian pacifist movement known as The Fellowship of Reconciliation.

The career of Maude Royden, who lived from 1876 to 1955, contains written into it so many of the different aspects of women's developing Christian service that it assumes almost archetypal significance. She was one of the first to benefit by the struggle for higher education for women and, as a student at Lady Margaret Hall, Oxford, she is linked with the Lady Margaret Beaufort who had in her day been among the first women to benefit by the new learning of the Renaissance.

Next, the Settlement Movement, starting at the turn of the century, drew her into its orbit and she worked so hard in the Liverpool slums that her health gave way. This sent her into the country where she lectured on literature for the newly formed Oxford University Extension Delegacy and subsequently for Women Suffrage under the direction of Mrs Fawcett. Her work so far had been determined by social, educational and political interests, but now, at the same time as she was discovering in herself unsuspected powers through this constant challenge of public speaking, she felt a strong leaning towards a religious vocation. She was a faithful Anglican, but the Church of England could find no use for her special gifts. A breakthrough, however, was made, not only for herself, but for the future, when the Congregational Church invited her to become a regular preacher at the City Temple. She had a fine voice and, like most successful orators, a sense of drama (she had once had an ambition to go on the stage) and her sermons soon became famous. Perhaps Dr Johnson if he had heard her preach would have revised his opinion of women's preaching.

Maude Royden was not only a preacher, she was also a good organiser and debater and, with Percy Dearmer, she founded undenominational services which allowed time for discussions after the sermon and from these services the Guild House Fellowship was started. Though she had suffered for her pacifist activities in the First World War, she felt, in 1939, that Nazism was an evil that could only yield to force and, after much inward conflict, she abandoned her uncompromising pacifism though continuing to work for ultimate peace by her support of the League of Nations. She had travelled widely on behalf of the League between the wars. In her later years she took advantage of the opportunities offered through the BBC and in her programme "The Silver Lining" she was one of the first women to speak regularly on the air upon religious subjects. She was very lame all her life but, like many another woman with whom this book has been concerned, she disregarded poor health and with fortitude and determination won through. She was intellectually brilliant, humorous and compassionate. Her approach was always intensely personal (sometimes, especially in old age, bordering on the sentimental) but she was the first woman to preach regularly from a church pulpit and she put the question of ordination on the map.

In the "Lift up Your Hearts" programme in 1962 there was a series of talks entitled "A Scientist tries to answer some of her own questions about religion." There were two arresting features here — that the speaker, a woman, was also both eminent in science and religion. Kathleen Lonsdale (1903-71) was a DBE, one of the two first women to become Fellows of the Royal Society and the first woman ever elected President of the British Association for the Advancement of Science. Less eminently she had also served a sentence as a convict in Holloway Prison. Brought up by a Baptist mother and an agnostic father (from whom she inherited her scientific leanings) she felt her life as a research student at Cambridge under Sir William Bragg was at first entirely satisfying. But her gradual realisation that "there were many scientific concepts that could not be satisfactorily defined", together with her growing admiration for the life and teaching of Jesus as a man, rather than as the second person of the Trinity, led her away from atheism. Then came the war and a challenge which she felt she could not evade. She decided to go to prison rather than register for war service, though by doing so she was risking losing her absorbing job and accepting separation from husband and children. But

> "I had wrestled in prayer and knew beyond all doubt that I *must* refuse to register, that those who believed that war was the wrong way to fight evil, must stand out against it, however much they stood alone."

She felt that however hard it was to leave her children, they would be more harmed if she was unfaithful to her principle. Mothers of strong convictions and equally strong family feelings have sometimes in times of crisis to face this conflict. An exactly opposite view, but one which involved the same agony of decision and parting, was that of Odette Hallows, a French Resistance fighter who felt it was *her* inescapable duty to leave her children in England and to return to France, because she believed it was wrong to allow others to fight so that her children might be free. But both mothers would have agreed on the two premises: that expressed by Kathleen Lonsdale that for one's children's sake also one must be true to what is felt to be the truth and Odette's declaration that what is done should be done "in the spirit of sacrifice and love".

This was the hardest trial for Kathleen Lonsdale for the prison experience itself, though unpleasant enough in some ways, she always maintained was a most useful experience. Characteristically the two books she took with her, and which she had to fight to retain, were Clark's *Applied X-rays* and Peake's *Commentary on the Bible*. She made friends with her fellow convicts — drunks and disorderlies, thieves and prostitutes — and conceived a respect for the prison officers though a profound dissatisfaction with the system. In the true succession of women prison reformers, she longed for more respect and concern for the individual, both during and after imprisonment. For herself, she declared: "My husband said it had done me a world of good . . . it had made me more human, more interested in other people.' Perhaps it brought out the woman in her which had possibly before suffered at the expense of the scientist. As a Christian, however, she seems to combine the practical outlook noticeable in many Christian women with the experimental attitude of the scientist. She was not much interested in theology or organised Christianity. In serving God she wrote:

"We are not concerned most of the time with major problems of the meaning of life. We are simply asking God's help in our constant battle with a quick temper, or a poor digestion, or a failing memory."

And again:

"If we knew all the answers there would be no point in carrying out scientific research. Because we do not, it is stimulating, exciting, challenging. So too is the Christian life, lived experimentally."

Kathleen had a great concern for the moral and religious education of children, for which she felt women had a special responsibility; but she also thought that women were much less effective than they might be because they were too unorganised and too much absorbed by domestic life. She wanted to see a more fruitful association of men and women in working out new ways of bettering the world.

The closer relationship of the sexes in all community life, arising out of the growing emancipation of women, has led to a quickening of the movement for their ordination to the priesthood. By the years following World War II, Congregationalists and Baptists had been ordaining women for some time and later the Methodists followed suit, though the numbers in all denominations remained small. In America, the nonconformist churches threw open the ministry to women at about the same time; as far as Anglicans were concerned, things moved more slowly but no less definitely towards ordination, although there was also much opposition. At the time of writing, fifteen women have been ordained by a rebel bishop in Philadelphia. At Boston University a priest chaplain, James Carrick, spoke out strongly in favour, stung by the proclamation of an all male Pastoral Research Committee's condemnation:

> "How long will members of the Church, men and women, bishops, lay people, deacons and priests, tolerate a situation that is quite plainly corrupt? Women are tired of the violence done them at every eucharist liturgy, which announces via the priesthood that they are less than persons."

The World Council of Churches in 1970 pointed out that theological argument and sociological change favoured ordination, and in 1975 the General Synod of the Church of England declared that there was no fundamental objection to it — as well they might, considering that two women had already been ordained in the diocese of Hong Kong and that Canada has also ordained women priests into the Anglican Church, and Australia has approved in principle.

The changing attitude towards ordination in the Anglican church called forth two letters of expostulation from Rome to Canterbury pointing out that this was a serious obstacle to reconciliation This was followed in January 1977 by an official papal proclamation against the ordination of women. The chief objections put forward to women priests are first, that Christ chose no women to be His disciples; it seems obvious that in the particular place and time of His mission such a choice would have been quite impracticable. Both the Jewish tradition and the whole Eastern attitude towards women were insuperable obstacles to such a choice. (Incidentally, neither did Christ choose any uncircumcised nor any from the wealthy or the influential in society.) Such an objection, then, though apparently a stumbling-block to many sincere Christians, seems untenable on an unprejudiced examination. More subtle and therefore most difficult to refute is the symbolism by which the officiating priest at the Eucharist impersonates Christ and the

Church, His bride. The claim is made that women are not degraded by such symbolism, but only that the difference of their function in worship is maintained. For all Catholics and for some Anglicans, Mary is the symbol of femininity in its highest form and "the Christ-Mary relationship is held to be similar to the Christ-Church relation — where the Marian principal is denied the Church becomes inhuman."[21] It is interesting in connection with this admission for the *need* for the feminine principal that those churches furthest from Mariology are those that have first admitted women to their full ministry.

This symbolic argument against ordination is linked with the belief that to allow women to become priests might devalue their special spiritual gifts. In taking over the duties of men, they would lose and not gain influence, for women's contradiction is "to be a supporting ministry giving strength and stability to men".[22] This argument has been advanced (by men) whenever and wherever women have aspired to wider fields of service such as in medicine, the law or commerce. A different view was put forward in the General Synod's latest report on women's ordination by Christine Howard, who said:

"A new situation exists in which women by increased education and opportunities to share in a wider range of skills are now capable as never before of exercising priesthood."

This characteristic practical argument is dismissed as utilitarian by the symbolists.

Acceptance into the priesthood for Anglican women in Canada and the USA has certainly brought it nearer to realisation in England. In November 1976 a Canadian celebrated the Eucharist in London, the first time a woman has conducted this service according to Anglican rites in this country, but she had to borrow a Unitarian Church in which to officiate. Still, it was a step forward and it was followed up by a symbolic occasion at St Martin-in-the-Fields, when Deaconess Baker offered the bread and wine to the Bishop of Winchester for his blessing, which he refused to give, as a public avowal of his disapproval of the ban against women priests. The service was thus brought to a dramatically unconsummated close. Deaconess Baker had, for thirty years, performed all the duties of a parish priest at her church except those denied to her — the consecration of the elements, the granting of absolution and the marriage service. The unfinished Eucharist at St Martin-in-the-Fields symbolised the waste of the sustenance and new life that women priests might bring to the Church at a time when its need is urgent.

The ordination of women to the priesthood is a contemporary and significant matter, but it is also an issue which has already been decided in women's favour by many Christians. Even in the Roman Catholic Church the signs are there that it will eventually come to pass. The Orthodox Church, perhaps the most impersonal of the Christian sects, alone is entirely unsympathetic, at present. In the future ordination for women will take its place in the changing pattern of life and will be accepted as normal.

What women have asked for and found in Christianity through-out the ages (however obscured by the heresies of the Church at different times) is reverence for the individual. The teaching of Christ stressed this in a society careless of such a valuation and indeed oblivious to it in the case of "a woman or a slave" (a classification from Aristotle's *Poetics*). The importance of the totally insignificant was epitomised in the patently absurd state-ment that the death of a sparrow mattered to the Supreme Deity. That everyone in her or his own right is valuable in creation is so apparently ridiculous a concept that, though it is at the heart of Christianity, it has never been fully accepted. Yet where and whenever the individual has been held of less value than an idea or an object embodying an idea, Hell eventually takes over.

It can be argued that women are biologically biased in favour of the child, the individual, the small, the particular. It is their job to sustain and protect life (notwithstanding the existence of a small number of women terrorists, an exception which emphasises the above generalisation). The aspect of Christianity that "exalts the humble and meek" should be especially dear to them. The Peace Movement in Ireland was started by two women, driven by the death of children to make an individual protest, and what they did was to meet other women on the opposite side of the barrier of hate as people and not as symbols. The thousands from both sides that followed those two women failed to make a political impact, but nothing can destroy the fact that, through them, men and women who had before only thought of each other as bitter symbols of hated beliefs then recognised their common humanity for the first time. The initial enthusiasm has inevitably died down, but the women's work of emphasising the sense of a common humanity and of the growing desire for peace continues behind the scenes. During the year after the movement started the situation improved and it is recognised that this was due in no inconsiderable measure to the groundwork done by the Peace Movement, though it is not possible to assess their influence with any precision. It is significant that their leaders have found it advisable to break up their membership into small active groups. Perhaps this is one of the portents of a radical change in society, for there are other movements of all kinds springing up elsewhere whose battle-cry is "small is beautiful". This reaction against too-large and de-humanising organisations in favour of a more individual approach appears to belong more naturally to women and is also surely more truly Christian in outlook.

Speaking generally, the male element in creation seems to be concerned primarily with abstractions. It possesses the urge to dominate nature and to create new worlds. Marvellous and terrible these have been and continue to be, but continually doomed through lack of balance, common sense, wisdom — call it what you will. Endurance and adaptability seem to be qualities more often possessed by women than men, perhaps forced upon them by centuries of social pressure as well as by biological necessity; and these are qualities essential to the development of a balanced whole. The great religions of the world have often lacked this balance. "Without vision the people perish", but with the wrong sort of vision they also perish. The old Earth Goddess was too static and atavistic; she had to be succeeded by the rampant Lord of Hosts. Christianity, owing to Jewish tradition and a perverted Pauline influence, has evolved as a predominantly male religion, though actually its early differentiating characteristic was that its founder was concerned neither with temporal power nor with knowledge but with love, and love involves personal relation-ships which begin with the mother.

It is not an accident that throughout the centuries women have provided the core of Christian worship. Although, in order to fulfil the Divine Will at that particular place and time, Jesus was born as the son of Joseph, when he passed out of Time into eternity surely sex was transcended. Might not we gain also if the male image of the Lord Almighty were replaced in our imagination by a conception more in line with Julian's vision of the Mother-Christ, the dual emblem of the mystery of creative love?

Notes

1. Thucydides II.45 (Benjamin Jowett's translation, 1881).
2. R. E. Wallis, *The Writings of Cyprian*, Epistle LXL.
3. *The Ancrene Riwle*, Kings Classics.
4. G. G. Coulton, *Five Centuries of Religion*.
5. Richard a Sancto Laurentio, *A Work in Praise of Mary*, quoted by Hugo Rahner in *Greek Myths and Christian Mystery*.
6. C. G. Jung, *Psychology and Religion*.
7. Henry Adams, *Mont-Saint-Michel and Chartres*.
8. Coulton, op. cit.
9. Charles Williams, *Descent of the Dove*.
10. R. P. Nicholas, O.P., *Marie Co-redemptrice*.
11. Translated by Fr Sebastian Bullogh, O. P.
12. Lord David Cecil, *Hatfield House and the Cecils*.
13. Quoted in G. M. Trevelyan's *English Social History*.
14. C. Fell Smith, *Mary Rich, Countess of Warwick*.
15. Sewel, *History of the Quakers*, Vol. 1.
16. Quoted from A. M. Stirling, *The Richmond Papers*.
17. Pusey House Record.
18. *English Women*. Collins, 1947.
19. Norman Goldsmith, *Housing Happenings*, St Pancras Housing Association, 1976.
20. Quoted by Una Kroll in *Flesh of My Flesh*.
21. John Saward, *The Case Against the Ordination of Women*.
22. Ibid.

Select Bibliography
(in chronological order)

1 Introduction
H. L. Goudge, *The Place of Women in the Church*, London, 1917.
T. B. Allworthy, *Women in the Apostolic Church*, Cambridge, 1917.
J. Harper, *Women and the Gospel*, London.
Charles Williams, *The Descent of the Dove*, London, 1939.

2 The Saxon Period
G. F. Browne, *The Importance of Women in Anglo-Saxon Times*, London, 1919.
G. F. Browne, *Women under Monasticism*.
Margaret Deanesly, *Sidelights on the Anglo-Saxon Church*, London, 1962.
Sister Ethel Mary, *Life of St Hilda*, St Hilda's Priory Publications.
Bede's *History of England*, translated by Leo Sherley-Price, Harmondsworth, 1955.
A. Hamilton Thompson, *Bede: His Life, Times and Writings*, 1930.
Sister Margaret Gordon, *St Margaret, Queen of Scotland*, Edinburgh and London, 1934.
Eadmer's *History of Recent Events in England*, translated by Geoffrey Bosanquet, London, 1964.

3 From the Conquest to the Reformation
Lina Eckenstein, *The Monastic Order in England*, London, 1896.
Alan Maycock, *Malling Abbey*, Malling, Kent, 1953.
David Knowles, *The Monastic Order in England: History of the Development, 943-1216*, Cambridge, 1940.
Eileen Power, *Medieval English Nunneries*, Cambridge, 1922.
The Ancrene Riwle, Camden Society, 1853.
George Gordon Coulton, *Five Centuries of Religion*, Cambridge, 1923.
Thomas Hodgkin, *History of England from the Earliest Times to the Norman Conquest*, London, 1905.

4 Julian of Norwich and Margery Kempe of Lynne
Julian of Norwich, *Revelations of Divine Love*, Harmondsworth, 1973.
The Book of Margery Kempe 1436, edited by S. B. Meech, 1940.
Walter Hilton, *The Scale of Perfection*, translated by Leo Sherley-Price, London, 1975.

5 The Virgin Mary
Giovanni Miegge, *The Virgin Mary*, translated by Waldo Smith, London, 1955.

Hugo Rahner, *Greek Myths and Christian Mystery*, London, 1963.

Henry Adams, *Mont-Saint-Michel and Chartres*, Boston, 1913.

Of the Tumbler of Our Lady and other Miracles, translated by Alice Kemp-Welch, 1908.

John Langdon-Davies, *Sex, Sin and Sanctity*, London, 1954.

6 The Reformation

L. J. Suenens, *New Pentecost?*, London, 1975.

Richard W. Dixon, *History of the Church of England*, Vol. II, London, 1893.

Narratives of the Days of the Reformation, Camden Society, Series LXXVII, London, 1859.

E. M. G. Routh, *Lady Margaret Beaufort*, Oxford, 1924.

Hester W. Chapman, *Lady Jane Grey*, London, 1962.

Elizabeth Jenkins, *Elizabeth the Great*, London, 1958.

Lord David Cecil, *Hatfield House and the Cecils*, London, 1973.

Ronald Bayne, *Shakespeare's England*, London, 1916.

Margaret Potts, *The Parson's Wife*, London, 1950.

Foxe's *Book of Martyrs and the Elect Nation*, edited by William Haller, London, 1963.

Arthur Geoffrey Dickens, *The English Reformation*, London, 1964.

7 The Growth of Puritanism and the Civil War

Katherine M. Briggs, *Pale Hecate's Team*, London, 1962.

Lucy Hutchinson, *Memoirs of the Life of Colonel Hutchinson*, 1806; edited by James Sutherland, Oxford, 1973.

C. Fell Smith, *Mary Rich, Countess of Warwick*, London, 1901.

John Evelyn, *Life of Mrs Godolphin*, Pickering, 1847.

John Bunyan, *The Pilgrim's Progress*.

Richard Baxter, Autobiography, 1696; edited by N. H. Keeble, London, 1974.

8 The Quakers

W. Sewel, *The History of the Rise, Increase and Progress of the Christian People Called Quakers*, 6th edition, London, 1834.

Rufus Jones, *The Later Periods of Quakerism*, London, 1921.

The Journal of George Fox, edited by Norman Penney, Cambridge, 1911.

Lucy Violet Hodgkin, *A Book of Quaker Saints*, London and Edinburgh, 1917.

9 The Age of Reason and Methodism

Anthony Armstrong, *The Church of England — The Methodists and Society 1700-1850*, London, 1973.

Henry Bett, *The Spirit of Wesleyism*, London, 1937.

Henry Bett, *The Hymns of Methodism*, London, 1945.

Rebecca L. Harmon, *Susannah, Mother of the Wesleys*, London, 1968.

J. A. Newton, *Susannah Wesley and the Puritan Tradition in Methodism*, London, 1968.

10   Women and the Evangelical Movement

Mary G. Jones, *Hannah More*, Cambridge, 1952.

E. M. Forster, *Marianne Thornton*, London, 1956.

Kathleen Bartlett, *Elizabeth Fry*, London, 1960.

11   The Victorian Age

A Chaplet for Charlotte Yonge, edited by Georgina Battiscombe and Marghanita Laski, London, 1965.

Betty Asquith, *Sisterhoods and Charlotte Yonge*, an unpublished paper written for the Charlotte Yonge Society, 1973.

Cecil Woodham Smith, *Life of Florence Nightingale*, London, 1950.

L. Mosk Packer, *Christina Rossetti*, Berkeley, 1963.

The Poetical Works of Christina Rossetti, London, 1904.

Edith Sitwell, *English Women*, London, 1942.

Augustus Hare, *Memorials of a Quiet Life*, 3 vols, London, 1872, 1873, 1876.

12   Women in Missions Abroad and at Home

Curryer and Moore, *The Story of Walthamstow Hall*, London, 1938; Sevenoaks, 1973.

Carol Christian and Gladys Plummer, *God and One Red Head*, London, 1970.

Cecil Howard, *Mary Kingsley*, London, 1957.

Daisy Bates, *The Passing of the Aborigines*, London, 1938, 1966.

Harold Begbie, *Life of William Booth*, London, 1920.

Josephine Butler, *Personal Reminiscences of a Great Crusade*, London, 1896.

Arthur S. Butler, *Josephine Butler*, a portrait, London, 1954.

Enid Bell, *Josephine Butler*, London, 1962.

Mrs H. Barnett, *Canon Barnett. His Life, Work, and Friends*, London, 1918.

13   Christian Women in Nineteenth-Century America

Elizabeth Blackwell, *Pioneer Work in Opening the Medical Profession to Women*, London, 1895.

Henrietta Buckmaster, *Women Who Stamped History*, New York, 1966.

Katharine Moore, *Women*, London, 1970.

14 From the Edwardian Age to the Present Day

Christopher Armstrong, *Evelyn Underhill, 1875-1941*, London, 1975.

The Letters of Evelyn Underhill, edited by Charles Williams, London, 1943.

Benedictines of Stanbrook, *In a Great Tradition*, London, 1956.

Dorothy Musgrave Arnold, *Dorothy Kerin — Called by Christ to Heal*, London, 1965.

Canon Raven and Rachel Heath, *One Called Help: The Life and Work of Beatrice Hankey*, London, 1937.

Maude Royden, obituary in *The Brown Book*, Lady Margaret Hall, Oxford, 1906.

Kathleen Lonsdale, *The Christian Life*, an anthology selected by James Hough, London, 1976.

Una Kroll, *Flesh of My Flesh*, London, 1975.

John Saward, *The Case Against the Ordination of Women*, London, 1975.

Index of Names

219